From This Day Forward

From This Day Forward

Memoirs of an Attache Wife

Helen Rodman

*To Jane de Frietas
with warm regards and
love —
Helen Rodman*

BRANDYLANE PUBLISHERS, INC.
White Stone, Virginia

❋ Brandylane Publishers, Inc.

P.O. Box 261, White Stone, Virginia 22578
(804) 435-6900 or 1 800 553-6922; e-mail: brandy@crosslink.net

Library of Congress Cataloging-in-Publication Data

Rodman, Helen, 1921–
    From this day forward: memoirs of an attache wife/Helen Rodman.
      p.   cm.
    ISBN 1–883911–33–8
    1. Rodman, Helen, 1921– . 2. Diplomats' spouses—United States
Biography. I. Title.
CT275.R5744A3 1999
973.91'092—dc21
  [B]   93–30577
                                            CIP

For Bill,
with whom I shared this adventure,
and
in loving memory of
Joni.

CONTENTS

ACKNOWLEDGMENTS

I'd like to extend my thanks to Margaret Daniel, Martha Leys, Wes and Cindy Robbins, Bud Bryant, Langhorne Gibson, Marti Bastido, Mary Lou St. Clair, and Bill Rodman, Jr. for the help and encouragement they have so generously given me during the writing of this book. Most especially, I am grateful to Jeanne Siler, my editor and friend.

INTRODUCTION

The course of history throughout my lifetime has been highly charged. My peers and I were of a generation born just before the Great Depression of the thirties. We were torn apart by a world war, learning early to survive tremendous sadness, and to come face to face with the uncertainty of a long separation, while at the same time assuming the armor of courage. We did not question what had to be done. We simply assumed our roles. Husbands, fathers, lovers and brothers went off to the hell of war while wives, mothers, and sisters and all those who loved a soldier waited anxiously at home.

This book is about those years, and the three decades that followed while traveling the world with my family in the United States Foreign Service.

In the best biographies that I have read, the dark side is recorded next to the light with no apologies. The writer does not rationalize the bad nor glorify the good. I have had my share of self-doubt, frustration and regret, but prefer to share the more treasured moments of my life— my happiness, my adventures, my family.

At the same time, I also feel a compelling need to pour from my heart my greatest sorrow.

"Where am I going? I don't quite know.
Down to the stream where the king-cups grow-
Up on the hill where the pine trees blow-
Anywhere, anywhere. I don't know."

From *When We Were Very Young*
A. A. Milne

· —— Chapter One —— ·

FROM THIS DAY FORWARD

WHEN BILL RODMAN AND I WERE MARRIED, I was just twenty and thrilled to be the bride of such a handsome and charming man. I was captivated not only by his spirit of adventure, but by his desire to do things just a bit differently from the other young men I knew while growing up on the Main Line of Philadelphia.

As an example, Bill was the only man I knew with a tattoo. At age fifteen, he and his two best friends considered themselves modern-day musketeers. During a rash and quixotic moment, they had had themselves marked for life with a tattoo—a skull, a sword, a star and the number thirteen on their left forearms. The skull attested to the death that comes to us all, the sword stood for man's right to defend his honor, the star signified that man's reach should exceed his grasp, and the number thirteen stood for one for three and three for one. In later years, Bill would wish many times over that this idealistic emblem of youth were not so conspicuous.

৵   ৵   ৵

3

Bill was a soldier, a private in the First City Troop Philadelphia Cavalry, stationed at Indiantown Gap Military Reservation, Pennsylvania. When he asked if he could have my hand in marriage, my father said, "Not until you get a promotion. How do you expect to support my daughter on twenty-one dollars a month?" (I was glad that Bill was in uniform and the tattoo did not show.)

So my beloved went off to camp and concentrated on being an exemplary trooper. A few weeks later, when he was promoted to corporal, he returned for my father's blessing. That gentleman had meant a promotion to second lieutenant, but had not spelled it out and had to agree to the union. Four months later we were wed on a sweltering 12th of July, 1941.

ᢣ   ᢣ   ᢣ

Our wedding night was to be spent in the bridal suite of the Princeton Inn in Princeton, New Jersey. We had borrowed a family car. Sometime before we got there, a summer storm broke, and the rain came down in torrents. It was 10 P.M. when we finally arrived. Dripping raindrops and rice, Bill approached the reception desk and announced grandly, "Mr. and Mrs. Rodman of Philadelphia."

We were suddenly deflated to find that the sleepy clerk did not jump to attention and show us to our promised haven. Instead, he thumbed through a file of papers looking for our name. Bill's father, his best man, had called just the day before to confirm the reservation and had ordered champagne and roses. Finally, the little man arose and led us down the hall to a very ordinary room with dust covers on the furniture, and horrors: Twin beds! No champagne! No roses! My dashing new husband exploded and chased the clerk back down the hall to the front desk, where the poor devil took refuge behind the counter.

Bill told me to go out on the porch, but through a window I

4

could see him shaking his fist at that trembling little man, whom he had grabbed by the collar and pulled halfway across the counter so that his feet were kicking up and down in the air like a puppet's. Bill disappeared momentarily only to reappear with roses under one arm and champagne under the other. We got in the car and drove off, but not a word was spoken. I wasn't about to interrupt the thought processes of my irate bridegroom.

Finally the ice cracked and we both started to laugh. Here we were at 11 P.M. in a rain storm, heading for New York City, and nowhere to go on our wedding night. I believe I said, "Why don't we call the Waldorf Astoria?"—probably the only hotel I had heard of in New York, so we stopped at a Howard Johnson to call. Bill sat me down at a table and went off to telephone the hotel. He came back grinning. Evidently there was a night manager on duty who had been married just two weeks previously, and after hearing Bill's story, he warmed to the situation. He told Bill not to worry—just come along and leave it to him.

We pulled into the underground garage at the Waldorf around 12:30 A.M. It must have been a slow night, for as we entered, bellboys and charwomen, with crossed mops, West Point style, were lined up to clap us along. The night manager himself showed us to Suite 16. There in the sitting room were fresh red roses, and champagne in a cooler. The bridal chamber had the appropriate double bed.

The next morning we were ravenously hungry and called room service to order breakfast. As we loved bacon, we decided that one order would not be enough, only two pieces, perhaps three, so Bill asked for four rashers of bacon, plus eggs, toast, juice and coffee. A waiter soon appeared pushing a large, shining, stainless-steel trolley which, when the hood was rolled back, revealed thirty-two pieces of bacon!

We were to spend our honeymoon at a friend's cottage in Southwest Harbor, Maine. To get there, we had reservations for

5

ourselves and the car on one of the old Eastern Steamship Line ships which sailed from New York at noon, and arrived Boston sometime the next day. After breakfast, Bill went down to settle the Waldorf bill. As we had only $200 for our entire trip, Bill was more than a little nervous. After all, Suite 16 at the Waldorf could be costly! Our friendly night manager was still on duty, and bid my husband into his office.

"Was everything all right, Mr. Rodman?"

"Oh yes, everything was wonderful. Thank you."

The young manager removed the bill from a drawer and started to hand it to Bill. Suddenly, with a flourish, he tore it in two, and said, "Compliments of the Waldorf."

We gratefully waved good-bye to Manhattan and set off on the adventure of a lifetime.

July 12, 1941

Chapter Two

THE WAR YEARS
1941–1945

FORT KNOX, KENTUCKY

IN THE AUTUMN OF 1941, while Bill and I were enjoying the first weeks of marital bliss, Germany continued to rattle its military armor in Europe. As his armies invaded further and further into Russia, Hitler shook his fist at the world and carried out a relentless persecution of Jews and other non-Aryan people. Because daylight air raids had proved too costly during the Battle of Britain, he now concentrated on night bombing and U-boat attacks on British shipping. Although the draft was in effect, and the United States was mobilizing, the U.S. had not entered the war. As we listened to Churchill's famous words of "blood, sweat and tears," we worried about our friends the British, and prayed that God would save the King and his subjects.

Then, on December 7, 1941, the scales were tipped. Japan attacked Pearl Harbor, and President Roosevelt made his grave declarations of war against Germany, Italy and Japan. Soon after, Bill went to Fort Knox, Kentucky, to Officers' Candidate School (OCS), and I followed in our little rattletrap black Ford, the "Willywog," which we had bought for $40. Upon arriving in Louisville, a 780-mile trip, up, down and around the mountains of Virginia, West Virginia, and Kentucky, it sputtered and died.

No amount of coaxing could make it go another inch. I had been safely delivered to my destination, and that was it.

In Louisville, I rented a small second-floor apartment in a vintage Victorian house. The landlady, a tiny white-haired woman named Mrs. Boney, lived downstairs and cooked pancakes every morning, sending a pleasant aroma throughout the house. This was our first married home. I spent a good part of the week preparing for Bill who would come in from camp on Saturday afternoon. My first dinner was a disaster. I burned the steaks and cooked the peas in the top of a double boiler, turning them into B-B shot. I also failed army inspection. My soldier husband, a bit carried away with the spit and polish of OCS, would run his finger over the woodwork as was done in his barracks by an officer with white gloves. And so I learned the rudiments of housewifery. We were grateful for the few moments we shared.

CAMP POLK, LOUISIANA

Bill graduated from OCS on July 4, 1942, and was assigned to the Third Armored Division stationed at Camp Polk, near Leesville, Louisiana. As he was given a short leave before reporting for duty, my spanking new second lieutenant and I took a train to New Orleans where I was pop-eyed at the night life of Bourbon Street. I am still pop-eyed at the memory of a woman standing on a ledge behind a bar twirling her naked breasts, one clockwise, the other counter clockwise, with golden tassels attached to her nipples. At a night club called the Puppy House, a young lady did a strip show on stage; then, entirely naked except for the briefest of G-strings, proceeded to walk among the tables greeting customers. At our table, she sat down. I did a lot of growing up that first year of our marriage.

Before leaving New Orleans we made an advanced booking at a hotel in Leesville. As it rated one star, we guessed it would be OK. We would journey over night by train to Lake Charles, Louisiana, then a long bus trip to Leesville. The only accommodation available on the train was a single upper birth. If you, the reader, are not too young, you will remember the Pullman trains of yesteryear. The sleeping cars had a narrow center aisle with upper and lower births along each side. For privacy, and to keep passengers from falling out, heavy green curtains snapped onto the side of each bunk.

Being young and in love, we survived that trip and the succeeding long, hot bus ride through the arid flatlands of Louisiana. Leesville was a dusty little town, bulging at the seams with soldiers from Camp Polk. We checked into the hotel and went to our room on the second floor. I remember it as being stuffy, scruffy and spacious with a lumpy double bed and a large ceiling fan—a far cry from the Waldorf Astoria. Bill had to leave me almost immediately to report at camp. I had developed a huge sty on one eye, so did not venture out of my room which may have been providential. I vividly remember heavy footsteps going up and down the hall all night long and the sound of knocking on doors, but being naive, I thought nothing of it. Therefore, the following morning when my agitated husband came storming through the door, I was surprised. I had not expected him until the weekend. He had gone to Camp Polk, reported for duty, and had met some of his OCS mates who were bemoaning the fact that they couldn't bring their wives.

"Why not?" asked my blue-eyed second lieutenant. "I brought mine."

"Oh," said a friend. "Is she staying with friends in Leesville?"

"No," answered Bill. "She is staying at the . . . hotel."

After a pause, Bill caught the drift.

"It's not?" said he.

"It is!" said his friend.

"Oh, my God!" said Bill.

He sweated out the night, and the next morning requested

permission to go to Leesville, explaining the reason to a sympathetic first sergeant who told him to take a jeep and be off.

I cannot recall Bill's words when he burst into my room at a very early hour of the morning. I can only remember panic packing, and running hand-in-hand to the railroad station where a troop train was in the process of being loaded. Hundreds of soldiers milled about the platform. Somewhere in my past, I had been advised to latch onto an officer in such a situation, and quickly found a handsome second lieutenant whose little brass nameplate said Taliaferro. He explained to me that in Virginia his name was pronounced Tolliver, a strange throwback to early settlers, I suppose. Bill was unhappy over this arrangement, but could do nothing under the circumstances, and Lt. Taliaferro and I boarded, found two seats together, and waved good-bye to my unsmiling soldier husband.

THE MOHAVE DESERT, CALIFORNIA

Before long I was again on the move. After only a few days at Camp Polk, Bill's division was sent to the Mohave Desert in California for maneuvers, and I followed by train from Philadelphia to Chicago where I boarded a tourist sleeper for Palm Springs, California. The cast on board included draftees, a group of young Polish pilots-in-training, military wives—some with babies—musicians and entertainers of varied talent, poker-playing businessmen, a wrestler and his entourage, and a group of soldiers who had been wounded at Pearl Harbor and were returning home from a hospital in Springfield, Illinois. Everyone mingled and shared experiences. I had never traveled west of Pittsburgh and was thrilled to see the great western plains and cities as I counted off Illinois, Missouri, Kansas, Oklahoma, Texas, New Mexico, Arizona, California. Again I had an upper bunk, but the train was not as modern as the one in Louisiana;

the partitions between the upper bunks did not go to the ceiling, leaving a two-foot space at the head and foot between you and your neighbor. As I was nodding off on the first night out, a little balled up wad of paper landed on my chest. It was not an invitation to tea. Frightened, I climbed down from my bunk, and spent that night sitting up with the Pullman porter as security guard. The following evening, I was given a safer lower birth.

જી   જી   જી

Bill could not get leave to meet me at Palm Springs, but had sent a fellow officer who took me to the lovely little *Casa del Camino* that Bill had rented. I had never seen anything so beautiful—living room, bedroom, bath, kitchen and veranda, all in a neat semi-detached adobe unit with red tile roof and a profusion of pink bougainvillea climbing the outside walls. Compared to Mrs. Boney's dowdy apartment, this, our second home, was vibrant and shining like a seashell.

Today, Palm Springs is awash with celebrities, but in the summer of 1942, it was still a sun-baked, sleepy little town, surrounded by desert with a backdrop of purple mountains. Only a few of the rich and famous had begun to dribble in. Outlying areas were already developing rapidly with groupings here and there of attractive one-story houses and condominiums, all with the ubiquitous red-tiled roofs, flower-filled courtyards, and swimming pools. In July and August, a temperature reading of 115 degrees was not unusual, but we cooled off in the pools and thought of the poor men out on the desert where it would go as high as 135 degrees. When the sun went down, it was cooler and the sunsets blazed across the desert. Creepy-crawlies abounded, as well as rattlesnakes, coyotes and lizards. I was less than happy the day I found a scorpion in my kitchen.

Among the officers' wives and children, instant friendships developed. No one had a car, so we rented bicycles, went horseback riding over vast stretches of sagebrush, read, sun-

11

bathed, swam, and chattered the hours away. Occasionally we lunched and swam at the beautiful Desert Inn. Living was reasonable. We paid $55 a month for our bungalow, fifty cents to hire a horse, and a number of swimming pools were open to army wives for as little as a nickel. The men had leave about every other weekend. We never knew when they would appear, dirty and tired, with desert sand in every pore.

♪   ♪   ♪

One day, a group of wives rented a car and drove about 120 miles to the maneuver area near Blythe, California, where we had an inside view of big mechanized troop movements. I had not even guessed how tough it was to be a desert soldier. Sand and thirst were the two worst enemies. Each man's water was rationed, but no amount quenched the thirst.

A sudden sandstorm caught us in a convoy between two heavy tanks. The inside of our car became so filled with sand dust that, from the back seat, I could barely see the driver. By staying two or three feet behind the tank in front, she could just make out its outline to use as a guide. At one point, the driver of the tank behind us didn't see that the convoy had stopped and might have demolished our car had he not swerved off the road at the last second. In a sandstorm, visibility is clearer looking back than ahead, so I spotted that monstrous thing long before he saw us and was frightened beyond the telling. In addition to the racket of the armored vehicles, airplanes flew so low over the convoy that men in the turrets of tanks could almost shake hands with pilots of planes. The storm and noise lasted for about twenty miles, but all the way back to Palm Springs, the sand in the air invaded our sensory organs.

Remembering this experience, I have had more sympathy and understanding for the men and women of Operation Desert Storm during the Persian Gulf War in January, 1991.

ॐ   ॐ   ॐ

On one occasion, Bill was put in charge of a convoy of trucks carrying enlisted men on weekend leave to Riverside, California. He stopped the convoy in front of Casa del Camino just long enough to tell me to rent a car and meet him there. During the war, hotels were more than willing to accommodate soldiers and their wives at very reasonable rates. We spent the night at the beautiful Mission Inn, once a monastery, enjoying untold luxury. I remember flowers and wine in the room, compliments of the management, and walking through the ancient catacombs. I still have a bill from the Mission Inn. The room, including breakfast and dinner, was $9. But, in addition to giving special treatment to soldiers, a warm feeling of unity and camaraderie existed everywhere in the United States. We were pulling together, proud of our soldiers and country.

Coming back to Palm Springs, Bill drove with me at the head of the convoy, and for fifty-three miles, I felt very much a part of the army.

At another time, we rented a car and drove to Los Angeles where we saw the new Lillian Hellman play, *Watch On the Rhine,* with Paul Lukas, then dined and danced the night away at Hollywood's famous Coconut Grove. A skinny Frank Sinatra was at a nearby table. The following morning we were given passes to Paramount Studios where we were free to roam the make-believe sets, and watch the filming of the sleeping bag scene in *For Whom the Bell Tolls* with Gary Cooper and Ingrid Bergman. They repeated the same scene over and over and I thought it miraculous that they could work up the prerequisite passion for every take. During a break, they both sat outside the studio on a bench studying lines while we sat admiring them a few feet away. I was tempted to ask for their autographs, but restrained myself at Bill's urging.

ॐ   ॐ   ॐ

After the blistering heat of July and August, Palm Springs unfolded like a flower in early October. Shops reopened, rents went up, and movie stars returned to their exclusive desert homes. Within a football kick of our adobe, William Powell had his rambling ranch style house. (He was a big box office attraction in 1942 along with Myrna Loy, his partner in the popular *Thin Man* series.) And a bit further on, the actor Adolf Menjou returned to his elegant retreat.

CAMP PICKETT, VIRGINIA

In October, maneuvers were over and the division was ordered to Camp Pickett, Virginia. Because of my past train experience, Bill decided it wiser to put me on a plane. At the last minute, however, when I found that Kay, another army wife, was going east by train, he agreed that two ladies traveling together erased some of the risk, and that it would be less costly. The day before I left, I was sitting on my veranda and looked up to see two airplanes flying dangerously close. In the next horrific second, they collided and went down in a ball of fire, crashing into San Jacinto Mountain only a mile or two away. One was an American Airlines transport. I had been scheduled on that plane.

᯾   ᯾   ᯾

Unlike my trip west three months before, a clean modern train carried Kay and me eastward. A kind porter gave us a vacant compartment for the nominal sum of $1 each. This was more than compensated for in an intense poker game with three army officers who didn't guess my wily ways at gambling, and thought a twenty-one-year-old unsophisticate would be a pushover. I cleaned them out of $35, a fortune to me.

During those early years of our marriage, I had to carry proof of my age in order to get a drink. No amount of play acting could convince anyone that I was a ripe twenty-one years old.

Our ticket took us to Richmond, Virginia, where Kay and I boarded a Greyhound bus for Blackstone. We hopscotched from there to every little town in the area of Camp Pickett, knocking on doors, and found it impossible to find accommodation of any kind. We were amazed at the plethora of Jezebels who converged on army camps during war time. As we of decorous upbringing were anxious to have a place before the men arrived, we had to settle for a large downstairs apartment in an old brick house in Farmville, Virginia, thirty miles from camp. There were two bedrooms, and we would share the kitchen, living room and bath.

ॐ   ॐ   ॐ

Two memorable events happened during this period. Bill was promoted to first lieutenant, and I became pregnant. We knew it wouldn't be long before his division would be sent overseas, the future uncertain. I only knew that we were very much in love and that I wanted his child, whether or not he returned. We had been trying to conceive for several months without success, and while on Christmas leave in Philadelphia, we went to see a lady gynecologist, a colleague of Dr. Rodman's, to be examined. Bill still blushes at the thought. When this ordeal was over, she sat us down in her office and said, "Children, your only problem is that you are trying too hard. You need to relax. I suggest you buy a half pint of whiskey and drink it down. Then, go to bed."

Nine months later, a son was born.

INDIANTOWN GAP MILITARY RESERVATION, PENNSYLVANIA

In April, the division was again transferred, this time to Indiantown Gap, Pennsylvania, the very place where Bill had started his military training two years before. We had gone full circle and had ended up eighty or so miles from our homes on the Main Line of Philadelphia.

We found a small apartment over a garage on a farm near the military reservation. I had recovered from bouts of morning sickness and was busy sewing handmade garments for the baby whom we dubbed "little Bimbo" after a storybook monkey. I remember laboriously featherstitching in blue, figuring that girls could wear blue but that boys could not wear pink. What a special time it was to be pregnant with a much wanted child! I felt exalted, and set apart from the rest of the human race, as if Bill and I were the only ones who could have been so clever as to transact this miracle of impending birth.

In June, when the weather became warm, we moved a short distance to a summer chautauqua called Mt. Gretna. The pretty resort area was situated on a lake, with cabins nestled here and there in a large pine forest. We bought a spirited brown-and-white setter puppy to keep me company during the long hours when Bill was at camp, and named him Roddy. As he ran back and forth along the pine needle paths sniffing and exploring, I did not realize the danger posed by the long rope which I used as a leash. One day, in his puppy exuberance, he wound the rope around my legs and I suddenly found myself two feet off the ground. I was not hurt, only frightened that I might have jarred the baby loose. We did not have a telephone, but good sense told me to get on our bed with my legs elevated, and this is how Bill found me upon returning from camp. When he heard my story, he raced back to the base to fetch one of the division doctors who reassured us that "little Bimbo," at five-and-a-half months along, would not likely be dislodged by a bump, but to be on the safe side, to stay in bed and quiet for a few days.

CAMP KILMER, NEW JERSEY

In late August, 1943, the Third Armored Division moved to Camp Kilmer, New Jersey, the final staging area before going overseas. Bill's very pregnant "bride" moved to his family home in Wynnewood, Pennsylvania, to await our baby's arrival. Even now, some fifty-eight years down the road, Bill still calls me his "bride."

I saw Bill one more time before his division embarked for England. On a six-hour pass, he met me in Philadelphia and I was stunned to find him with a shaved head. The order had come down from headquarters that every man in the division should have a crewcut of no more than a quarter of an inch. Four of the men in Bill's platoon turned up at reveille with shaved heads. As the lieutenant had bragged that he would have a shorter haircut than any man in his platoon, they challenged him to do the same. I mourned his beautiful blond wavy hair for days.

At dinner, feeling sad and anxious, we held hands across the table and listened to the sad strains of "I'll Be Seeing You." A woman in the cafe was going from table to table reading palms. After examining Bill's, she glanced at my billowing shape, and said with a smile, "Don't worry, darling. He will be here when the baby is born."

Three days later, Bill was on the high seas. Six weeks later, William Louis Rodman, Jr. was born on Oct. 16, 1943.

THE LONG WAIT

Our son's birth was difficult, but not only because my husband was overseas. At that time, "caudal" or "spinal" anesthesia was in the experimental stage, and a young doctor at the Lying-in Hospital in Philadelphia was one of the pioneers. Having my baby would be a breeze, he explained. I would feel nothing, and would be able to sip a chocolate milkshake while listening to a baseball game on the radio during the delivery. He was so persuasive that I innocently agreed and signed a form. What he did not explain was that the baby had to be in perfect alignment for delivery before the anesthetic could be administered into my spine. Bill, Jr. was not entirely in the breech position, but close to it, and it took forty hours of difficult labor to straighten him out. I was so worn out and desperate toward the end of this long ordeal that had someone opened the window of my room, four stories up, I might have gone out. Under the circumstances, the doctors should have realized that I was not a good candidate for their experimentation. Also, the actual delivery was botched. A rectal fistula developed which caused painful spasms until I underwent surgery two months later. It is interesting to note that my fashionable,

Bill Rodman in England before the invasion.

but alcoholic Philadelphia obstetrician committed suicide some three or four months after our baby was born.

Although my father was fifty-one years old and had been wounded during World War I, he applied for and received back his old commission of captain, and went off to Officer's Training School somewhere in Florida where one of his barracks' mates was Clark Gable. He loved military life. When Bill, Jr. was born, my father was working in an Air Force Intelligence Unit in Washington, D.C. and he and my mother had moved to Alexandria, Virginia. This is where I went with our new baby whom we called "Chip" or "Billy." This healthy, happy boy with blue eyes and blond hair became my friend, my life, my joy, my little love.

જ્ર   જ્ર   જ્ર

At 4 A.M. on the morning of June 6, 1944, we awoke to shouting in the streets. D-Day! The Americans had stormed the coast of France and we were now fully involved in the war in Europe. I cuddled our baby even closer and prayed. I did not know whether Bill was among the first troops to land. As it turned out, his division was prepared to cross the Channel on D-Day, but this plan was aborted because of a storm. Whereas landing craft carrying infantry could make it in rough weather, landing craft carrying tanks, could not. Later, I found out that he did land at Omaha Beach on D-plus-3, and soon after was appointed a company commander with the rank of captain.

જ્ર   જ્ર   જ્ર

During the summer of 1944, my father developed a breathing problem. He was sent to Walter Reed Hospital for tests which indicated a serious heart condition, and was medically discharged from military service. The doctors further advised him not to return to his investment business in Philadelphia, but to retire

19

and take it easy. As he had grown up in Richmond, he had dreamed of retirement in Virginia. He and mother drove to Charlottesville where he had graduated from the University of Virginia in 1912. When they returned to Alexandria, they were all smiles. They had found a beautiful house to rent called "Orchard House" in Ivy, Virginia, seven miles west of Charlottesville.

We moved in the autumn of 1944 when little Bill was just a year old. He was now walking in his new brown shoes. Among other things, "shoe white" had gone to war. To this day one little brown shoe hangs on our Christmas tree. I fell in love with the lush green countryside of Albemarle County and the Blue Ridge Mountains rising in the distance. I remember thinking that this was a place where someday I would like to settle, a wish that came true thirty-seven years later.

As a war effort, I volunteered to work on a farm, Clay Hill, six miles west of Orchard House. For the most part, I drove a tractor, plowing the rich red clay soil. This entitled me to claim coupons for gasoline so that I could drive back and forth. As Charlottesville was not a likely target, we did not need air raid shelters, sirens or blackout curtains. We did have rationing of sugar, tobacco, liquor, gasoline and other commodities needed for the military, but, being seven miles from the city and the nearest bank and market, gasoline was the only major problem.

My dear friend, Mary Cam Wilde, lived about two miles away. Her husband was overseas and her son, Jimmy, was a year older than little Bill, whom I would push in his stroller over the bumpy dirt roads to her farm, "Westleigh." While the little boys played, we mothers played penny-ante poker and talked about our husbands. War widows needed someone in similar circumstances with whom to share their fears and dreams, and we found that outlet in each other. Copying the farm hands, three-year-old Jimmy adopted the strange habit of calling his mother "Mrs. Wilde." One day he appeared in the doorway of the living room where Mary Cam and I were talking. It must have been a conversation we did not wish interrupted, as he kept repeating, "Mrs. Wilde?" with more and more urgency in his voice. When his mother finally said, "What is it, Jimmy?" the little boy answered, "the tat's in the fridgerfrater, Mrs. Wilde." And sure enough, that is just where the cat was.

ᔓ   ᔓ   ᔓ

On Christmas morning, I awakened feeling very uneasy. Anxiety continued to build within me to the absolute bursting point and I ran out of the house sobbing. I ran on until exhausted, and fell under a clump of bushes where I lay for some time. All of a sudden a sense of peace came over me which I did not understand any more than my feeling of despair only an hour before. I returned home calmly, and confided in my aunt who was visiting over the Christmas holiday. That evening while we were having dinner, the telephone rang. A friend in Philadelphia said, "Isn't it wonderful about Bill?" I did not understand. She then explained that his picture was on the front page of the *Philadelphia Evening Bulletin* accompanied by a story of heroism during fierce fighting in the Battle of the Bulge. He and remnants of his company, surrounded by the enemy in the small Belgian town of Hotton, had fought off a superior German force, denying them an important bridge and crossroads leading to Liege. The fighting had continued for four days and nights until relief arrived on Christmas Day. Bill received a serious back injury which would plague him for the rest of his life, and later he would be awarded a Silver Star for heroism, but he was spared. God must have had a hand in my strange extrasensory experience on Christmas Day.

ᔓ   ᔓ   ᔓ

On April 12, 1945, the world was stunned by the news of President Franklin Delano Roosevelt's death at Warm Springs,

Georgia. Although he had appeared drawn and tired of late, his death was nevertheless unexpected. This famous American had been in the White House for an unprecedented three terms of office and was well into a fourth. Many young servicemen could hardly remember another president. As a young man, he had been afflicted with polio, and for years had propelled his body painfully but valiantly on crutches until confined to a wheel chair. Roosevelt's years as president had been racked with The Great Depression, unemployment, and war. His popularity was controversial, but even those who didn't like his manner or politics, admired his courage, and mourned his death.

The new president, Harry S. Truman, was a little-known enigma to the American people. As vice-president he had seemed a retiring small town politician from Missouri, hardly worth a second glance, a complete contrast to the aristocratic, articulate and compelling personage of Roosevelt. But, as president, he became a man of wisdom, decision, and good sense, growing in stature with every passing day.

With the coming of spring, the Allied Forces were forty miles from Berlin. The war in Europe was drawing to a close, and the war in the Pacific was close behind. On May 6, 1945, President Truman spoke his famous "Victory in Europe" triplet over the radio—"Peace is Here, Peace is Here, Peace is Here."

And nineteen-month-old Billy Rodman helped his grandfather place an American flag in the middle of our garden.

꙳   ꙳   ꙳

For the first time in twenty months, I knew that Bill would come home and that our little son would know his father. The once sad song at parting, "I'll Be Seeing You," now became my happy theme song. I prepared and planned our reunion, feeling like a bride all over again.

Around that time, Billy got into trouble. He was now big enough to climb out of his crib. One afternoon while having his nap, he toddled into his grandmother's dressing room where an assortment of little perfume bottles attracted his attention. He carried several to his room in a plastic sandbox bucket, and climbed back into his crib. When I found him, all had been emptied, or swallowed—or both. It took weeks to rid Billy, the crib and the room of the mixed aromas of Chanel No. 5, Arpége, and My Sin.

At another time, my parents were entertaining friends and three or four cars were parked in the driveway. At gas stations, Billy had carefully observed how tanks were filled. It was a beautiful summer evening and he was playing outside. To be helpful, he managed to remove the gas caps of two of the cars, then took the garden hose and filled the tanks. When the guests tried to depart, their cars wouldn't start, and the culprit was soon identified. I heard a commotion and looked out the window to see my father dragging little Bill by the ear and sputtering, "I want this child spanked!" When it came to my father's disciplinary measures, mother and son had an understanding, but I took him upstairs to carry out the sentence.

Besides, in this case, the little boy had thought he was being helpful. So I put him over my knee, and with one hand palm up on his rump, I clapped. Billy knew what to do. He yelled.

چ   چ   چ

In mid-October, the long awaited telegram arrived. My parents were not at home and Billy was napping. Bursting with the good news, I dashed out of the house and found Sylvester, the yard man, working in our Victory Garden. He must have had a few moments of alarm wondering what had prompted this joyous outbreak.

When the magical time arrived, I left Billy with my parents and went by train to New York City to meet my beloved. More than two years had passed, during which time he had endured a terrible

23

war. I tried but couldn't quite conjure up his face, his smile, his laugh. Would he be the same? Had I changed? Had time pulled us apart? What would he think of the son he had never seen? I imagine these same questions pass through the minds of every young couple who has lived through a long separation.

I arrived at Grand Central Station at 5:30 A.M. where returning soldiers and their wives made hotel bookings. Even at that hour of the morning, the queue was long. Several desks had been set up and behind them was a large blackboard. On this was written the names of hotels with vacancies. They were an impressive lot—the St. Regis, the Plaza, the Waldorf, the Ritz, and more. Remembering our wedding night, I hoped for the Waldorf, but by the time I got to the head of the line, it was sold out; I chose the St. Regis. In normal times we could not have afforded such luxury, but returning soldiers were treated like conquering heroes and offered huge discounts. The tab was $6 a night for servicemen.

I settled into our room. The arrangement was that when Bill reached Fort Dix, New Jersey, he would phone his mother, whom I would have already called, and she would relay the message as to which hotel I had selected. Not knowing what time Bill would arrive, I was afraid to venture out. Television had not yet intruded upon humankind, and I was too excited to read, so I passed away the hours taking bubble baths and primping. At five o'clock in the afternoon, I heard a knock on the door and my heart skipped a beat. It was only a bellboy carrying a tremendous duffel bag. A touch miffed, I tried to understand why Bill had not accompanied his luggage. I gave the bellboy a tip and tried to collect myself. In a few minutes, another knock. It was Bill. Later, he explained that he had sent his bags ahead because he didn't have money to tip the bellboy, and didn't want his first words to be, "Have you a quarter?" During a ten-day delay at Camp Lucky Strike in France while waiting to board a victory ship for home, a shrewd major had taught Bill how to play gin rummy; the unhappy result was that Bill was skinned of his few hundred dollars of combat pay, and his German pistol collection. He had borrowed just enough cash for a train ticket to New York from Fort Dix, where he had been discharged on terminal leave. For lack of taxi fare he had lugged his duffel bag from Grand Central Station to the St. Regis.

That evening, as we were waiting to cross the street to go to dinner, an automobile backfired, and my soldier husband hit the pavement—flat. This was the first indication that there would be readjustment and nightmare problems ahead.

After a brief visit with his parents, Bill and I left Philadelphia by train for Charlottesville and the long awaited meeting of father and son. Billy was now a sturdy two-year-old. As we drove through the "Orchard House" gate, he was playing in the rose garden in his little navy blue coat and red Eton cap. When he saw us, he came running across the lawn, gave me a hug, then looked up at the tall soldier by my side. His first words to his father were, "Read me a story—please?" Then he took his father's hand and led him into the house and up to his room to find a favorite book.

And so we started a new chapter together as a family of three.

October 1945 at the Glass Hat restaurant in New York City,
Bill Rodman's first night home after two years overseas.

· —— Chapter Three —— ·

THE COLLEGE YEARS
January 1946 to September 1948

WHEN BILL AND I WERE ENGAGED, he suggested that after the war we might acquire a government land grant in the Matanooska Valley in Alaska. This sounded fine to me. I was so in love and starry–eyed, I would have settled on Devil's Island. When, however, he learned that he could continue a university education under the G. I. Bill of Rights, he began to have second thoughts. He also felt increasingly the responsibilities of husband and father. We were both sports enthusiasts, loving nature and the great out-of-doors. As he could not bear the thought of a career behind a desk, he decided on an agricultural career— someday, he hoped, on a farm of our own.

In January 1946, Bill enrolled in the School of Agriculture at Virginia Polytechnic Institute (V.P.I.) in Blacksburg. We found a little upstairs apartment for $40 a month if Bill stoked the furnace and mowed the lawn. We could hardly afford more on $90 a month from the government, and a small allowance from "Poppadoc," Bill's father. To enhance our income, we both grabbed whatever odd jobs we could find. Bill washed dishes at the Gobbler Grill, and I peddled Merrimade paper products door–to–door with our son in tow. We both corrected freshman themes for 25 cents an hour.

One opportunity that came along was "beets." That summer beets were a glut on the market in our area and were being given away to poor students. We acquired two or three bushel baskets full, took them to the local cannery, canned them ourselves for a pittance, and ended up with enough beets to feed a battalion of starving men. Years later, we were still struggling to eat through this noble effort.

In November, I again became pregnant. A favorite recreation in the months that followed were Saturday afternoon picnics with fellow married G. I. students. To reach one of our picnic spots, we had to walk through a pasture where cattle were grazing. On one occasion, when I was about eight months along, we did not notice a large bull who picked me out as easy prey. As he came charging toward me, I dropped my bundles and ran for dear life. When I reached the bank of a stream, I jumped about eight feet across it, and, after catching my breath, looked back. The animal had stopped. He was pawing the ground and bellowing on the other bank. This experience is proof of what one can do when the adrenalin is pumping. I seemed to have my jolts when pregnant, but again the baby within me held on.

Bill had studied throughout the previous summer, but in 1947 it seemed best for me to be at "Orchard House" in Charlottesville, so that I could be close to the University of Virginia Hospital where our child would be born. There was a swimming pool at "Orchard House" where friends congregated on hot summer days, and where Billy, now nearly four, learned to swim. Because of the difficulties encountered with our firstborn, I was apprehensive. I need not have been. Channing's birth at the end of July was a breeze. We named her after my father, Channing Williams Daniel, figuring that the name was so unusual that it could be used for boy or girl. Had the baby been a boy, we had promised to name him John Stewart after Bill's father who was very verbal about wanting a namesake. Therefore, in order to realize a male Channing, I would have to produce three sons, and this possibility seemed remote. Thus, our beautiful baby girl with reddish fuzz atop her head and big brown eyes acquired a very big name for a very little lady. I felt quite clever to have birthed a boy and then a girl. Our family now seemed complete.

For $65 we had bought an old, gray, four-door Plymouth which struggled to stay alive for almost six more years. We called her the "Old Gray Mare." The rear right door wouldn't close so we had to leave a crack in both front and back windows in order to secure an old leather belt around the two doors.

When we returned to Blacksburg for the fall semester, we moved to a larger apartment in the same building. It was a busy life. For starters, Pampers were not yet on the scene. For months I washed diapers and clothes in a tub on the back porch in all kinds of weather, and hung them out to dry. In winter they would freeze on the line. Small wonder that our introduction to the installment plan was a Maytag washing machine. We paid $4 a month, and were still paying long after we had departed from both Blacksburg and the Maytag.

Billy was four and went to preschool that winter. The little school house was across town so I must have taken him there in the "Old Gray Mare," with Channing rattling around in the back seat. Car seats for children had not been invented, and I often reflect on the dangers involved, especially when I see young mothers of today strapping in their little charges for safety. I recall a morning when there was a loud knock on the front door. A very tall policeman was holding a little boy's hand. "Is this your kid?" he asked. It was. Billy had decided he didn't like school that day and had somehow escaped. He was in the middle of town and halfway home when picked up. I often wonder if he would have found his way to the apartment two miles distant like a small human Lassie.

An early father–to–son gift was a pair of very small boxing gloves. I observed with interest a father's reaction to a son whom he had not known as a baby. The little boy would stand on his bed while Bill, who was on his knees on the floor, encouraged his son to tuck one small mitt under his chin and jab with his right while bouncing up and down on the mattress. Next, Billy was coached to attempt a sudden strike with the left. Bill figured that the way for a boy to get along in this world was to be strong and tough, to eat everything, clean his plate, and control tears— perhaps an obscure reaction to the war and the hell he had been through. Like his nightmares, filial problems had to be worked out and it would take time, but little Bill did not have an easy time growing up. Being tough was contrary to his nature. As a result, he later shunned bodily contact sports, and turned his attention to books. A firstborn child is as loved as any succeeding child, but, having no former knowledge of raising children, parents must experiment on their eldest. They read a lot of how-the-twig-is-bent-so-grows-the-tree books and then bend away until the little twig breaks. By the time a second or third child comes along, they throw away the books and use common sense.

ೲ   ೲ   ೲ

Bill's back was giving him increasing problems during these years. His discomfort stemmed from the time he was injured in Belgium. At times, the pain became so acute that he had to wear a brace and walk with a cane, often struggling to get to classes. On several occasions, only a shot of novocaine into his back would relieve the agony. At other times, the pain would subside, and he would be fairly comfortable for a few months until the pain would again hit him full wallop. During such an attack, his professors were very understanding and would allow him to take exams at home on the honor system. A graduate student brought the papers to our apartment and returned for them at the appointed time. Each recurrence of his back problem seemed a little more severe.

As Bill became better educated in the agricultural sciences, he realized that without a sizable savings account, it would be impossible to purchase a farm of our own. In any event, the wisest course would be to manage someone else's, thereby gaining practical experience and building a reputation. Therefore, when he graduated in the spring of 1948 with honors, he was pleased to be selected from a list of applicants to manage a purebred Aberdeen Angus farm in Brandy, Virginia, owned by Admiral Lewis L. Strauss, then head of the Atomic Energy Commission.

• —— Chapter Four —— •

BRANDY ROCK FARM
September 1948 to January 1951

BRANDY ROCK FARM, NEAR CULPEPER, VIRGINIA, encompassed an area of 1,700 acres of beautiful rolling Virginia countryside with well-fenced pastures for cattle, and productive arable fields of alfalfa, corn, soybeans, and barley. The manager's house was at the south end of the property near the little village of Atlanthus, where the farm hands lived. Painted white with green shutters, it nestled in the center of a half acre of lawn, surrounded by a cross-board white fence. Looking from our porch on that clear September afternoon of our arrival across the expanse of open fields to distant barns, I thought I had never seen a lovelier sight. Billy, now five years old, and Channing, two, all too ready for sweet release from the confines of an automobile, pranced about like happy little goats.

I soon learned the ways of a farm wife. Other wives, living on the property, showed me how to churn butter, pasteurize milk, make sausage, and preserve fruits and vegetables in season. After the children were asleep, I often found myself in the kitchen surrounded by three or four bushel baskets of apples or peaches, and enormous boiling pots on the gas stove. Part of Bill's pay, $2,500 a year plus house and utilities, was a side of beef and a hog. The prepared cuts were kept at a commercial freezer in Culpeper where I would select the week's meat supply each Friday, my shopping day, while Idella, the wife of one of the farmhands, took care of the children. My budget was $13 a week for food and gas, and $2 "mad money." Part of the mad money was spent at Newberry's Five and Ten Cent Store where I bought a trinket for each of the children. Channing called it her "sprise."

Another portion went for a milkshake and sandwich at Lewis Drug Store where I loved to sit on a counter stool and chat with the locals—my weekly social outing. Nowadays, it seems incredible that I could manage on so little, but we did not have to buy meat, milk, or butter, and our larder and freezer were well stocked with farm grown fruits and vegetables.

To add to our family tableau, we had a black mongrel named Brandy, a tiger cat named Nicodemus, and briefly, a pet raccoon which the children found as an abandoned baby. As Brandy had the unlovable habit of chasing heifers and killing chickens, he became unacceptable as a farm dog. We then got a more placid little cocker spaniel named Spring Fever. The inherited cat was also hopeless because he wasn't housebroken, and chose the far reaches of the hall closet as his depository. I tried, but at times was unsuccessful in keeping the closet door closed. One day, Nicodemus was sleeping under the car and Bill backed over him. We mourned and buried him under a maple tree, and I felt guilty in my relief.

Finally, Billy had a brown and white Chincoteague pony whom we named Apple Blossom. She was foaled in Frankfort, Kentucky, and sent to us as a gift by relatives. I will never forget her arrival at Brandy Station where she was off–loaded from a freight train. Encased in a wooden crate, we put her onto a truck for the four-mile journey to the farm. Had she been able to speak, I'm sure she would have told a harrowing tale. The poor little creature was only a baby, about three feet high. Billy and Channing were thrilled. From then on Apple Blossom lived within the fenced area of our yard. She could climb the three steps onto our porch, and many a morning I would awake to find Apple B looking at me through the window of our first floor bedroom. Her disposition was somewhat volatile. When in the right frame of mind, she would lie down and let the children climb on her back. At other times, she would kick and raise a rumpus.

We kept a big galvanized tub full of water for Apple Blossom in the yard. This fascinated our small daughter. One Sunday afternoon, Channing was happily sailing little twigs in the tub. While trying to reach one of her "boats," she leaned too far over the rim. Her feet went off the ground and her head into the water. I shudder to think of it, but had we not glanced in her direction as we were burning trash in an incinerator close by, she might have drowned.

One day, soon after we settled at Brandy Rock Farm, Billy went to the barns with his father. As he reached out to pat a small mongrel dog belonging to one of the men, the animal attacked him and savagely tore the flesh from eye to chin on the right side of his face. Charlie, one of the farmhands, held Billy while Bill, with his hand on the horn, sped home to pick me up. I remember literally holding Billy's face together with a terry cloth towel as we rushed thirteen miles to Culpeper in the pickup truck. We briefly discussed driving fifty miles to the University of Virginia Hospital in Charlottesville, but the child was bleeding so profusely that it was critical we find a local doctor and stop the flow. The first doctor we tried was not at home, but his wife came to the door and told us of a new doctor who had come to town that very day. When we arrived at his house, Dr. Jones was still carrying in furniture from the sidewalk, but it only took seconds for him to size up the situation, grab his doctor's bag, and rush Billy into the house and onto the dining room table. I could not bear to watch and sat outside listening to our son's screams. Bill had the difficult task of holding Billy down, and trying to stabilize his head while the doctor worked for what seemed hours sewing together torn muscles and flesh. It was a terrible moment for Bill and me, and worse for our little boy. The only fortunate part of this episode was that Dr. Jones had been a plastic surgeon during World War II, but had later decided to become a general practitioner in a small Virginia town.

Billy's wounds healed, but we had an anxious wait of three months to be certain the dog, who had been taken off the farm and caged by health officials, did not develop rabies. Had the animal been rabid, we were told that it would have been useless to administer the Pasteur treatment. The wounds were so close to the brain that there would not have been time for the serum to take effect. Like many traumatic experiences, that day is somewhat of a blur. I can't remember what we did with Channing who was just under two. We probably left her with Charlie. I do vividly remember the morning and evening ritual of gently rubbing Billy's scars with Vaseline in hopes they would be less noticeable as he grew. Dr. Jones had done a splendid job and the scars that remain give our son a slightly craggy appearance, quite attractive in a man.

Billy turned six years old on October 16, 1949. He was ready for school, but the law in Virginia stated that a child could not attend first grade unless he had turned six by October 1. I found a solution to this dilemma by ordering a first grade home–teaching course from the Calvert School in Baltimore, Maryland. Our son was already a reader, having been a bookworm since about the age of two, and was more than ready for expanding his academic horizons. Had Channing not been a child that could amuse herself for hours with dolls and toys, teaching Billy at home might have been tricky, but she was used to "Shhh, Daddy's studying," and now it was her brother's turn. At the end of the morning lesson, she was allowed to join in for art work and poetry. I remember both small-fry piping up with "Someone came a-knocking at my wee small door" by Walter de la Mare, and "There was a little turtle. He lived in a box" by Vachel Lindsay. Channing still treasures that little green poetry book called *Silver Pennies.* The following year, Billy went to school in town.

The school bus route from the farm to Culpeper took an hour over dusty winding country roads. Channing and I would walk with Billy to the cattle guard where the bus would pick him up at seven o'clock in the morning, and we would meet him there at four o'clock in the afternoon. In the wintertime, it was dark in the morning and road conditions could be hazardous. Even though Billy was now almost seven, I remember my anxiety at sending him off on such a long day's journey. I also felt completely deflated when, after working so hard to accomplish first grade, I was informed that the Culpeper school system would not accept him into second grade because I was not an accredited teacher. However, Mrs. Bragg, the first grade teacher, explained that as a child could be promoted after the first term, Billy was jumped up to second grade after the Christmas vacation. A favorite story in our family comes from the short period he was in the first grade. Mrs. Bragg called me to say that she had been discussing health habits with her class that morning, and asked Billy what he should do before eating dinner? The somewhat embarrassing answer that popped out was, "Well, last night I went upstairs while Mommy and Daddy had a dry martini!"

ॐ   ॐ   ॐ

Atlanthus, a small village of black families, was comprised of a cluster of clapboard houses, a general store, a church, and a one room schoolhouse. The store was stocked with staples— sugar, flour, molasses and salt in large barrels, bushel baskets of seasonal fruits and vegetables, piece goods, canned food, and penny candy in the glass counter. Customers warmed themselves in front of the pot-bellied stove in cold weather. Sitting on our porch on Sunday evenings, we could hear gospel songs of praise and longing bursting forth from the small Baptist church.

Occasionally, Bill and I attended a funeral. I remember the congregation parading solemnly by the open casket, interjecting "Amen, brother" after each sentence the preacher uttered, and the childlike abandonment of the mourners in their outpouring of grief. The tiny schoolhouse was often without a teacher. Many of the "colored folk" didn't take schooling seriously. Some children only attended long enough to be able to sign their names. Several of our farmhands couldn't read or write and still signed for their checks with an X. One man's name was "Knot" Jasper. His father was Ormsby. Knot came by his name as a young boy when a stranger called at his house looking for his father and asked the child, "Is you Ormsby Junior?"

And the little boy answered, "No, sir, I is *not*." And Knot he was from that day on.

Saturday night in Atlanthus was the night to hoot and holler, gamble the week's earnings, and drink moonshine whiskey. Tempers flared and people were often hurt with knives and guns. Two murders occurred while we were there. The most notable happened at dusk one summer eve. Willie, a slightly retarded farmhand, killed Alice, a laundress who worked for Admiral and Mrs. Strauss. He then tore through the village broadcasting that he had a few more to kill that night. The alarm was sounded and the police arrived with blood hounds. Bill ordered that two men would go to the big house on the hill to protect Mrs. Strauss who was alone, while another two patrolled the farmhouses on our road. As Bill was one of the two to go to the big house a mile away, he took the precaution of sitting me in a chair facing our front door, and handing me a gun with orders to shoot anyone who came onto the porch on foot. The two men patrolling the road would be in a farm truck so I would know not to shoot them. There was a full moon that night and the children were asleep upstairs. I will never forget listening to the bloodhounds yelp their eerie cry which sounded like, "whoop, whoop, whoop," sometimes close, then fading, and back again. When Willie was caught, the prearranged signal was three gunshots into the air. It seemed an interminable time before I heard those shots and could relax. Willie had gone full circle around the neighborhood and the woods beyond. When the bloodhounds caught up with him, he was sitting on his own back porch.

ᔕ   ᔕ   ᔕ

We celebrated Christmas, 1949, at Orchard House in Charlottesville with my parents. Although Bill had to return to the farm the day after Christmas, the children and I stayed on for another week. When my father put us on the train for the short trip to Brandy Station, the hug he gave me seemed a little more special than usual, and the sad look in his eye foreboded something I did not understand at the time. Looking back, I realize that he knew that he might not see us again. He died a few days later of congestive heart failure on January 8, 1950. He was fifty-nine years old. As I knew that mother would need me for a few weeks, we parceled out the children, Channing to Bill's parents in Philadelphia, and Billy to friends in Alexandria. It was the start of a difficult year.

As time went on, Bill's back pain became more acute. There were frequent trips to the University of Virginia Hospital in Charlottesville, but the doctors there finally admitted there was nothing more they could do. Upon hearing this discouraging report, Bill's father, Dr. Rodman, called a colleague, Dr. Alan Bennett, a noted orthopedic surgeon at Johns Hopkins Hospital in Baltimore, for advice. Recently retired, Dr. Bennett had specialized in back problems and had pioneered research on fusing injured vertebrae of the spine with bone taken from the ilium. He recommended we contact a disciple of his, Dr. Josephus Hoover, at the Medical College of Virginia Hospital in Richmond. Although still in experimental stages, Dr. Hoover had had a high rate of success with this operation. We contacted Dr. Hoover with the result that in early October, 1950, we again sent the children to relatives, and went to Richmond. The operation was long and tedious involving both neuro and orthopedic surgeons, but Bill was strong and withstood it well. I became a surrogate farm manager of sorts, and went back and forth between Richmond and Brandy Rock Farm where I tried to oversee operations, and pay the men. At the end of a two month hospital stay, the forty pound body cast was removed and Bill was fitted with a lighter one that laced down the middle for removal at night. He returned to the farm by ambulance and I followed in the car. We retrieved our children just before Christmas, and heralded in the new year, 1951.

For several months, Bill could walk, stand, or lie flat, but could not sit. Dinner was served on the mantelpiece. Finally in the early spring, this second cast was replaced with a smaller one which allowed him to drive and sit down for meals. It was a long painful period for Bill, but also one of relief. The operation had been a success, but the signal was loud and clear that he could not continue a farming career.

One day Bill stopped at a diner for a hamburger and lying on the counter was a little magazine called *Quik*, published, I believe, by the Time/Life Corporation. As he was browsing through it, his eye hit upon a sentence under the heading of "Quik Predicts." It said that the U.S. government planned to hire people trained in agriculture to serve overseas, but no further explanation. The following week Bill drove to Washington in the farm pick-up truck to investigate. Having no idea how or where to start, he first inquired at the State Department. From there he was sent to the Department of Agriculture where he was directed to the Office of Foreign Agricultural Relations (OFAR) on the fifth floor. When he asked to see the administrator he was told that he needed an appointment, and was handed an application form. Still determined, he said he would wait, hours if necessary. Bill is a very charming guy and of course he pulled out all the stops and flirted with the secretary, a Miss Nellie Lee, who later became a dear ally and friend. Finally, the administrator, Dr. Eric Englund, came out of his office and Bill introduced himself, explaining that it was urgent that he talk to him. I'm sure Dr. Englund was taken with this eager young man, and they returned together to his office. The hoped–for interview was in progress.

Bill returned to the farm that evening with high hopes. He felt certain that he had found what he wanted to do with his life. We had often talked about how we would like to travel, and the Office of Foreign Agricultural Relations, which later became the Foreign Agricultural Service (FAS), seemed the answer. Before he had left the office that day, he gave Nellie Lee his application which took about three months to process. (All federal employees are checked by the F.B.I.) Then, sometime in September, we were sitting on our porch enjoying a golden sunset when the phone rang. It was Dr. Englund with good news. Bill had been accepted into the foreign service.

At that time, there were only a few agricultural attache posts overseas. Today, there are sixty-five or more, plus a large office staff in Washington. The attaches are always attached to the United States Embassy, and essentially do market development and trade intelligence. This information is published worldwide with the primary purpose of stabilizing commodity prices and gathering information on the distribution of U.S. agricultural products overseas.

I had enjoyed our three years on Brandy Rock Farm, but was thrilled with the prospect of this new career, and a chance to see the world. As success on a farm is so often controlled by the elements of nature, I looked forward to having more control over our destiny. In a lighter vein, I could hardly wait to escape a three-party telephone line which drove me crazy.

ॐ   ॐ   ॐ

In November, when Bill arrived in Washington to report to OFAR, he was surprised to learn that he was scheduled to go on a late morning plane to Ottawa, Canada, as a member of the American delegation to the Dominion Provincial Agricultural Conference. He did not have a chance to call me until he got to Ottawa.

During his week in Canada, Bill attended a large diplomatic reception at the Chateau Laurier, Ottawa's time–honored hotel. Feeling very alone, and awkward in his wrinkled suit, he was standing in a corner surveying the massive sea of unfamiliar faces when a kindly–looking elderly gentleman approached.

"I've been observing you, son," said the small, white-haired gentleman, " and you look a bit forlorn. Can I do anything for you?"

Bill explained that he had just arrived in Ottawa, felt very out–of–place, and didn't know anybody.

"You do now," said Bill's new friend, "I'm Louis St. Laurent. What is your job?

"I'm new in the U.S. Foreign Service, sir, and attending the Dominion Provincial Conference," Bill replied. "And what do you do, sir?"

As he touched Bill on the shoulder in a friendly gesture, the old man answered, "I'm the Prime Minister of Canada."

కో   కో   కో

After a week in Canada and another in Washington, Bill returned to the farm with the news that he had been assigned to Ottawa as assistant agricultural attache. We took out a loan to buy our first new car—a green four-door Ford—packed up, begged furniture from our parents to be sent ahead, and were on our way just after the first of the year, 1952.

Before we left, the men who worked on Brandy Rock Farm gathered on our porch one evening. Clarence, the spokesman, said they had something they wanted to give us and handed Bill a big box. He opened it to find a three–masted square rigger with chrome sails and a clock in its plastic hull. I'm sure they thought it was the most beautiful farewell present they could possibly find for the boss. I know that there were tears in our eyes as we thanked them.

Billy, Channing and Apple Blossom at Brandy Rock Farm.

· —— Chapter Five —— ·

CANADA
January 1952 to September 1953

THE SNOW FELL HEAVILY AS WE DROVE NORTH FROM BRANDY, a foretelling of things to come. Billy read as always, and Channing played happily with her dolls and crayons. We stopped for the night at a motel near Albany, New York. This was the children's first motel experience, and they immediately went "exploring," a custom they were to repeat over and over in the years ahead.

We arrived at our destination to find that Ottawa was in the grip of a freeze that would make a penguin shiver. Someone told us the temperature had fallen to twenty below zero, an exaggeration perhaps, but, having come from the moderate climate of Virginia, we believed it. In such weather we were warned to cover nose and ears when out–of–doors, as they could freeze just waiting for a traffic light to change.

Our small house was a corner duplex on Springfield Road just below the affluent section of Rockcliffe Park where many diplomats lived, and where the U.S. Embassy residence was located. Although not what we would have chosen, we were grateful for the newly acquired furniture from our parents. One item was a monstrous Victorian mahogany sofa with blue velvet upholstery which had graced the surgery in Bill's grandfather's waiting room in Victorian Philadelphia. It occupied a large portion of the small living room and was insufferably uncomfortable.

Another was a grandfather clock which had appropriately been left to me in my grandfather's will. Throughout my growing–up years, this beautiful antique, circa 1810, had graced our hallway where I had been intrigued as a little girl with the rotating disk above the clock face depicting the four seasons. I was proud finally to have it in our possession. Its bold strike had a majesty all its own and its ticking gave rhythm to the passing hours. Bill's parents supplied us with beds, and my mother sent us a dining room table and chairs. In our thirteen years of marriage, it was the first time we had furnished a home. Up until that point, the only piece of furniture we had owned was a knee-hole mahogany desk. During our V.P.I. years, I had driven from Blacksburg to Richmond and had entered Talheimer's furniture department like a royal duchess. I bought the desk for $59, an extravagant sum which we could hardly afford, but it gave me an exalted sense of ownership. Since those days, Bill and I have become more affluent, but this first acquisition of a solid, material object was probably the most fulfilling purchase of my life. Fifty years later, the little knee-hole desk still occupies a corner of Bill's study.

I remember being perplexed by the upstairs windows of our Canadian home. In the frame of the outside storm window were several small holes covered by a piece of wood which could be swiveled open to let in air at night. But even with so little air, it was cold, making it difficult to get out of bed in the morning when the clock-radio burst forth with "The Maple Leaf Forever" at 7 A.M. Someone had recently composed this rousing song which was being pushed as the new Canadian national anthem. The beautiful "O Canada," however, would not be bullied into retirement and is still Canada's proud anthem.

Channing found a built-in playmate in Carol Jean, who lived in the other half of the house. I have two vivid memories of

Carol Jean who was a year older than our daughter. One occurred just before Christmas when Channing ran in from play dissolved in tears. Carol Jean had told her that there wasn't a Santa Claus, and I was unable to repair the damage.

On another occasion, Channing and Carol Jean were playing upstairs while I was entertaining a group of French Canadian ladies at tea. I suddenly noticed that the little girl conversation had taken on an urgent tone, and went to investigate. Somehow, Carol Jean had locked herself in the bathroom and my child was sympathetically supplying her with items slender enough to slip under the half inch space between door and floor. A box of animal crackers, administered one by one, was helpful, along with a few items retrieved from mother's dressing table. Try as I might with a screw driver and an assortment of odd keys, I could not open the door. Finally, I had to go downstairs to rejoin my friends who were making ready to leave with *toujours la politesse* and a few French idioms I did not understand.

By the time Bill returned from the embassy, the supply of half–inch articles had run out, and Carol Jean was in tears. An ambassador's reception was planned for that evening and members of the staff were expected, as always, to arrive fifteen minutes early—guests, 7 P.M., staff, 6:45 P.M.—no excuses. Present time—6 P.M. Bill was grubby and looking forward to a hot shower and change, but first he had to solve the crisis at hand. He tried the odd keys again to no avail and finally had to fetch an extension ladder from a neighbor. A small crowd gathered at the scene, plus an agitated mother whose child was now screaming bloody murder. As the crowd hooted encouragement, Bill ascended the ladder, wriggled his body head first through a tiny bathroom window, and released the hysterical child.

We made the ambassador's reception with less than a second to spare.

જ   જ   જ

When we first arrived in Canada, the embassy staff was still feeling the reverberations of a tragic small airplane accident in which the ambassador and two other embassy officers had been killed. The new ambassador was Stanley Woodward who had been chief of protocol under Truman. He was a handsome man of great charm who made a point of getting to know each of his staff officers and their wives, right down to the bottom rung of the diplomatic ladder, and that is exactly where the Assistant Agricultural Attache and Mrs. Rodman stood. Protocol dictated that I make a brief call on every American diplomatic wife who outranked me within the first forty-eight hours of arrival. Finding a sitter for the children and getting myself organized with white gloves and calling cards was a juggling act of sorts. I had not had a chance to unpack. Fortunately, an embassy chauffeur drove me on my series of fifteen ten-minute calls on the first two afternoons I was in Ottawa. Knowing which corner of the calling card should be bent up for ladies who were at home, and which for those who were not, was of critical importance.

In the last twenty-five years we have made strides in the United States towards women's liberation which has eased the role of embassy wives overseas. At mid–century, however, a diplomatic wife was expected to toe the mark, and, along with her husband, put her best foot forward as a representative of the United States of America. Her performance had an impact on his advancement. I therefore quickly learned to entertain and be a gracious hostess, jump if I was needed for an embassy function, attend embassy wives' meetings, serve on committees, pursue philanthropic endeavors, meet visiting dignitaries, escort visitors on shopping and sightseeing tours, and help new embassy arrivals settle in. We were also expected to be a source of knowledge about the government, history, and the culture of the host country. A few wives simply couldn't cope, and returned to the United States, but the majority accepted this role without question.

As the Canadian winter progressed, we became accustomed to the snow and cold, a dry cold that left the snow crisp under foot. Years later, when we experienced winter snow and ice in Washington, D.C. or Charlottesville, Virginia, I would continue to marvel at the snow removal system in Ottawa. The big plows worked efficiently all night long so that when daylight came, the roads were clear, and one could drive safely without chains. Snow tires had not been invented.

Ottawa was very much a church–going city. Being Episcopalians, we chose the Anglican Cathedral where Bill became a junior warden. Quite often, the governor general, Vincent Massey, would attend services, and Bill and another warden would usher him down the aisle with their warden's wands. Channing stole the show on one occasion. She had brought along a little plastic pocketbook filled with red, white, and blue poker chips—her "money." While Bill and I were at the alter rail celebrating the Holy Eucharist, there was the unmistakable clatter of poker chips on a tiled floor, followed by a commotion caused by a small child crawling underneath pews to retrieve them. When we returned to our pew, Billy was alone looking very embarrassed. Then, a little reddish-blond head popped up about three rows behind us startling a few worshipers.

In addition to collecting family memories, Bill and I were learning the ways of diplomatic life. For the Queen's Garden Party, given by the governor general, Bill looked dashing in a rented swallow–tailed coat and striped pants, and I wore the prescribed hat and gloves. We observed Canada Day on July 1, attended diplomatic receptions, served hot dogs to Canadians at the traditional Fourth of July picnic at the ambassador's residence, called on new arrivals, learned the protocol of seating guests at dinner, and where not to sit in living rooms or automobiles when others of higher rank were present. Our mentors were Lucy and

Dick Kleinhans, the commercial counselor of embassy. They guided us patiently, and became lifelong friends.

I enjoy the challenge of a new language, and Canada seemed the perfect opportunity to hone up my schoolgirl French. I had several French speaking friends who encouraged and helped me along, plus a French conversation group. But best of all, we had a most delightfully animated teacher, a Swiss Roman Catholic priest named Jean Hulliger, who, in exchange for supper and a very small fee, came to the house twice a week. Channing and Billy adored these sessions peppered with little stories, poems and songs— "En passant par la Lorr-ai-ne avec mis sabots" they would sing. After the children went off to bed, it was our turn. I have always felt that almost any subject can be learned and enjoyed if taught by the right teacher. Father Hulliger fit that bill.

When I was a child, my mother took me and my older brother to the Philadelphia Ice Skating Arena every Saturday morning during the winter months. He and I learned to waltz together around the rink under the proud gaze of mother and other spectators who I'm sure found this team of miniature waltzers amusing. We even did our little act at one of the big carnivals and made the rotogravure section of the Philadelphia Sunday Inquirer. Now, some twenty-two years later, I bought a new pair of figure skates and joined the Minto Skating Club of Ottawa. It didn't take long for the feel of the ice to return. Bill tried, but never overcame weak ankles, and Ambassador Woodward became my waltzing partner. As his wife was not a skater, he would often stop by our house alone for a simple dinner, then drive me to the rink. This was unusual in the formal world of a busy ambassador, but skating was his favorite form of exercise. I became very involved in the Minto and helped stage a presentation of Peter Pan performed at the annual ice carnival. Billy was a pirate and Channing a fairy. He wore a tricorn hat over a red bandana and sported big mustachios, while Channing wore a little white net costume sprinkled with silver stars and carried a wand. She even had her own billing on the program as "The Littlest Fairy" because, unknown to her, she had a solo act. She was only four at the time and still very shaky on her tiny skates. At one point in the show, when all the other fairies made a fast exit, Channing tried to follow but could not keep up. As the crowd cheered her on, she would fall, pull herself up, skate a few strides and fall again. It was a very determined performance and the audience loved it.

In the fall of 1952, Harry Truman finished his second term of office, and the race was on for president of the United States between Democrat Adlai Stevenson and Republican Dwight D. Eisenhower. As the Republicans had not been in office since Franklin Roosevelt defeated Herbert Hoover in 1932, it was an exciting campaign. Although Stevenson was a very good candidate, Eisenhower had been the successful and popular Supreme Allied Commander of the European Theater of Operations during the Second World War and the "I like Ike" momentum reached fever pitch. A young Richard Nixon became Ike's running mate, but not without difficulty. He had to go on national radio to explain away the fact that he had accepted a little dog named Checkers as a pet for his children. I cannot imagine anything more harmless, but politicians and federal employees are not allowed to accept gifts. Even in our more humble role, we had to report any gift over twenty dollars. The saying was, "If you can't eat it, or it won't spoil in twenty-four hours, don't accept it." Eisenhower won the election in a landslide, and went on to serve two terms of office as a very popular president.

ᢞ   ᢞ   ᢞ

Elizabeth II of England was crowned on June 2, 1953, and Ottawa went wild with excitement. The Canadians started their joyous holiday at 7:15 A.M., the corresponding time of her crowning, with the pealing of bells from many churches, and above them, the carillon chimes of Ottawa's Peace Tower. Later that morning, the four Rodmans observed the ceremonies from the balcony of the ambassador's office, which faced Parliament Hill. We watched the Trooping of the Color and the reviewing by the governor general of his foot-guards, clad in their red jackets, bearskin hats and shining armor; later, a splendid parade representing every branch of military service, strode down the Duke of Wellington Street, each with its own marching band. Most colorful of all were the massed bagpipers and drummers in full Scottish regalia. Every time a new contingency of troops went by, the throng of people would cheer loudly and wave little Canadian flags. Channing never stopped jumping up and down with excitement. A more serious Billy scanned the parade with binoculars.

After the parade, there was a pause while the mounties formed a human chain to control the crowd. All of a sudden, Vincent Massey, the governor general, in an open golden carriage surrounded by cavalry, came swiftly down the street and entered the great iron gates of Parliament Hill. A small, handsome man with piercing blue eyes, he looked like a character from *H.M.S. Pinafore* in his black uniform with gold braid, and a Lord Nelson-type hat with billowing white plumes. The carriage stopped in front of the Peace Tower and he took his place on a platform. A sudden quiet fell as he addressed the people in English, then French. Next a recording of the Queen's speech was followed by "Oh Canada" and "God Save the Queen" with both carillon and combined military bands. The grand finale was a forty-two gun salute, used only at coronations, as a hundred saber jets tore through the sky in E II formation.

ᒫ   ᒫ   ᒫ

In the summer of 1953, we coordinated plans with four other young couples to rent an abandoned logging camp on Lake

Fauquier, an hour's drive from Ottawa. Just as the winters in Canada are long and severe, the summers are short and delightful. While we fished for lake trout, Bill told the children "happily ever after" stories about beautiful maidens, wicked witches, and ugly crocodiles who turned into handsome princes. After dark, we went frog-gigging with flashlights. The bright beam of light would stun the frog for a second and Billy would pop it into his net. I can't imagine myself nor Bill killing the poor little creatures, but we must have, as we learned to enjoy frog's legs for dinner. I also recall skinny-dipping off the dock but being careful of leeches, playing cribbage by firelight in the evening, and spotting wildlife—black bear, deer, raccoon, and many birds. These were good holidays and the only kind we could afford. Bill was at the bottom of the diplomatic heap on an annual salary of $5,313 plus housing.

ꝫ   ꝫ   ꝫ

A policy of most new presidential nominees is to pledge a clean-up of the bureaucracy in Washington by scaling down the government. Dwight D. Eisenhower called his pledge Operation RIF (Reduction In Force), and, with the zeal of a zealot, he promised a thirty percent reduction in government personnel. Excellent foreign service officers lost their jobs. Others not so worthy blundered on. The younger men and women who ranked at the bottom of the diplomatic pecking order were often the victims. *To RIF* became an active verb, and, along with others in American Embassies around the world, Bill Rodman became a candidate to be "riffed."

Then, one day in late August, 1953, Bill received a cablegram from Washington. Doug Crawford, the OFAR liaison officer, had this to say:

> Bill, you have good potential and we want to keep you. As you know, the situation in Washington is very

delicate. However, we have a plan for you. Pack up and leave Ottawa just as soon as you can clean up your desk. Make arrangements immediately to have your effects shipped to Buenos Aires, Argentina, where you will be the Assistant Agricultural Attache. If we can get you and your family en route, I think we can dodge this RIF fiasco.

Bill understood the urgency. Channing and I left the next day for Philadelphia by plane while the professional packing of our effects was going on. That same night, the two Bills drove to New York to leave our car at a designated wharf for shipment to Buenos Aires. They then joined us in Philadelphia where we rented a car. Doug had arranged a week's leave to say good-bye to our families and to attend my youngest brother's wedding in Staunton, Virginia. Under no circumstances were we to come to the Washington area. We felt a bit like fugitives. Immediately after the wedding, we rushed to New York City to board our Pan American plane for Argentina. The date was October 3, 1953.

Billy and Channing, ages five and eight

51

• ——   Chapter Six   —— •

ARGENTINA
October 1953 to July 1956

WE FLEW PAN AMERICAN FROM NEW YORK TO
BUENOS AIRES IN A DC 6—thirty-one hours with refueling
stops in Trinidad and Montevideo. Dr. and Mrs. Rodman gave
each of the children a "survival kit," a bag containing toys, games,
books and candy, and bid us farewell at the airport. What I
remember most about that flight was that it seemed never-ending.
The stewardess gave the kids Pan Am wings to wear on their
shirts and the captain invited Billy into the cockpit. In this modern
day of jet travel, I can't imagine a young boy being accorded the
unbounded pleasure of "helping to fly a plane." Bill and I were
given little books of Spanish words and phrases which I tried to
memorize. During our early days in the small Argentine hotel
called the Nogaró, where no English was spoken, my efforts
may have helped in spite of what must have been atrocious
pronunciation. It was baptism by fire.

When we arrived at the two rooms reserved for us, we were
confused, exhausted, and dying for a bourbon-on-the-rocks. We
had the bourbon with us, but how to get the rocks? I looked up
"ice" in my Spanish/English dictionary, picked up the phone,
and shouted "hi-ello" into the receiver. I was not understood. A

few minutes later, there was a polite knock on the door. It was a tall, handsome bellboy who, in broken English, asked what it was that Madam wished? I pointed to the word in the dictionary and he exclaimed, "Ah,—*hielo!"* and off he went. In a few minutes he was back with a saucer containing two rapidly melting pieces of ice!

Eduardo Rodas was that bellboy and he proved an invaluable friend. A highly intelligent young man, he was striving to learn English in hopes of emigrating to the United States. Our conversations became a beneficial language interchange for both of us. He practiced his halting English with me and I practiced my even more halting Spanish with him. Soon after we left Argentina in 1956, Eduardo did emigrate, served in the U.S Army, and became an American citizen. He continued in hotel work, and rose to the top, managing a large Chicago hotel when last we heard.

But my poor little Billy! Those first days in Buenos Aires were very hard for him. He was full of normal boyish energy, and a hotel on a busy city street in a huge Latin American city was not a good playground. One way he amused himself was by running the self-service elevators up and down. Of course, the management objected and this had to be stopped.

A week after our arrival, we were introduced to a family with two boys near Billy's age, one of whom happened to be having a birthday on October 16 when both he and our son would be ten years old. There was a party and our little misplaced person was included in the festivities. The two brothers attended an anglo-Argentine boarding school called St. John's, and without further thought, we bought a school uniform and entered Billy, even though it was close to the end of the school year. (In Argentina, as in other Latin American countries, the school year runs from March to December.) Off he went as a new boarder to an unknown school in an unknown country, a prime target for his devilish little peers. As starters, they gave him a Mohawk haircut and blocked him when he tried to take a shower. Bill and I were appalled when he was allowed to come to the hotel for a few hours on a Saturday afternoon. Our young Mohawk was so dirty that it took two baths and three rinse waters to get him clean. Perhaps we should have pulled him out of that school right then, but I guess we were trying to teach him "grit." We sent him back at the appointed time, and our unhappy little boy sweated it out for the few weeks left before the summer vacation. When school resumed in March, we sent him to another anglo-Argentine school called St. Andrew's as a day student, a much happier situation. Sometimes I wonder how Bill, Jr. ever turned out so well. Before he was through high school he had attended nine schools in four countries.

I vowed to learn the language as quickly as possible and first tried the Spanish lessons given at the American Embassy. Progress was too slow. Then I heard of a teacher who lived five or six blocks from our hotel and off I went. On the door was a brass plate—*Madam Lopez, Professora.* I knocked and an abundantly bosomed Señora, with masses of blond hair piled high atop her head, answered the door and ushered me into her charming little apartment. She was an excellent teacher, and after six weeks of intensive study, I was almost dreaming in Spanish. As I walked to my lesson, I remember repeating over and over "mil novecientos cincuenta y tres" (1953), thinking that if I could get my tongue around that mouthful the rest would come easily.

With this concentration on Spanish, plus attending diplomatic functions and calling on embassy wives, it was necessary to find someone to take care of six-year-old Channing. Eduardo Rodas suggested his sister, Vicky, who was young and pretty and spoke no English. She proved to be a perfect *niñera.* Soon Channing was chattering away in Spanish without an accent.

I found Buenos Aires a magnificent city with sweeping tree-lined avenues. To walk its streets is to be in a jumble of noise and traffic and exquisite aromas of good Argentine beef emanating from an abundance of restaurants. Storefronts display goods from all over the world along with beautiful Argentine products of leather and wool. And everywhere there are parks— big ones with grand monuments, little ones tucked into corners. The architecture is steeped in history, some dating back to Spanish colonial times, some to the British who introduced their own style and set up the railroads, and on to the French who built lovely mansions with mansard roofs and intricate wrought-iron balconies. Buenos Aires is in part a combination of Paris, Rome and London. The rest is strikingly Argentine.

Toward the end of November, not having found a house, we were still living at the Hotel Nogaró. This was probably a boon to learning Spanish, but we were anxious to get settled. I vividly remember the breakfasts which were served in my room—fruit, hot croissants with honey, and *cafe con leche* which was poured simultaneously from a coffee pot and a hot milk jug by the waiter who brought the tray. Considering my recent farm wife status and the gentle breaking-in to the foreign service that I had experienced in Canada, I had to pinch myself and wonder, "Is this really me?"

Bill discovered that our room was bugged. Each time we used the phone, there was a noticeable "click, click." He took the receiver apart and there it was. In 1953, "bugs" were not as sophisticated as they are today. Eva Perón had died less than a year before we arrived, and her husband, Argentina's president, Juan Domingo Perón, in his drive for power, was becoming more and more despotic. All new arrivals had to be tested to be sure they were not C.I.A. agents posing as embassy personnel. We did not disturb the "bug," but were very careful about what we said in our room. Once in a while we pretended to make noisy, passionate love to give the "goons" a treat.

Perón was a dramatic and charismatic speaker, although his words were those of an agitator rather than a ruler, and Argentina acquired increasingly the characteristics of a police state. All forms of freedom allowed to political opponents gradually disappeared. He loved to hold mass meetings for the working class whom he called his *decamisados* (shirtless ones). On these occasions, thousands of Argentines were ordered to the Plaza de Mayo, and from a balcony of the Casa Rosada (Government House), he would rant, rave, and even cry to arouse them to near hysteria. They idolized him and his dead wife, and misguidedly thought of them as saviors from the wicked oligarchy who were waiting to pounce, taking everything from them and turning them into slaves. As well as being an eloquent orator, there is no doubt that Perón had an extraordinary sense of mass psychology. From the balcony of our room at the Hotel Nogaró, we witnessed this spectacle. It was frightening. His followers looked and acted more like savages than human beings, and in the days ahead they would prove as ruthless.

꙳   ꙳   ꙳

One morning I awakened with a terrible pain in my gut. A doctor was called and ten minutes later I was rushed to the hospital with appendicitis. It was Thanksgiving Day.

Meanwhile, Bill found a suitable house in Accassuso, a pretty northern suburb about eight miles from Buenos Aires. We could move in immediately if we didn't mind an unfinished stairway and a non-functioning furnace, both of which, according to the landlord, would be taken care of within a month. Our personal belongings had arrived and Bill must have worked hard to reach a semblance of order before I came home from the hospital. Those were the days of extended hospital stays, and I was grateful for the opportunity to regain my strength. Christmas was upon us.

Although Bill's title was Assistant Agricultural Attache, he was in charge of the office at the embassy. His boss, Bob Tetro, did not arrive with his family until sometime after the first of the new year. While they were trying to find a house, we took in their ten-year-old son Bobby, a sweet but solemn little boy whom we tickled just to make him laugh. He put catsup on everything— scrambled eggs, pancakes, ice cream, macaroni. His parting gift was a case of the mumps which he passed on to Channing and Billy.

In Argentina, as in most Latin American countries, servants were the norm, not the exception. I was unaccustomed to this luxury and had no idea how to interview prospective girls. The first one I took on was incapable of boiling an egg. She also was a thief and was particularly partial to my lingerie. Poor kid, I'm sure she had just come in from the country and had never seen a nylon slip. I wear rather plain undergarments, but to Angelica, they were irresistible. I find it very hard to fire someone, and this was a first. I think I gave her some money and underwear and told her to scat.

The most oft repeated story of those first months in Buenos Aires is one of Bill's favorites. As mentioned, our house was not finished. The stairway was only blocked in, and the furnace was not in working order. As winter approached, Bill contacted the Argentine colonel who owned the house and told him that he must fulfill the contract or that he would have the embassy withhold the rent. Still nothing was done, so Bill wrote him a polite note saying that the current rent check was being held in escrow at the U.S. Embassy, and would be remitted as soon as the work on the stairs and furnace had been completed. The next day, two grim-faced men, dressed in black suits, came to Bill's office. One, slapping a glove onto the desk, stated that the colonel's honor had been questioned; therefore, the colonel challenged Mr. Rodman to a duel in Palermo Park. He would expect a reply as to weapons within twenty-four hours. Bill was stunned! We were learning that the Argentines can take themselves very seriously.

Bill went immediately to the DCM (Deputy Chief of Mission), and explained his predicament. Thirty minutes later, he was in the office of an Argentine lawyer who explained that, as Bill was the one being challenged, he had the right to choose weapons. Bill answered that the only weapons he would be willing to use were his fists. And so it was that the lawyer contacted the colonel's representatives, and told them that his client was willing to meet His Honor at dawn in Palermo Park, and that the chosen weapons would be bare knuckles. That was the end of the affair. As Bill had met his challenge, the colonel's honor had been upheld. The lawyer added that most duels were settled in this manner in the 1950s, and suggested that we find another house as quickly as possible.

The happy ending was that just a few blocks away we found a nicer house, surrounded by a large yard and high hedge, being vacated by a departing embassy family. Best of all, it came with an excellent Paraguayan cook named Fernanda.

༄   ༄   ༄

About this time, Bill and I decided to have another child. Billy was at St. Andrew's and Channing had started first grade at an anglo-Argentine girls' school called Northlands. We had a lovely home and Fernanda to help. It seemed a perfect time to enlarge our family and try to present Bill's father with a much desired namesake.

One rainy night, there was a knock on our door and Elena entered our lives. Having just arrived in Buenos Aires from Asunción, Paraquay, she had no place to go, and was looking for her older sister, Fernanda. She was seventeen years old. With our baby now on the way, she was heaven sent. We put bunk beds in Fernanda's room, and made her a part of our growing family. Fernanda was quite plain, but Elena was a beauty. She had intelligent dark eyes, black hair, a beautiful olive skin, a wide smile, and a shapely figure. In her uniform she looked adorable.

Elena had a burning desire to become a registered nurse. She could read and write, but had little formal education. I had always wanted to teach and this was a golden opportunity. We purchased suitable text books and went to work on the kitchen table. A bright and conscientious student, at the end of three years Elena passed a national high school equivalency exam enabling her to enter into nurse's training at the Anglo-Argentine Hospital. Bill and I guaranteed her tuition for the first year. After that she would be on scholarship if she proved capable of the work. She left us in March, 1956, and graduated three years later as a registered nurse. While in training, she attended an Anglo-Argentine patient whose family owned a large *estancia*, and in time our little Elena became Doña Elena Legizamon–Pugh. In the years ahead, Bill and I would collect a coterie of "littleones" as we called them. Elena was our first.

ᕕ   ᕕ   ᕕ

Joan Stewart Rodman was born on December 31, 1954, at The Little Company of Mary Hospital in Buenos Aires. She was a tiny five pounds, but perfect. Her birth is a fond memory. The American Roman Catholic nuns, in light blue and white garb, achieved a zenith of care and efficiency in tending their patients. My large, comfortable room with chintz curtains and well chosen paintings on the walls was bright and sunny. The food was excellent. Morning coffee was served at 11 A.M. and afternoon tea at 4 P.M. Dinner was at the civilized hour of 7:30. The average length of stay was ten days. I always think of this euphoric birthing experience when I observe the young women of today being rushed in and out of hospitals in forty-eight hours or less. Perhaps I hold an old fashioned notion, but to me, giving birth is a very big deal.

The advent of J.S.R. was happy all around. Billy, twelve, was a proud big brother, and Channing, seven, was over the moon. Even Dr. Rodman never let on his disappointment that she was a girl. The initials were the same, and so was the name except for an "a" where an "h" might have been. The nuns called her *Pimpollita* (little rosebud) because she was so fair, with blond peach fuzz atop her head. It was easy to find her in the nursery—one little Caucasian blond baby amidst a dozen or more Latin babies with shocks of black hair. We called her "Joni."

♫   ♫   ♫

Political unrest mounted in Argentina during the early months of 1955. Anti-peronistas disappeared, newspapers succumbed to threats and stopped honest reporting, robberies were rampant, and the pumped-up propaganda was incredible. As a result, there were demonstrations which were ruthlessly put down by Perón's army of thugs, or "bullyboys" as we called them. Several demonstrating students were killed. The police did not attempt to keep law and order, often looking the other way during the mindless burning of a church, or a robbery. A recognized fact was that policemen would accept loot or "hush-money" to keep quiet.

In February 1955, we awoke with a start at a very early hour. Elena was screaming, "*Ladrones!*" (robbers!) We dashed downstairs to find utter chaos. During the night, robbers had come in through the terrace doors and ransacked the living and dining rooms taking all of our beautiful Towle sterling flat silver, as well as sterling dishes and platters. They knew what they wanted; plated silver items were discarded or thrown across the room. They also must have known that they could make plenty of noise and that we would not wake up. The reason became clear to us later in the day when a detective arrived on the scene. He told us that of the many robberies taking place at the time, most were inside jobs. Two methods were used. One was that food was drugged by the inside help. The other was that a maid lent out her house key to be copied. The robbers then entered the house without breaking in, as in our case, and somehow sprayed chloroform in the sleeping area upstairs to guarantee that the family did not awaken. I shudder to think of drugs in the children's food or the baby's bottle, but equally disturbing is the chloroform theory which I believe was the correct one in our case.

The aftermath of the robbery turned comical. As Lloyds of London would not write insurance policies during the last years of the Perón regime, we had taken out Argentine insurance. (It was practically worthless, but we did not realize it at the time.) After reporting the crime, we were told by the insurance company that the adjusters would call to assess the damage. Our hearts sank when Argentine friends told us that the way insurance representatives worked was to add up everything that was left in the house and deduct this amount from the policy amount of $3,000. As we never considered someone might rob the upright piano or the dining room table, our insurance was far less that the value of our belongings. Therefore, I had to swing into action to remove everything that could be easily moved out of the house, leaving only the basics.

While Fernanda, Elena, and I packed up glass, chinaware and other items in large laundry baskets and cardboard cartons, two friends with station wagons pulled into our driveway and carried them off in relay fashion. We even got rid of most of our clothes, leaving only a couple of suits and dresses and two pairs of shoes in each closet. While this operation was in progress, (my friend Jean, had just pulled out of the driveway), I spotted two men in black suits at our gate. My tummy must have flipped because on the kitchen floor were two large laundry baskets ready for relay. I quickly told Fernanda to put the contents back on the shelves while I ushered the men upstairs to begin their inspection. When we got to the kitchen, the crystal and china were not on the shelves! What Fernanda had done was to hide our valuables in an old top loading washing machine filled to brimming with soap suds. Furthermore, she was busy washing dishes in the kitchen sink which was equally billowing with suds! My effort, however, was of small consequence. The final adjustment on the stolen property was a paltry $700. As a compensation prize, Bill and I bought a handsome pair of antique silver stirrups, such as *gauchos* wore, which still adorn our dining room wall. Eventually, we bought new flat silver, but it was not as handsome as the original pattern which I had chosen as a bride.

The police insisted on taking Fernanda and Elena's fingerprints, but this proved nothing. Bill and I felt certain that they were innocent. As time went on, however, we had second thoughts about Fernanda. She had a boyfriend, recently arrived from Paraguay. I had met him briefly and had not like his looks. Possibly she had loaned him her key which he had duplicated. Also Fernanda and Elena had asked to go to a late movie that night and I believe they were out when the robbery occurred. This theory was substantiated three years later when we were in San José, Costa Rica. An embassy friend from Buenos Aires came to visit. When our conversation turned to the robbery, she said, "Everyone but you and Bill believed it was an inside job. Did you know that your silver was seen in Asunción, Paraguay, in a pawn shop? It was recognized because of the initials."

I was stunned. Elena, I feel sure, was an innocent bystander, genuinely startled when she discovered the robbery that morning, but I now believe that Fernanda and her boyfriend were guilty. To this day it hurts me to think about it.

჻   ჻   ჻

Buenos Aires was our first experience with Latin American city traffic and Latin drivers. Avid horn-blowers, they thought driving a car was a game of bluff. It fanned their *machismo* to be reckless behind the wheel, and they considered their opponent a coward if he or she gave in before the crash. Aliens, like Bill and me, who treasure our lives, did a whole lot of "giving in" while driving in Buenos Aires. In spite of the fact that our government retained diplomatic relations with Perón's government during this period of unrest and revolution in Argentina, Americans were not always popular with the Argentines. One game these crazy drivers played was to see if they could drive past a parked car close enough to remove the door handles; in the '50s, these were not flush. Our beautiful green Ford which was shipped to Argentina from New York was de-handled twice. Another favorite trick was to walk with a key or sharp instrument concealed in a hand and scratch along the length of the offending car. Cars of diplomats were easily identifiable by their license plates with CD, for Corps Diplomatique, and the numbers that followed indicated the country. This licensing practice became more and more dangerous as terrorism increased on a worldwide scale.

Because of the unrest in Argentina, and our new baby, I did not have a chance to see as much of this large country with its mountains, pampas, and coastal areas as I would have liked. On the other hand, Bill traveled widely, including a 5,400 kilometer trip through the southern territory of Patagonia. On one occasion, he and I drove to the beautiful mountain area of Cordova, and when my mother visited in 1955, she and I flew to Barilochi, the "Switzerland" of Argentina. Snow-capped mountains overlooked crystal clear lakes where large trout were so plentiful that an amateur fisherman, such as myself, could catch a fish by simply dropping a line over the side of a boat. Our return to Buenos Aires was one of my most vivid airplane experiences. About half way along, one of our plane's twin engines failed. I remember looking down almost longingly at air strips on private *estancias* as we flew over them at very low altitude. When one was behind us, we would look ahead for the next. The pilot quite obviously was doing the same. Several times I thought he was going to try to land. We limped along in this manner for what seemed an interminable period. There was a corporate sigh of relief when we finally landed, long overdue, at the airport in Buenos Aires. Having been informed of the plane's distress, Bill, who was there to meet us, was a nervous wreck.

જ જ જ

As a family, we often visited Los Puestos, a cattle station owned by friends, about forty-five miles from Buenos Aires. There we would ride horses across the pampas, Channing on a pony. At midday we stopped for an *asado* or cookout, an Argentine custom whereby the *gauchos* (cowboys) slaughter a steer, and stretch one half of the carcass on iron stakes to cook slowly during the night over the heat of quebracho coals. (*Quebracho,* meaning ax-breaker, is a very hard Argentine wood.) Billy had a gaucho outfit—*bombachas* (baggy white pants), white shirt, red scarf, boots, and wide brimmed hat— and like little boys everywhere, he loved to follow the gauchos and play cowboy.

One time we took the family, including Joni, to a seashore resort called Villa Gesell. Most memorable about that trip was my gambit in the famous gambling casino in Mar del Plata. I admit to an affinity for gambling, on a nickel-and-dime scale, and could not resist trying my luck. Bill went along with my whimsy, and gave me five dollars, or its equivalent in pesos, and off I went while he and the older children pushed the baby stroller up and down the boardwalk.

The grandiose, gilded interior of the casino with its crystal chandeliers, and plush red carpets was impressive. On the first level were the money–changers behind little barred windows, similar to a bank. The exchange rate was about twelve to one, so I must have changed about sixty pesos into chips, a sum so small as to be absurd in this playground of the rich. As I walked up the splendid staircase to the gambling rooms, I felt the personification of "innocence abroad." I watched for a while, then gingerly placed one chip on the red at a roulette table. That one turned into two, so I placed both on the black. That made four, and so on until there was quite an astonishing pile of chips in front of me. But all too soon Cinderella had to depart this make-believe world (the golden coach was becoming more pumpkin-orange by the second), so I cashed in and returned triumphant to the fold, fluttering my small fortune on high.

My only sojourn outside of Argentina was to Asunción, Paraguay. Bill and I went on a U.S. Air Force plane which made regular trips to this land-locked, poverty stricken country to deliver supplies to the American diplomatic corps. We stayed with the U.S. army attache and his wife in their rambling one-story house which had a red tile roof, colorful tile floors, archaic plumbing and many servants. In the bathroom, a hole in the floor and two large indented footprints indicated where to place my feet; hanging from the ceiling was a rope to hold onto. I have met up with some memorable plumbing systems, but this may have been the most unique. To add an air of the comic, outside of our window was a twenty-foot cage of tropical birds and monkeys who twittered and screeched, especially in the early morning.

One afternoon we rented a dilapidated taxi and drove to a pueblo where the women made *ñanduti,* an intricate Paraguayan lace. In every hut, women, both old and young, were tying the myriad of little knots that end up as beautiful tablecloths and shawls. They worked in a squat position on the earthen floor just inside the doorway, so that the rare passing tourist would notice them. The extreme poverty that we saw in Paraguay was heart-breaking. Clothing, though often colorful, was ragged, and, in the country, rarely did you see a child or woman with shoes. The men seemed better off. They rode horseback while the women walked beside them carrying expertly balanced loads on their heads. Once in a while we would see a man on a horse followed by a woman sitting side-saddle fashion on a small burro with a baby suckling at her breast. Other assorted children scrambled behind. The head of the Paraguayan household was definitely the male.

ॐ   ॐ   ॐ

During the early months of 1955, the political situation in Argentina had become increasingly foreboding. On June 16, it exploded. The Argentine navy was in full revolt, attacking the Casa Rosada and other strategic buildings from both air and sea with the express purpose of dislodging Perón. The day started rainy and cold, normal for that time of year. That anything unusual might happen was not even rumored. (Later, we learned to live on rumors; for wrong or right, they were almost our only source of information in a country which had not known the "four freedoms" for twelve years.)

At 1:30 P.M., an excited embassy secretary called to tell me not to leave the house under any circumstances because there was trouble in the city—ambassador's orders. That was fine by me, but what about Billy and Channing who were in school four miles away? I turned on the radio and heard, as we were to hear hundreds of times in the days to follow, "Absoluta tranquilidad reina por todas partes del país." (There is absolute calm throughout the country.) Mournful music was played intermittently with this monotonous announcement. A short time later, Bill got through to me on the telephone and I knew then that the situation was very serious. Due to widespread wiretapping, he spoke in euphemisms such as, "It's hot in town," and "The overhead picture is grim." Soon after, our friend, Carlos, a ham radio operator, called. I then learned for certain that the "overhead picture" meant that bombs were being dropped on Plaza de Mayo and the surrounding buildings.

As planes flew over our home that afternoon, it was hard to believe that they were about to bomb the city. I never knew who brought them, but Channing and Billy both arrived home around four o'clock in private cars, both terribly excited, though little Channing was completely bewildered. Because it was safer, we never mentioned Perón in front of the children. Billy, however, being older, and a student in a very anti-peronista school, had some idea of the situation. Bill and I deplored the fact that Channing had to be taught glaring propaganda, immortalizing Eva Perón and glorifying her husband. Primary school readers were full of garish pictures of both Peróns with benign expressions on their faces, hugging little children, and doing great and glorious deeds for the homeland. The children referred to Eva as Santa Evita. When books were handed out, the teacher would ask each little girl, "Who gave you this book?" and the child would answer, "Santa Evita gave me this book." One of Channing's first-grade readers stated: "Peron is the leader. Everybody loves Perón. Everybody sings – Viva Perón!" And the children would repeat, "Viva Perón! Viva!" This type of brainwashing of children, designed to implant totalitarian principles into young minds, was the same as in Germany under Hitler.

In addition, Argentine children were being taught to worship Juan and Eva Perón instead of God, and each night, Channing would kneel by her bed and pray to *mi general* (my general) to bless her and her family. Although frustrating, it was wiser to say nothing except to remind her that Eisenhower was her president and the United States her country. Her first question on that memorable day was, "Mommie, has anything happened to *mi general?*"

When the first deluge of bombs fell about 1 P.M., Bill was having lunch at the London Grill, six blocks from the Plaza de Mayo. He was so absorbed in a new *Saturday Evening Post* that he wasn't aware of other customers hastily leaving the restaurant. When he finally looked up he noticed that the heavy metal blind, used after hours on stores and restaurants for protection, had been pulled down. To exit, a person had to crawl through a little metal doorway cut out in the blind and locked by the last man out. As Bill crawled through this small door onto Calle Florida , someone shouted that the Casa Rosada had been bombed. He hurried toward the embassy, dodging masses of excited people running in the opposite direction. Close by, he could hear machine gun fire. When he turned the corner at Diagonal Norte, he could see the terrible scene in which hundreds of people were killed and wounded. Many were civilians just strolling in the Plaza, or on their way to lunch. One bomb exploded, killing and wounding three bus loads of passengers, as well as bystanders. As embassy offices were located on the second and eighth floors of the Boston Bank Building, no more than a city block from the Plaza de Mayo, it was a marvel that embassy personnel and others of the American community escaped unharmed.

When Bill arrived at his office, he found that the ambassador had ordered all personnel down to the second floor, but shortly thereafter, thinking the air raids were over, Bill, the ambassador, and a marine sergeant went up to the fifth floor of the building to have a better look. Just as they stepped through a window onto a small balcony, a second wave of bombers came over, and they dove back inside. On that raid, the office building next door was hit, causing extensive damage.

Later, Bill decided he would try to leave the city. Our car, which had been parked on the street, was undamaged, while others nearby were a heap of twisted metal. He was not stopped until he reached a point where buses had been placed bumper to bumper to cut off exit from the city. In this case, our diplomatic license plates were a godsend; he was allowed through while others were trapped for hours.

On the evening of June 16, the rebels were forced to surrender when army tanks captured their air base east of the capital, depriving them of a place to land and refuel, and fled to Uruguay, a long time haven for enemies of Perón. They also blamed their defeat on heavy fog that hindered both planes and warships. The next day Perón made a speech advocating pacification and calling on both his comrades and adversaries alike to put down their arms and work together in harmony. This sounded phony. However, the beaten rebels gave him ninety days to prove his words by releasing political prisoners and restoring freedom to Argentina. After two weeks, he lifted the "state of siege" and repaired the bomb damage, but tension mounted and rumors were rampant. Increasingly, the peronistas started bogus uprisings and demonstrations so that they could be put down by peronista policemen. This proved how strong they were and gave them the opportunity to arrest those who disagreed with them.

It seems inconceivable, but has since been brought to light, that Perón was out to eliminate the Roman Catholic Church in Argentina. He would then set up his own Religion Justicialista (Religion of State), whereby he and Eva would be sainted and worshipped. Even as she lay dying of cancer three years before, her husband had commissioned Pedro Ara, a famed Spanish anatomist, to embalm the body with his special process, guaranteed to produce "absolute corporeal permanence." Ara was on hand at Evita's deathbed, reportedly to make sure that the doctors gave her no drugs that would affect the embalming. Perón announced to the country that Evita's body would eventually lie in state at the base of a monument bigger than New York Harbor's Statue of Liberty. This monument had already been constructed and was later found in the province of Mendoza. Plans called for it to be placed at a strategic spot on Avenida Reforma, the beautiful avenue leading into the city from the north. Smaller replicas would be placed in the restored churches, then to be called "temples" of the new religion. The monument depicted a huge standing figure, similar in character to the Virgin Mary, but with the facial features of Eva Perón. At its base was a very much smaller kneeling figure of Christ looking up at her adoringly with his hands folded in worship. This, more than any other irrational act on his part, demonstrates how crazed Perón became in his struggle to survive as dictator.

While this desperate man was bellowing pacification, he was amassing military strength for the final coup in which he would decimate the oligarchy and emerge triumphant. The oligarchs were his sworn enemies and he vowed to fight until he had annihilated them. It was later revealed that this bloodbath was to start on October 8. His "goon" squads, led by the Alianza Nationalista, an organization of highly paid fanatics, were to march on Barrio Norte, an affluent section of the city where the aristocracy lived. They would drop incendiary devices down the oil chutes of apartment buildings, exploding the storage tanks, and destroy the entire area. Then they would work their way out to the northern suburbs kidnapping, looting, murdering. Certain houses were targeted with a black X, and in some, domestic help had been bribed and ordered to murder their employers when the signal came.

The peronistas calculated that this attack would be successfully completed by October 17 when Perón would announce his new doctrine and new religion. October 17 had been the date in 1946 when, after an earlier revolution, the workers brought Perón back into power after he had been briefly imprisoned. Ever since, it was observed as a peronista holiday. Had the siege been successful, a terrifying and bloody period of civil war would have ensued.

During the ninety-day period between June 16 and September 16, tension mounted. Under President Perón's direction, the Alianza Nationalista murdered, kidnapped, tortured, looted, and burned the churches, inciting so much fear that no one dared raise a voice in protest. On August 31, Bill called to tell me to pick up the children at school and return to the house. Perón had sent in his resignation and trouble was expected. This was a bluff, but we didn't know it at the time. As planned, the C.G.T. (General Confederation of Labor), called a work stoppage and sent out word to all workers to come to the Plaza de Mayo. If necessary, they were to commandeer private cars, holding them up at gun point. When these mass demonstrations took place, trains, trucks, and buses were jammed with workers. Some were on roofs, or hanging onto the sides brandishing sticks and weapons. All were shouting. I wondered how so many dirty, crude men and women could appear so suddenly!

With car doors locked, I drove off to collect the children. The schools, now accustomed to these emergencies, were well organized. A line-up of senior students, waiting at the entrance, ran relays to fetch and sign out a child whose name had been given. All along the streets were long queues of people trying to buy bread and food before the shops closed, and I wondered with a slight feeling of panic what provisions were at home should a real emergency arise.

That evening, Perón made an inflammatory speech in which he stated that because of demonstrations and uprisings (these instigated by his own party), and other unlawful acts, it was obvious that the country did not want peace. Therefore his so-called "pacification policy" was over. Violence would be met with greater violence and for every peronista harmed, "five others would fall." He told his howling mob that any man defending the cause of Peronism could take up arms and kill. He was turning countryman against countryman, and giving any hoodlum the right to take the law into his own hands. Although we realized that his speech was like the last desperate cry of a dying animal, we were frightened. With the supports under him weakening daily, Perón believed his only path was to dispose of everybody and everything that stood in his way. His police arrested scores of priests and hundreds of Catholic laymen for showing "disrespect;" he bolstered his campaign to "Peronize" the minds of school children; thousands of upper class Argentines were jailed and tortured; he decreed that no more than two adults could meet together at any time on streets or sidewalks, in cafés or automobiles, and any violation of this was punishable by death. As a result, *Time* magazine made the astute statement that, "It was a pretty stupid Argentine that couldn't manage to get himself shot."

As promised, on September 16, 1955, the second revolt began. Again I was called to get the children from school, and Bill came home from the office early, but this time, nobody went back to work for nine days, and the schools were closed until further notice.

The first uprisings started in the provinces, with the main battle taking place in Cordova city. While the radio reported that loyalist troops had repressed the rebels in all sectors, we soon learned that the rebels were actually beating the daylights out of Perón's loyalists. From our ham–operator friend, Carlos, we got first hand reports of the fighting. He called day or night with updates which Bill would relay on to the ambassador.

On Monday, September 19, with navy ships in the harbor and guns trained on Buenos Aires, Perón resigned. Political asylum is generally given without question in Latin American countries, even to despots. Perón was first granted asylum in the Paraguayan Embassy. Later, he was transferred to a Paraguayan gunboat which bobbed up and down in the harbor for twelve days before arrangements could be made to fly him to Asunción, Paraguay's capital. There he made hysterical remarks to the press predicting his triumphant return to Argentina.

On the days immediately following Perón's resignation, the revolutionaries did a thorough clean-up job and made many arrests. A military junta of generals was appointed to negotiate with rebel leaders. This junta was peronista infested and nobody knew what might happen. The red arm-banded Alianza Nacionalista and their "goon squads" were now desperate as well as fanatical. The headquarters of the Alianza were located at the corner of Corrientes and San Martin in the heart of Buenos Aires. On the night of September 20, the day after Perón had been overthrown, the revolutionary army drew up tanks in front of the Alianza building and, giving them a two-hour grace period, demanded that an estimated six hundred members inside surrender. There was no response. When the army gave them an ultimatum of five minutes, they held out a white flag. A young lieutenant and three enlisted men entered the building. On their way up the stairs they were machine-gunned to death. With that, the tanks opened fire and within a few minutes the building had been demolished.

Nobody dared guess what might happen if the C.G.T. decided to take up arms and start a counter-revolution, hoping to restore their fallen idol. So far, the fight had been between the divided armed forces. Furthermore, the police force appeared to be pro-Perón. What would their reaction be to his downfall? While such atrocities as the burning of the churches were taking place, they had looked the other way.

Although we did not think it right, the United States had maintained diplomatic relations with Perón's government throughout the crisis. Now, there was a blackout of communication between the State Department and Buenos Aires. Several families in our neighborhood quietly formed a protection group. We checked the background and leanings of our domestic employees, built up stocks of food and water, and memorized each others telephone numbers. Only certain key words and phrases were to be used. We also planned escape routes to places well out of Buenos Aires, some to *estancias*, others to designated spots along the banks of the Tigre River for escape in boats. But at the peak of our most anxious moments, providence stepped in. Whatever action the hoodlum gangs might have taken was thwarted by heaven-sent torrential rains lasting two days and two nights.

As the revolutionary army continued a systematic mop-up of peronista strongholds, people were beginning to relax and celebrate the new Argentina. From his office window, Bill witnessed a group of civilians attacking the headquarters of the Partido Peronista Feminino (the Women's Peronista Party) located on the third floor of the building opposite the American Embassy. First they knocked down the six-foot high pictures of Juan and Eva Perón on the facade of the building, then threw everything out of the windows—pictures, papers, letters, furniture. They accumulated it all and made a tremendous bonfire on the sidewalk below, while spectators watched and cheered them on. The two big metal backed pictures were not burned. They were left face up for people to trample on. Similar incidents were widespread. It only took two days to remove every trace or reminder of Perón, his wife, and his dictatorship. Towns, provinces, ships, streets, buildings, parks, railroad stations and airports that bore their names were changed back to the original. The ubiquitous signs, busts, statues, portraits, inscriptions, and slogans were destroyed. They had been used for brainwashing at its most eloquent.

The students at Billy's school made a bonfire of copies of Eva's book, *La Razon de Mi Vida*, which every boy was required to read. At another school, the children symbolically planted a little oak tree where once a statue had stood. At Channing's school, under teacher supervision, the little girls either crayoned over or tore out the pages of their readers that referred to the ex-president and his "immortal" wife.

On Friday, September 23, Provisional President Lonardi arrived in Buenos Aires from Cordoba to take the oath of office, and the day was declared "Dia de la Libertad" (Day of Freedom). Bill and I went to the city to join in the celebration. The throng that marched proudly down Diagonal Norte to the Plaza de Mayo had not been ordered to do so. They came of their own free will and in no way resembled the rabble of the peronista aggregations. They were well dressed and orderly. Engraved on their faces were mingled looks of pride, hope, relief and joy. They waved flags, sang the national anthem, and shouted, "Viva La Libertad." The buildings were bedecked with flags, banners and streamers of light blue and white, the national colors, and everywhere was the revolutionary symbol, a V with a cross for Victory and Christ. It was the first day of spring in Argentina, and after the recent heavy rains and the long period of fear and unrest, the sun was shining brightly.

Billy and Channing joined bands of marching children, singing and waving small flags. First came the older children followed by diminishing sizes down to the tiny ones, just barely keeping up, and after them a few straggly dogs. Almost every house flew an Argentine flag, and many flew the yellow and white Vatican flag as well. Some had signs draped across the doorway saying *Bienvenido* (welcome). These were the houses of prisoners and exiles who would now be returning home.

During the ensuing period, the Lonardi government opened the presidential residences to the public so that people could see evidence of the graft and corruption of the former regime. It was mind-boggling to observe first hand the enormous wealth that Juan and Eva Perón had amassed for themselves by mishandling public funds—the priceless jewels, solid gold telephones, fur coats, an enormous number of shoes, dresses and suits, automobiles and motorcycles.

Also on view was Perón's bombproof "love nest" or "hide out," hidden deep below the city streets with secret tunnels and safes full of jewels. One of his quirks was a liking for teenage girls. Passing in a train or car, one could see them playing on the lawns of the presidential palace. News accounts reported that Juan Perón had millions of dollars in Swiss bank accounts, and had stashed away

124,000 United States gold eagles in Switzerland by means of sensational black market deals.

After the successful September revolution, and until the end of the regular school year in December, elementary schools were closed. There were no books. By March, the beginning of the next school year, the new books had been printed, and Billy and Channing finally returned to school. As we were scheduled to leave Argentina in July for Washington, D.C., we decided to send Billy to the American School to give him a few months of the American system of teaching. This would be his third school in Buenos Aires.

We left Argentina in late July 1956 on the S.S. *Del Mar,* a Delta Line ship. Channing had her ninth birthday on board; Joni was seventeen months, and Billy twelve. With us was a teenage Argentine girl named Margarita who would help with the children in exchange for the opportunity to learn English. The voyage lasted three weeks and the children loved the pool and other shipboard activities. On one occasion, Joni escaped Margarita's watchful eyes and made her way into the bar where she spied her father sitting on a bar stool. When he felt a tug on his pants, he looked down into the blue eyes of a tiny daughter in pink pajamas.

Upon arrival in New Orleans, after three years in the Argentine, we checked into our hotel, mustered our forces, and marched across the street to a Walgreen Drug Store for American hamburgers and chocolate milkshakes.

Joni's christening in April 1955.

· —— Chapter Seven —— ·

FALLS CHURCH, VIRGINIA
August 1956 to October 1958

AFTER A SHORT HOLIDAY AT A FISHING CAMP IN
MAINE, we bought a house on a wooded lot in a quiet cul-de-
sac at Lake Barcroft, on the Virginia side of Washington. As the
house was liveable but unfinished, Bill, with a lot of determination
and the *Handyman's Do-It-Yourself Guide Book,* set about
finishing the roughed-in spaces—an effort which resulted at times
in strong language and smashed thumbs.

Bill's Washington assignment was Director of the Meat and
Livestock Division of FAS. He was unhappy with the shackles
of Washington: the duplicity of effort, the endless red tape, the
confinement of a small office, the traffic jams. We both looked
forward to going into "the field" again.

With Joni in the shopping cart, it was a thrill to wander
through the U.S. supermarkets observing the fantastic display of
packaged, frozen, tinned and fresh products. I overbought and
overspent until I became accustomed to this culinary affluence. The
Argentine marketplace was more picturesque with meats, including
innards, hanging out in the open on an iron hook, but, I found the
sanitized, plastic, saran-wrapped U.S. foods more tempting to buy,
although not necessarily better to eat. I was also pleased to drink

tap water with a feeling of safety, and not to have to wash fresh fruits and vegetables with halazone tablets. But perhaps best of all, I was comforted to be on peaceful soil after living with political corruption and revolution in Argentina. I felt safe.

When a foreign service officer is posted to Washington, he loses his housing allowance as well as other perks such as a school allowance and commissary privileges. This sets him back to base pay which can prove a financial hardship, especially while in the early civil service grades. During this period we struggled to make ends meet.

The children settled into their various schools, and I subscribed to the Famous Artists Correspondence Course in Westport, Connecticut, headed by such well-known individuals as Norman Rockwell and Stephen Dehanos. I had always loved to draw.

Our prime source of entertainment was a small, black and white television set. We had never seen TV; it was magic. Thinking back, the programs seemed far better than today. Joni learned her ABCs from Captain Kangaroo. The sex and violence of today's programs did not exist. The late 1950s was a wholesome, peaceful period. The Korean War was over, and the drug problem had not surfaced in mainstream America.

In August of 1958, we learned that Bill had been approved for assignment to the regional post of Costa Rica, Nicaragua and Panama. He would start immediately on a schedule of briefings and a trip to Central America to survey the area he would cover. Finally, we would take three weeks of annual leave during which time we would sell our house, bid farewell to our families, buy clothes for the tropical climate, pack, and depart for our new post in late September.

We were thrilled except for one thing. After one year at public school, we had sent Bill, Jr. to Episcopal High School, a boarding school in Alexandria, Virginia, to enter ninth grade. We would be leaving him behind.

· —— Chapter Eight —— ·

COSTA RICA
October 1958 to January 1962

TUCKED BETWEEN NICARAGUA AND PANAMA IN
CENTRAL AMERICA is the tiny country of Costa Rica. As
opposed to its sultry and humid neighbors, it has an ideal climate,
especially on the wide central plateau where the capital city of
San José is located at an altitude of about 3,500 feet. A naturalist's
paradise, its beauty is unsurpassed. Strategically located between
the Atlantic and Pacific Oceans, Costa Rica is very important to
the United States, an oasis where our country is free to carry on
important projects in research, experimentation, ecology. Private
industry is welcomed. Costa Ricans are easy–going, friendly
people who, because of unique historical and political
development, have avoided marked social class divisions. Driving
through the countryside passing one small well–kept *finca* (farm)
after another, you are aware that these are relatively prosperous
people who proudly live in a democratic country. In contrast to
the politically unstable countries surrounding it, Americans come
to Costa Rica not only for short periods, but also to settle or
retire. This is where we would be posted for the next three happy
years.

With a sad farewell to Bill, Jr. at Washington's National

Airport, Bill and I and the two girls flew to Miami. The following day, we took a small twin–engine plane belonging to the Costa Rican airline, LACSA, to San José, a five hour flight, where we were met by the minister of embassy and his wife, and whisked off to an apartment on the top floor of a tall building overlooking the city.

Fortunately for our family, the problems of relocating in Costa Rica were not as difficult as in Buenos Aires. This being our second Latin American posting, not only could we speak Spanish reasonably well, but Costa Ricans admired North Americans, and were generally polite, congenial, and helpful.

ぢ　　ぢ　　ぢ

The first few weeks in a foreign post can be baffling when you find yourself in a strange hotel or apartment in a strange land. Until becoming familiar with your new surroundings, culture shock can set in. In a small post such as Costa Rica, however, the embassy wives helped me through that initial period of orientation and resettlement. Our car had not arrived and they took me shopping, provided playmates for the children, gave me tips on schools and housing, helped me make calls, and introduced me to others in the diplomatic corps.

In my first letter home, I wrote:

> The only redeeming feature of this fifth floor apartment is that it overlooks San José and has a beautiful big terrace where Joni can ride her tricycle. Looking down on roof tops and narrow streets where busy little people bustle hither and yon, we feel very aloft. Encircling all are the mountains. At night the sky is brilliant with stars and the city speckled with lights. A very dominant Texaco sign reminds us of home. The day, already brilliant with sunshine, starts about 5 A.M. when the city noisily

awakens—church bells, sirens, horns, street vendors, and traffic all compete. Bill and I lie in bed and moan but are gradually becoming immune to the city's sounds. The night the Pope had a stroke they blew the air raid siren at 3 A.M. which had us both leaping for the telephone.

Near noon, the storm clouds gather; around 2 P.M. the rain comes down in torrents. Sometimes it rains for an hour or less, and other times for most of the afternoon. During the rainy season, May to November, an umbrella is standard going–out attire after midday. In the morning, the sun never fails to shine and the sky is electric blue. At night it is cool enough for one blanket. All year long the temperature on the central plateau is constant, ranging between 55 degrees Fahrenheit at night and 75 degrees in the daytime. Perpetual springtime. We have all had a little trouble adjusting to the altitude and feel quite listless, but this will pass.

Although there are only two months left of the school year, (March to December), Channing has already started at the Lincoln School which combines an American system of teaching with a tremendous dose of Spanish, especially for those students who are not fluent in that language. I think she is the most adjustable child in the world, taking life as it comes, never complaining, and making the best of every situation. She loves new sights, new sounds, new adventures—our little gypsy.

Joni goes to nursery school every morning. There is only one other American child in her class, but she plays happily with all the little Ticos as the Costa Ricans are called. Two afternoons a week she takes ballet lessons and seems to take to them naturally. I will be so glad to move into our permanent home in November.

જ્જ   જ્જ   જ્જ

We were fortunate to find a large Spanish colonial house in a very pretty neighborhood, Barrio Jimenez, but had to delay moving until our effects arrived. The girls were dying to get out of our confining rooftop quarters, as were we. In the meantime, a highly recommended Jamaican cook, Alberta, came for an interview. She was a big, handsome black woman with gray hair and beautiful white teeth. I was reminded of Bloody Mary in *South Pacific.* With her imposing figure and commander-in-chief personality, I felt awed in her presence, and soon realized that she was the one doing the interviewing. Yet there was something about her that gave me a feeling of security and confidence, and I hired her at a salary of $28.50 a month.

Alberta stayed with us for the three years we were in San José, and we grew to love her. Underneath an austere exterior was hidden a heart of gold. When she was busy, invasion of her kitchen domain was unacceptable, and the children were often expedited with a loud "Hout, hout of my kitchen!" There was a lilting quality to her voice and her accent was such that the letter "H" was put before vowels, and dropped for "H" words. House became "ouse" and oven became "ho-ven." If she made cookies, she would hide them from Bill whom she referred to as a "cookie monster," and on one occasion she chased him from the kitchen with a butcher knife—and a chuckle. Having to search surreptitiously for cookies did not altogether please the master of the house.

As time went on, we realized that Alberta was highly intelligent and that she resented her lack of an education. One day she complained to Bill that white people had all the breaks. He explained to her that none of us had control over how we would be born, that he did not choose to be white, nor she black; it was all a part of God's great plan for His universe. Being an ardent Seventh Day Adventist, this simple explanation appeased her to a certain degree, but I agree with her that God's great plan for his world doesn't always seem fair.

We moved into our new home in mid November. It was a handsome Spanish style house of white stucco with a red tiled roof and large arched windows with iron bars. Downstairs was a recreation room. A smaller room with excellent natural lighting became my studio. When I announced that I was going "to the mountains," the family knew that Mom was holed up in there and not to be disturbed. The maids' quarters were also downstairs.

Upstairs was where we lived. Channing and Joni were delighted each to have her own big room, and Alberta was equally pleased to leave the roach-ridden little apartment kitchen for a larger kitchen area which she scrubbed until it sparkled.

Our big yard was surrounded on three sides by a tall wrought iron fence, and in the back, by a high cement wall between our property and a coffee finca. Flowers grew in profusion along the fence and driveway, and in beds in front of the house—bougainvillea, poinsettias, hibiscus, oleander, Spanish bayonet, and blue hydrangeas. We even had orchids growing in notches of trees in our backyard. Jacaranda trees, with their lovely lavender blooms, lined the one street of our neighborhood. A night watchman guarded the seven or eight houses at night, and a gardener tended the lawns and flowers by day. The *barrio*, owned by the Jimenez family, was very private.

We quickly settled into our new home. The rainy season was over and we could count on unfailing sunshine until May. We joined a country club in a lovely area called Escazu, the site of an old Indian village, established long before Columbus discovered these shores. (History books tell how the Indians living in Costa Rica were annihilated when the Spaniards came because they preferred death to surrender.) Here we joined friends for tennis and a swim. This is the only place where I can remember having ball boys. Like caddies of old, they were poor kids who picked up balls for a few colones (the Costa Rican currency), as well as being so talented with a tennis racket that they could fill in if the fourth for doubles didn't show up. Unlike many communities, social life did not revolve around the country club. Entertaining was done at home.

Maids were customary in all middle and upper class houses in the late 1950s, and as we needed someone to help Alberta, we hired a prim, little woman named Ninfa to do the housework and wait on table. She was decorative to have around the house as she not only wore her black uniform and organdy apron on her trim figure with style, but insisted on a jaunty organdy cap perched atop her gray head. Each week she would collect all the small soap pieces in bathrooms and kitchen, melt them down, and reshape them into a large cake which she would take home on her day off. After a few months, however, I had to let her go as she became increasingly eccentric and I worried that she might do something irrational in regard to the children. Also, for peace in the kitchen, it was just as well. Her Victorian prissiness was abrasive to big, pragmatic Alberta.

We then engaged Maria, a pretty girl with a son named Toñito, a little older than Joni. This gave Joni a built-in playmate as well as a guardian. Maria was sweet and accepted her role as subordinate to Alberta, so harmony was restored. She also sang in a clear soprano voice as she worked, and taught Joni little songs. Each evening at bath time, it was a delight to hear them singing together—"Arroz Con Leche," "La Cucaracha," and others. In addition, Maria would sing for our guests at parties, and we became known as the family with "the singing waitress."

ぅ   ぅ   ぅ

I doubt if the beauty of Costa Rica could be exaggerated. Only the finest artist could capture the lush green of the countryside with its kaleidoscopic shade, and changing colors. A tree called the Royal Poinciana or *llama Del Bosque* (Flame of the Forest) was indescribably resplendent with its bright orange blossoms. In its brilliance it seemed to be on fire. Plants and flowers grew so rapidly that stakes, used as fence posts, took root and grew into trees which served as windbreaks on the mountainsides, protecting the animals as well as the crops. The rural areas were dotted with privately owned farms of not more that a few acres, each having a small stand or two of coffee, bananas, cacao or sugar, the four crops on which the economy depended. The little homes were gaily painted and surrounded with flowers. People smiled and waved as you passed. Costa Rica was remarkable in that it was perhaps the only country in Latin America where class discrimination did not exist. Completely democratic, it boasted more schools than soldiers, more teachers than policemen. The literacy rate, about 98 percent, was by far the highest in Central America.

Costa Rica is also a bird lover's paradise with reportedly some 725 species of bird life in the various zones, compared to about 850 in all of North America. An ornithologist wrote, "There is no need to claw your way through the jungle to see birds. Just drive out into the country and sit quietly for half an hour and they come to you." Like the flowers, many have brilliantly colored plumage such as the ubiquitous parakeet. One day, Bill and I were lucky enough to see a quetzal, a bird of resplendent plumage unique to Central America. The early Mayan and Aztecs named this bird after the god, Quetzalcoatl, the plumed serpent, and only emperors were permitted to use the tail feathers to adorn their clothing. During the eighteenth and nineteenth centuries, its beautiful plumage was so sought after in Europe that thousands of skins were smuggled across the Atlantic. As a result, the quetzal was threatened with extinction.

Although the intricately painted ox cart has now been replaced by more utilitarian conveyances, at mid century the carts could still be seen along country roads laden with wood and other products of the soil. An art form unique to Costa Rica, no two designs were said to be the same. Natives claimed that a neighbor could recognize another man's cart before it came into view by the sound of the wheels as it clattered down the road.

꒰   ꒱   ꒱

When Bill, Jr. came home for the Christmas holiday, we detected that all was not well at the Episcopal High School. He obviously had not had a good grounding in the fundamentals of grammar and math and was stumbling scholastically. Also, from the tone of his letters after he returned to Alexandria, his spirits were as low as his marks and we became increasingly concerned. Fifteen can be a difficult age, and in the case of our boy, it may have been a mistake to wean him from the security of home. He had been shuttled from one country to another, and had had to cope with two languages and eight different schools in nine years.

When his April report card had not shown improvement, we decided to bring him to San José to repeat the tenth grade at the Lincoln School. This, we felt, would give him a chance to gain confidence and do well in his studies. He was a bright kid who devoured books and knowledge, and we knew he had it in him to succeed academically. The school year had just begun in Costa Rica and he would therefore start almost from the beginning with his class.

Once this decision was made, Bill and I felt a certain relief. We would have him home again where we could watch his progress more closely, and help him find his footing. We also felt that there were certain benefits for him at the Lincoln School. His class was small; we could have him tutored in subjects where he was floundering; and two or more years in Costa Rica would give him the opportunity to become fluent in Spanish. He would also have a chance to travel with his father to other Central American countries.

We wrote of our decision to his school and to him at the same time, and worried about his reaction to our letters. We knew that it would be tough leaving school and friends in mid term, but more than that, we worried that he would feel that he had let us down. Hoping to convince him that he should not blame himself and that his return to the fold would be for the best, Bill wrote him an exceptionally loving letter in which he said:

"At various times in life, one is faced with difficult decisions . .

I believe that you will agree with us that you are out of your depth this year. We do not feel that it is your fault, nor the fault of the school. It is just one of those situations in which we sometimes find ourselves. No person ever lived who didn't get into that position every once in a while, and the only honest thing to do is to face up to the problem and find a solution . . . You have what it takes to make a mark in life for the good, son; I am willing to stake my life on that. So, don't doubt yourself, and don't let yourself get mired down in useless self–recrimination. Worry is a waste of time. Remember that what has happened is no disgrace. It would be a disgrace, however, if we didn't face the situation squarely, and we are going to do just that. It will be wonderful to have the whole family together again. I love you."

We are indebted to our friends, Margaret and Charlie Pearson, who helped Billy pack up and get off. He was not a happy boy when he arrived in San José on April 6, but within a few days, his smile returned and he settled into his new life and school with enthusiasm. The jolt to his ego seemed to have given him an "I'll show the world" attitude and he took off like a jet. He enjoyed his school, his friends, his home, and his little sisters who adored him. We arranged tutoring in math and chemistry and his academic problems melted away. In a very short time, he became an excellent and popular student, and a very happy teenager. To give him his own space for privacy and study, we converted part of our garage into a pleasant bedroom, adding a big window, closet, bookshelves, and a built-in desk. We gave it a fresh coat of paint, hung pictures and put a rug on the cement floor. There was already a small bathroom. The result was a cozy and comfortable place for a boy, set off from the rest of the house, where he could practice his guitar, and study in quiet.

ᘚ   ᘚ   ᘚ

We discovered a lovely resort overlooking a wide valley called La Catalina. Only forty miles from San José, it became our favorite weekend spot for family outings. Charming little Swiss chalets perched precariously on the edge of a mountain and overlooked the San José valley. We rode the slow, dependable horses on trails through the tropical growth with Joni on the saddle in front of Bill, fed the tame deer in a little deer park, swam in the icy pool fed by mountain springs, and went to bed under three blankets. The children loved it, and one fond memory is of my two Bills having a father-son talk while sitting on a rock overlooking the valley as the sunset blazed across the horizon.

With the two older children, we took a transit steamer through the Panama Canal from Colon to Panama City. Once we had cleared the harbor at the end of our trip, we had arranged to debark on a small boat which would come to pick up the pilot who had guided us through the locks. Somebody goofed, however, as Bill, Jr. suddenly noticed the little pilot boat pulling away from the ship. Bill ran up to the wheelhouse to tell the Captain, who radioed the pilot boat, which then returned to collect us. It pulled along side bobbing up and down with the waves, and we descended perilously down a rope ladder. Had it not been for Billy's bright eyes, we would have been on our way to Ecuador!

ᘚ   ᘚ   ᘚ

In his four-wheel-drive enclosed jeep, provided by the U.S. government, Bill engaged in frequent travel into the interior of Nicaragua. His job was principally to develop markets for agricultural export, gather information on what commodities were being produced, and promote trade with the United States. To do this he needed reliable contacts at the working level in remote areas, which required travel down miles of unpaved and often muddy roads. When the terrain was impassable by jeep, he journeyed by Piper Cub, handrail car, banana barge, train, dugout canoe and even burro. He could not drive to Panama as the Pan American Highway had not been finished at that time. He therefore had to fly and sometimes do his Panamanian field work by riding a rickety local bus, or hitching a ride on a company plane that could land on jungle air strips. Although he was generally away only three or four days at a time, he invariably returned with a new story to tell which we filed into our store of memories. Being an adventurer at heart, he loved his work.

There were dangers such as the time he was captured. Bill had driven to Managua with Frank Irwin, a fellow officer from the American embassy in Costa Rica, and that evening had planned a reception for his Nicaraguan contacts at the suburban home of one of the junior officers at the American Embassy. Latin Americans are prone to be late, but when no one had arrived at the party by 10 P.M., Bill knew something was amiss.

He phoned the embassy and was told that the ambassador wanted to see him immediately. When he and Frank arrived on the outskirts of the capital, Nicaraguan tanks and foot soldiers had taken up positions at strategic road junctions, and the central district was in blackout. At the embassy, marine guards in battle dress were on duty both inside and outside of the building. Bill entered the ambassador's office and was handed a "top secret" cable directed to William L. Rodman from the U.S. Military Attache in San José. The cable said that an unconfirmed report had been received that Cuban troops had been airlifted onto an unidentified landing strip near the Costa Rican border with the intention of invading Nicaragua, and asked Bill to proceed with caution and verify.

Because of Bill's frequent travels into the interior of his three assigned countries, he had been asked before to keep his eyes open for any out-of-the-ordinary proceedings, so this request to do a small bit of military intelligence was not a surprise. Bill felt certain he knew the landing strip in question. It belonged to a rancher he had visited recently and was close to the border crossing.

A snag developed, however, when the ambassador insisted he proceed at once. This, Bill explained, was a foolhardy thing to do as it would be extremely dangerous driving at night on country roads without lights, and if it proved to be true that the Cubans were mounting an attack, it could be fatal. The ambassador flew into a rage and called the dictator, President Luis Somoza, who agreed that Bill should leave immediately, but for protection he would dispatch a Nicaraguan army officer, and an enlisted man with a machine gun to accompany him. This, Bill knew, could only make matters worse if he ran into trouble, but he realized that he and Frank were up against a stone wall. Civil servants do not disobey the orders of ambassadors and presidents. In all of our twenty-nine years in the foreign service, the above mentioned individual was the only ambassador under whom we served who could be called an unparalleled mistake.

Bill and Frank drove to the Gran Hotel to get their luggage and spent well over an hour ostensibly packing, while the lieutenant and the machine gunner sat impatiently in the jeep. If they stalled as long as possible, Bill reasoned, they would have daylight for at least part of the trip. They finally departed about 1 A.M. and drove down back-country roads at a snail's pace for close to four hours. Bill was familiar with these rough dirt tracks because of his travels, but, at night, without headlights, the going was slow and hazardous.

As they rounded a bend, they almost ran into two land rovers blocking the road. After quickly turning on the dome and headlights, Bill and Frank put their arms out of the windows and told the lieutenant and private to place their weapons on the floor and do the same. It was a tense moment. Not a sound. All of a sudden, the quiet was broken by a band of rough looking characters yelling and leaping out of the bushes brandishing machetes and guns. Although my blond husband and Frank were shouting, "Somos Americanos—Americanos!" the would-be attackers encircled the jeep poking guns in their faces and demanding they get out. Bill managed to open the door with his knee, hands still in the air, and they dragged both men into the glare of the headlights. Having eaten an ample amount at the aborted reception, Bill had undone his belt for comfort, and his pants fell down around his ankles. In spite of the crisis at hand, he said the thought flashed through his brain that a newspaper headline might read, "Diplomat Caught with his Pants Down."

Good fortune, however, was with them. One of the wild men suddenly yelled above all the ruckus, "Dios mio!—no son Cubanos—es mi amigo Americano—Señor Rodman!" Bill's savior was indeed a friend and the owner of a *trapiche,* a small sugar mill. The "wild" men were actually a group of small farmers of the area who had heard the rumors of a Cuban invasion, and had banded together to defend their country. A jug of local rum was produced and the story ended with *embrazos* and good cheer all around, giving a happy conclusion to a very small international incident in the hinterland of Nicaragua.

Bill's friend explained that when the *campesinos* had been warned of the Cuban incursion, he and his neighbors had rigged up a field phone running from the nearest pueblo to the roadblock, and, in their excitement, had heard the word *Cubanos* instead of *Americanos,* even though the little green jeep was going in the wrong direction.

By the time Bill and Frank reached the border, dawn was breaking, and still no Cubans, so they crossed and drove on to the air strip in question. Wagons, tractors, logs, and other impediments were strewn along the strip, put there by local "Ticos" who were not about to let the enemy land in their country.

ॐ　　ॐ　　ॐ

Whenever possible, I accompanied Bill to Nicaragua in the jeep. The country was rugged and beautiful, but the capitol, Managua, was dirty, poor, backward and insufferably hot. By some unfortunate misguidance, the city was established in a tropical basin instead of on higher ground as in the case of San José, and, just like hot soup in a bowl, steamed twelve months of the year. A rather off-guard saying was that "if the world could be given an enema, Managua was where they would insert the pipe."

A fanciful embellishment at our favorite lodging, the Gran Hotel Managua, was a array of rare tropical birds that roamed aimlessly around a swimming pool in the central courtyard. Hot water literally wasn't needed; the cold water was warm. When Bill called on city contacts or worked at the embassy, a suit and tie were the proper attire. In those days, tropical–weight suits were of the wash-and-wear variety, often made of non-breathing material. By the end of the day, they were limp with sweat, and common practice was to wear them right into the shower.

Commercial air service offered frequent flights of less than an hour from Costa Rica to its two adjoining countries. On the occasions that I went along with Bill by air, we traveled on separate planes. With three children at home, it seemed wiser. In the capable hands of Alberta, we could leave with a feeling of confidence. She would have picked up a meat cleaver and killed anybody who tried to break into the house, and was not rumpled by the frequent earth tremors, or the occasional earthquake.

For me, the fascination of Panama City was the duty free shopping. This city of 2,000,000 souls was truly a little Hong Kong and we bought many wonderful items including china, teakwood furniture, and linens. In addition to the shops, we were authorized to use the military post exchanges in the American Canal Zone. Our favorite hotel was the old Tivoli with its broad verandas, comfortable rooms, wicker furniture, ceiling fans, and delicious food. Reminiscent of a romantic movie set from a Somerset Maugham novel, it, alas, is no longer there. As with so many charming hotels of the past, in the cross-eyed name of progress, it was torn down to be replaced by fast food eateries. Spelled backwards, Tivoli becomes "I lov it," and love it we did. In fact, when we later acquired a new cocker spaniel, we named her Tivoli.

જ્ર   જ્ર   જ્ર

Bill became Senior Warden at the Church of the Good Shepherd where the Episcopal Church had its Central American see, the official jurisdiction of the American bishop. Both he and the new young bishop, David Richards, had jobs which took them to remote regions of Costa Rica and Nicaragua and they sometimes traveled together.

In Costa Rica there were nine missions, and as many in Nicaragua. These sites, located in the jungle and coastal regions, were extremely depressed due to the withdrawal in 1931 of the United Fruit Company as a result of Panama Disease. This root rot in bananas had spread like wildfire, completely destroying the thriving industry in both countries. At one time there had been 34,000 acres of bananas under cultivation in Costa Rica alone. Hundreds of Jamaicans brought in to work on the banana plantations had been out of work for decades. They clustered in small settlements where they could hardly scratch a subsistence raising cacao, coconuts, garden vegetables, sugar cane and corn. Coming from an Anglican background in Jamaica, they requested help from the church, and the missions came into being.

Anglican work in Central America was transferred from the Church of England to the Protestant Episcopal Church of the United States of America in 1947. At the First National Council meeting of the Episcopal Church in Costa Rica, I was elected secretary of women's work. With a committee of four, all black except me, we went by train up and down the old railroad line of Costa Rica visiting the missions, and trying to encourage the women to form auxiliaries, altar guilds, and youth groups. As secretary, I wrote a report to the bishop making observations and recommendations. We hoped that some of our advice would rub off, but in more cases than not, good intentions dissolved the minute we departed. As an example, in a report to the bishop regarding Holy Cross Mission in Guácimo, I wrote the following:

"Father Harrison met with the committee to present some of the problems involved in trying to set up either men's or women's church organizations in this area. He pointed out that previous attempts had failed and put the blame on the mental lethargy of the people.

A big problem is the custom of concubinage. This has been practiced by fathers and forefathers, and it is likely to be the exception rather than the rule that a man growing up in this environment would be able to grasp the reasons for changing a way of life that is age old. If they commit this sin, after having been confirmed at an earlier age, they are refused the holy sacraments. As a result, in their limited understanding, confusion develops, followed by indifference. The vows of matrimony or confirmation, not truly understood, mean little. In their daily existence, the future is of no consequence, only the moment itself.

Another problem is drinking, especially during the corn season when the people have a little money in their pockets and the cantinas stay open all night long ... Father Harrison, a black man in his seventies, said that he had hauled lumber and mended the church roof himself after giving up in desperation of finding help from the men."

Although this report was discouraging, there were occasions when our work seemed worthwhile. Sometimes all four of us traveled together; at other times, just Miss Britton, the chairman, and I journeyed out by train and slept in native houses. On occasion I took Channing with me. In raising our children, Bill and I felt it was important to expose them to the other side of their privileged existence at home. She slept with me in jungle huts, played with native children, ate the meager diet of rice and beans and coconut milk, endured the violent rains, mosquitoes, and near presence of termites, spiders, tarantulas, and snakes. Sometimes, we would accompany Bishop Richards on his rounds of the missions, and Channing, now thirteen, would walk with him down the railroad track and through jungle growth to act as acolyte in administering Holy Communion to the sick and disabled.

At the end of the day, hot, tired, and dusty, we would generally wind up in Puerto Limón for a comfortable night at the Park Hotel. One side of the hotel overlooked the Caribbean Sea; the other faced a little park famous for its colony of three-toed sloths—little animals that hang bottom side up in the trees. Once in Puerto Limón, a young parishioner left a package for Channing at the front desk. She opened it to find a child's white and pink plastic bureau set with mirror, pin tray, brush and comb in a heart shaped box, hardly a gift for a budding teenager. Nevertheless, she and I were greatly touched that the young man had probably spent his last cent to express his love.

ॐ   ॐ   ॐ

Engineers overcame the impossible when they constructed Costa Rica's railroad in the 1880s. They forced a path through a wilderness of mountains and swamps. The tracks rose 5,000 feet across rivers which flooded periodically, and along hillsides where it could rain as much as thirty-five inches within thirty hours. During construction, 4,000 or more lives were lost due to malaria and other tropical fevers. Recruitment, therefore, was continuous, especially from the West Indies. Black men were more resistant to the hazards of the tropics.

Riding the little train along the "Old Line" was a never-to-be-forgotten experience. It ran on a narrow gauge track from Alahuela, a few miles east of San José, to Puerto Limón, the Atlantic port, taking about an hour to go eight or ten miles—six hours total. The engine huffed and puffed up one mountain and down the next, sometimes riding the ledge, enabling passengers to look down into what seemed a bottomless chasm. Many of the curves were so sharp that the front and back of the train were in horseshoe formation. At one point, the little engine slowed down to ten miles an hour to cross a gorge on a spider bridge 1,000 feet in the air, and then wound its way along the rugged Reventazon River to Siquerres. Here, the railroad branched north to Guápiles and south to the sea at Puerto Limón. Along the tracks of the Old Line was where the Episcopal missions were located and where the jungle was often so dense that foliage smacked at the train in passing.

The train was the life-line in an area that was isolated from the world—no roads, no plumbing, no hospitals, and almost no electricity or schooling. Dotted along the tracks were small communities of thatched huts and one or two room wooden shacks with porches adorned by potted plants in tin cans. Whoever had something to sell, perhaps a chicken, some mangoes, or a stand of bananas, hopped aboard the little train and, walking up and down the aisle, loudly plied his wares. Once they were sold, the vendor would hop off the train at the next stop and sit on the platform until a returning train took him back to his melon patch or chicken coop. I have used the masculine pronoun, but many of these vendors were women in colorful loose fitting garments, a bandana tied around their heads.

The ribbon of track went by the front gate of Los Diamantes, a beautiful estancia and agricultural experimental station cut out of the jungle. Laybe Larsen, a ruggedly handsome man and a former bronco rider, managed the station. He, his wife, Catherine, and two sons lived in a house with wide verandas and ceiling fans in every room. In well-tended gardens, flowers grew in abundance. A swimming pool was built into a stream that flowed through the estancia. There were horses to ride, an assortment of dogs, and a pet monkey named Poncho who loved men but would not go near the ladies. Poncho was an aggressive pest who would put his wizened little face only inches from a man's nose, wrap his long hairy arms around the victim's neck and chatter raucously. The kids enjoyed

Poncho, but I was thankfully ignored. A veritable jungle oasis, Los Diamantes became a favorite spot for our family to visit. In 1960, the Larsens offered young Bill a summer job working on a dam-building project, and tutoring their young sons who were being schooled by the Calvert System. He went off with his guitar tucked under his arm and a happy grin.

After a day of visiting missions, I would often head for Los Diamantes. As it was not an official stop, the conductor would signal the engineer to slow the train down just enough for me to leap into the bushes alongside the track. At night it was somewhat frightening, but the Larsens knew when I was coming and would be standing near the jumping spot with a flashlight. To relax with them over a cool drink and dinner, plus a shower before bed was five-star luxury, a welcome contrast to the nights I spent at the church missions.

One night, after a hot rainy day of visiting missions, the three ladies of the committee and I stayed in Guácimo at the house of Mr. James Earl, a respected leader in the community. My three friends were shown to a room with one double bed and I was shown to a tiny room at the back of the house with a cot and a crib. (The crib would later accommodate two little black babies.) Before bed, I hid my medicinal half-pint flask of whiskey under my dress and asked where I might find the privy. Mr. Earl handed me a flashlight, an umbrella, and a piece of old newspaper, and pointed out the back door. Thinking of what might be lurking in the bushes, I made my way hesitantly down a footpath to a dilapidated outhouse. To this day, I have to grin at the thought of sitting there in the dark in the middle of nowhere with rain pouring through cracks in the roof, sipping whiskey, and holding an umbrella over my head.

At Holy Cross mission in Guácimo, Bill and I gave a brass altar cross in memory of our fathers. All the churches were simple wooden structures, falling apart and termite ridden. While kneeling at a service, my spiritual concentration would be addled by watching the termites kick up little clouds of wood dust.

I often wonder how I ever landed myself in the role of missionary. Although I grew up in an Episcopalian family and attended an Episcopal school, I was far from a dedicated church woman. I think now that my travels for the church in Central America fulfilled a deep-seated love of adventure, as well as a desire to reach out to other people.

Because of my peregrinations, however, I continually found myself in unlikely situations such as one I encountered in the small community of Rio Hondo at St. Peter's Mission. The grounds of St. Peter's were planted with lovely trees and flowering shrubs. A path led up a hill to the church that had once been the prettiest little mission in Costa Rica, but was now in dire need of paint and repairs. Miss Britton and I were met at the station by Mr. Mantle, a young cacao farmer, who escorted us to his home where we met his wife and mother, the only remaining members of the congregation. He explained that St. Peter's had been a thriving mission, but about a year before, the people began leaving due to antagonism with the lay reader. They were also annoyed with the priest-in-charge, who was based several stations away; he had not visited for a span of six weeks which included the Christmas season.

To locate the people who had left the church was an impossible task in the time allowed before our train left for Puerto Limón, so we asked Mr. Mantle to ring the church bell long and loud. As the lovely sound rang out over the quiet jungle, people left what they were doing and wandered up the hill, curious to know what was going on at the mission on a Monday morning. Soon thirty or so adults and children were sitting quietly in the church. Mr. Mantle, acting as spokesman, asked if Miss Britten and I might conduct a short service, so we read Morning Prayer and asked them to join in several rousing hymns to the strains of a rickety pump organ. Without question, the small congregation was happy to be reassembled.

Before our visit was over, a Women's Auxiliary had been organized, and plans made to resume Sunday School. When Miss

Britton and I saw the priest-in-charge later that day, we recited our story and asked him to get to Rio Hondo the very next Sunday—without fail.

Now, a highway has replaced the "Old Line," and sadly, "The Little Engine That Could" has disappeared into the archives of history.

֍   ֍   ֍

The citizens of San José went bananas when it came to decorating their city for Christmas. Lamp posts, telegraph poles, and store fronts in town were bedecked with tinsel, lights, and other forms of festoonery. Almost every house had a small lighted tree, and a little shrine with a nativity scene and a favorite plaster saint. A carnival atmosphere prevailed for a week featuring fireworks, masked parades, marimba bands, and concerts. People danced in the streets. Tacos, caramelized apples, and ice cream were sold in all-night stalls. To us, the lights looked a bit out of place adorning banana, palm and papaya trees. It also seemed strange that right after Christmas, we would go to the beach at Marbella on the Atlantic Coast for a short holiday.

Joni, being so much younger than her brother and sister, was the target of a great deal of both parental and sibling advice, but one subject which was truly a poser was "Christmas in the Tropics." Our intelligent four year old believer quickly figured out that reindeer could not land on red tile roofs, nor Santa gain passage into houses without a fireplace. December was the only time of year when I would have welcomed "the moon on the crest of the new-fallen snow."

Between Christmas and the New Year, bullfighting, Costa Rican style, was a tradition. A young bull was let loose in a bull ring and any youth who felt the urge could play matador. In free-for-all style, the bull chased everyone and everyone chased the bull. The end came when the bull was exhausted and several would-be bullfighters piled on top of him. The poor animal was just too tired to get up, but was not killed.

In contrast to Christmas, Easter Week was a time when a deep melancholia invaded the Costa Rican atmosphere. Villages and towns were strewn and garlanded with thousands of flowers. On small carts, grotesque statues were paraded mournfully along the appointed routes. Sometimes, rather than statues, favored citizens reenacted scenes of Christ being led to Calvary, or the crucifixion itself. I personally found these processions macabre; a strong accent was placed on the dead and bleeding Christ, and little on the risen Christ. It especially pained me to see the shrouded women, dressed in black, wailing as they followed the procession. Some were on their knees.

Little Dancer
Joni, age 3 years, 11 months
in San José, Costa Rica, November 1958.

Chapter Nine

EAST COAST OF NICARAGUA

IN 1960, THERE WERE TWO WAYS TO TRAVEL ACROSS NICARAGUA from its capital, Managua, to the eastern coastal port of Bluefields, on the Caribbean Sea. The practical and sensible way was by air. The other involved jeep, dugout canoe, river launch, and a pioneering spirit. This is the way we chose.

Very early one morning, with our friends Dick and Yvonne Johns, American missionaries in Managua, we set off down the Rama Road in Bill's jeep. When completed, this road would stretch 160 miles to Rama, a little town where the Escondido River, a navigable waterway to the east, meets with smaller tributaries, bridging the gap between the Atlantic and Pacific oceans. The project was started in 1943 as part of President Franklin D. Roosevelt's Good Neighbor Policy, and was scheduled for completion in 1967. But in July 1960, the Rama Road was still fifty miles short of its mark.

Like the Costa Rican Railway, the Rama Road, thrusting its way through primeval forest, craggy rock formations, and jungle, was a monumental engineering achievement. It bridged streams and rivers, and wound its way over heavy red *clay s*oil which quickly churned into a slippery bog during the incessant rainstorms. Here and there a little clearing of rough pasture or patches of cultivation

100

appeared, and small clusters of thatched dwellings brimmed with chicks, piglets, and babies. Much of the surface of the road was unpaved creating a washboard effect that forced you to hold your mouth tightly shut to keep your teeth from knocking together. For comic relief, we laughed at the misshapen trunks of trees, each with its own distorted personality, functioning as telegraph poles.

When we reached the picturesque hill town of Juigalpa, we stopped for breakfast at a forsaken little building with the grandiose name of Hotel Imperial. The elderly couple who greeted us was overjoyed to have customers, and, to our amazement, served us a breakfast of avocado, eggs, refried beans, rice, an unidentifiable meat, and cafe con leche. We briefly looked at their accommodations in case we might want to stop on the return trip. The rooms, dormitory style, were clean but primitive with a water basin and chamber pot by each canvas cot. Wisely, we bought broad brimmed hats which later became invaluable as umbrellas, although mine seemed contoured to drain down the back of my neck.

Around noon we arrived at the village of Muelle de los Bueyes, (Wharf of the Oxen) a muddy little settlement on the Rio Mico, where we would set out in a dugout canoe to cover the thirty miles to El Recreo. The dugouts, known as pitpans, are crudely made—a hollowed out trunk of a tree pointed at both ends. In performance, however, they move swiftly and silently, and will stay afloat even if half full of water. With two native guides, one at each end, we four settled ourselves in the bottom of our pitpan for a wet and hair-raising, three–hour journey.

We were told to wear rubber boots as we might have to walk around several of the more hazardous rapids. We never learned which of the 110 rapids were the so-called dangerous ones as this suggestion was never carried out, and we admired the calm skill and teamwork of our guides.

Along the banks, the jungle was alive with brightly colored birds, blue butterflies, monkeys, and flowering orchids. White and blue herons stalked in the shallows. Occasionally, we spotted a clearing with a lonely little thatched hut and barking dog. Natives washed their clothes in the river and children played nearby. Everyone grinned and waved. White men were a novelty to enjoy.

As we approached El Recreo, the tinkling bell of a small wooden church was a comforting sound in the remoteness of the landscape. The sound came from the headquarters of an agricultural experimental station, comprised of a bungalow for the resident officer, a guest house, little painted houses for the staff, and a colony of wooden huts for the native workers. After the excitement of the jungle river trip, we were relieved to gaze upon peaceful fields of grain, nurseries of young trees, and well tended fencing as far as the eye could see.

The guest house was cool and charmingly decorated in rattan furniture cushioned with explosions of chintz flowers. We enjoyed running water in our showers, followed by cooling drinks and dinner prepared by Ana, the housekeeper, before we fell into bed.

The following morning, Captain Willoughby Fenton, our host, drove us in his jeep to Esperanza, a private plantation of African palm trees where workers were processing the palm oil for export. The manager was Carl Thomason, a gentle and intelligent Texan. A civil engineer, he had originally come to Central America to work on the construction of the Pan American Highway. His wife was Nicaraguan. They had ten children and had lived at Esperanza for thirteen years. I marveled that this long period of isolation from the outside world had not made them apathetic and insular; instead they were charming, outgoing, and abreast of happenings outside of their small realm. The older children had gone off to colleges in the United States, while the younger ones were schooled at home.

We returned to El Recreo to find that the launch and crew, requested by radio, had arrived from Bluefields. Compared to the pitpan, the launch seemed the height of luxury. It took about an hour to reach Rama City where the little Mico River joins the mighty Escondido. We asked ourselves how such a diminutive ghost town could be referred to as Rama City? But perhaps it was destined to live up to its name once the road was completed and parts of the river dredged so that ocean going vessels could sail into the interior of Nicaragua from the Caribbean. Then, opportunities for increased trade with the outside world would be unlimited.

The tiny hamlets along the Escondido were essentially unchanged since the Spanish Conquest. Natives who shared both Indian and Spanish blood were called *mestizos,* but the Nicaraguans living in this area had pronounced Indian features. They lived in thatched or wooden huts and tried to eke out an existence on small banana or coconut farms. The government had built schools, but those we saw appeared closed. It would be difficult to entice teachers to these remote, forsaken little communities, and I would guess that the people themselves didn't see any need for learning. All traffic was on the water, and the ubiquitous pitpans went silently and gracefully to and fro in the lazy flow of the river.

Shortly after we left Rama City, we stopped to see a mission family named Jacobs who lived just over the rise of the bank in a cluster of ramshackle huts. A message had reached Dick at El Recreo that the matriarch was sick and in need of medicine. The rain was teeming down as we stepped onto an improvised dock. Suddenly, several rotten boards gave way and Dick fell through, badly scraping one of his legs. Nevertheless, in his kind and gentle manner, he tried to comfort the old lady and led the family in prayer. Although she was frail and ill, old Mrs. Jacobs was feisty, giving orders in a strange creole patois to her brood, and demanding her pipe back. As they had no timepieces and were illiterate, Dick carefully explained that the medicine was to be taken at sunrise and moonrise.

Between Rama City and Bluefields, as other rivers flowed into it on its journey to the sea, the Rio Escondido became a wide estuary. In order to take full advantage of the beauty of the setting under a full moon, as well as to celebrate Bill's and my nineteenth wedding anniversary, we four sat on the roof of the launch and sang old favorites, toasted each other with whiskey in tin cups, and dined on avocado, local cheese, and cold spam adorned with a small candle from Bill's "survival kit."

Upon arrival in Costa Rica, Bill had taken to heart the advice of a bush pilot to never leave home without a survival kit. Therefore, in his old army musette bag he carried anti-venoms for a variety of poisonous snakes, halazone tablets to purify drinking water, iodine, bandages, bug repellent, various pills, small candles, a metal mirror for signaling, matches in a waterproof case, a folding jungle knife, fish hooks and line, dehydrated army rations, some lightweight rope, a pocket size Bible, family pictures, and sundry other items, all of which weighed less than eight pounds. The children loved to watch him check his "survival kit" to make sure everything was in good order before setting off in his jeep.

When we reached Bluefields at 1:30 A.M., a single lantern, dangling on a pole, welcomed us at the dock. Dead tired, we shouldered our bags, and stepping over sleeping bodies which littered the dock, trudged up the dirt road to the Episcopal Church rectory and knocked loudly. The sleepy young minister in charge of St. Thomas's Church, Larry Walton, though not thrilled to see us at that hour, graciously showed us to our rooms in the guest house next door. As the generator had been turned off, we had no lights or running water. Nevertheless, before going to bed, we were grateful for a unique bucket-shower rigged on the outside of the house, and a drink of rainwater from a barrel under a downspout.

Bluefields was West Indian in appearance and seemed to have no connection to the rest of Nicaragua. The town was pretty, neat, and clean. White weatherboard houses were in the English cottage style—two stories, dormer windows, and red roofs. Each stood in a small garden surrounded by a white fence. This had been a flourishing port until the banana industry was virtually wiped out during the 1930s by Panama Disease. Hundreds of Negroes, brought in from Jamaica to work on the banana plantations, as well as coastal natives, were left without jobs.

જ   જ   જ

Our next stop was Corn Island which lay forty-seven miles out to sea from Bluefields harbor. We left at 7:30 in the morning aboard an old United Fruit Company tugboat, the Síquia, and rather than rough seas which were the norm, the crossing was as smooth as glass and took only six instead of the usual eight hours. The day was so crystal clear that we were still an hour out to sea when we first sighted Corn Island. As we approached the shore, we could look down into the deep, translucent water and clearly see the ocean floor.

At the dock, Bonnie Jean met us in her pickup truck, one of three vehicles on the island. She was a fat, unpleasant character whose occupation was killing pigs to send to market in Bluefields. We had no choice but to pile in the back and try to ignore the leftover stench of dead swine. For two miles, we bounced along a widened mule track to the Episcopal Mission House where we were to spend two nights with Father Davis and his wife. As we drove up, the Girls Friendly Society was grouped on the porch singing songs of welcome, one of which we recognized as "The Little Brown Church in the Wild Wood."

The Davis's house was immaculate. We were offered hospitality and a meal of fried bananas, lobster, and coconut pie cooked by Alan, a teenage orphan, whom Mrs. Davis had taken in and trained. Father Davis was proud of his collection of 78 RPM records, several of which he played for us on a old wind-up victrola.

Corn Island, seven miles long and one mile wide, had a population of about 1,500. Surrounded by an iridescent sea of constantly changing color, it was green and lush, with forests of waving coconut palms and fine white sand beaches. The Davises told us that at one time the island had been used as a safe haven for pirates, as well as a depository for sick slaves. It was therefore no wonder that many of the islanders were black–skinned with blond hair and blue eyes, or white–skinned with black curly hair. As in Bluefields, Anglo-Saxon names predominated: Quinn, Campbell, Macintosh, Downs. The islanders gained their livelihood from the prolific coconut palm which bore fruit all year round. Small boys scrambled up trees like monkeys to harvest the nuts. Dotted here and there were little mills which extracted the coconut oil. This was sealed in drums and sent to Bluefelds, then flown to Managua. The copra was also dried and the nuts exported to the United States. Despite its name, little or no corn was grown on the island. During the early twentieth century, Corn Island had been used as a jail, but incarceration in "paradise" could hardly be classed as punishment and the jail was moved to a more intolerable location.

Bill had brought along several varieties of beans with the idea that he would show the people how to prepare a seed bed, then plant. Dick and some young men helped with this project. Bill carefully explained that when the crop was harvested, some of the yield should be saved for replanting and expanding the bean crop; in this way their meager diet would be enriched by the protein in the beans. In case of a wash-out from heavy rains, he left several bags of beans for replanting. We heard later that they had not only had the wash-out, but that the natives had eaten the replacement beans. Discouraging, but not surprising.

In the meantime, Yvonne and I visited the school which ran from first through sixth grade. After our inspection, a holiday was declared so that the children could accompany Mrs. Davis, affectionately known as "Mommie," and her visitors to the sea to bathe. Amid squeals of joy, thirty little bodies bounced about like young porpoises in the delightful, clear water. A reef protected the swimming area from sharks.

At the end of the seventeenth century, a famous English navigator and writer named William Dampier recounted his adventures to the author, Daniel Defoe. Dampier mentioned joining some buccaneers, who, while sailing northeast from Bluefields in the Caribbean, had picked up a castaway on a deserted island. The man, guilty of some misdemeanor, had been put off the ship by an irate captain, not knowing that the captain would arrange for another ship to pick him up after a given length of time. The castaway story so appealed to Daniel Defoe that he wrote his immortal work, *Robinson Crusoe.* Corn Island, or its neighbor, Little Corn Island, may have been the setting for this famous tale.

ॐ   ॐ   ॐ

The crossing from Corn Island to Monkey Point, our next destination, was far from peaceful. After receiving a bad weather report, we left just before midnight in order to try to stay ahead of a storm somewhere out to sea. Nevertheless, the Caribbean became a churning cauldron. We and the Johns flipped a coin for the one tiny stateroom aboard the tugboat. Bill and I lost and had to spend a harrowing night on deck hanging on for dear life to whatever was within reach. As we approached Monkey Point, however, the sea grew calm and the dawn was breathtaking in its beauty. The captain slowed to half speed in order to have full daylight before maneuvering the tug between the coral reefs to find a safe spot to anchor. A dory came out to meet us.

Monkey Point was unique in that the forty people living there were all members of one family. The matriarch, "Ma" Presada, of creole origin, was eighty-two years old. She had originally come from Bluefields where she had met her husband, a sailor from Martinique. In 1906, they had settled at Monkey Point—surely one of the most isolated spots on earth—and had given birth to eleven children, only five of whom were living. These had married natives from the coastal region or nearby hamlets. Ma had a very sharp mind. She had instructed her clan in the ways of the Lord, and read daily from the Bible. All were literate as she had taught them how to read and write, a paradox considering the high rate of illiteracy on Nicaragua's east coast.

One of her sons, Luke Presada, led us up a path through jungle growth to his mother's house. As she was almost blind, Ma studied us closely with squinty eyes, and moved her wrinkled fingers over our bodies. She decided that Bill was the bishop that she had been hoping would come. Not wanting to disappoint her, Bill did not deny it.

A visit from the outside world was a prodigious event at Monkey Point and word was sent out over the jungle grapevine to members of the clan to assemble, properly attired, at Ma's house. This took a little time as young and old took care to present themselves in immaculate condition. After Dick had read the Episcopal service of Morning Prayer, hymns were sung while Ma swayed back and forth slowly clapping her hands, lost in her own euphoria.

Two stalwart sons helped Ma down the hill to say good-bye and, like children everywhere, the little girls and boys wanted to hold our hands. We were presented with a dozen turtle eggs and, as we departed in the dory, the entire family gathered on the dock to sing a touching farewell song.

࿓   ࿓   ࿓

Back at Bluefields, we somehow managed to acquire the slowest and dirtiest banana boat on the east coast for the next leg of our trip to the Pearl Lagoon. The *Muco* was a twenty-foot inboard motor launch with two natives as crew. We unaffectionately renamed her the *Mucus*.

For the next few days, this would be our home along with fleas, spiders, and rotten smells. As there were strictly no comforts, we and the Johns were forced to become intimate—at night the four of us cuddled up like puppies on two air mattresses placed crosswise on the ribs of the old tub. Coconut milk was the purest liquid we could drink; we even used it for brushing our teeth. Dinner was cooked on a Coleman stove by my husband, the chef, and consisted of Dinty Moore stew or Spam, avocados, and any other local fruits we could garner. Between a leaky roof and sudden downpours, we were soaked much of the time. It made sense to wear shorts or slacks on board our *African Queen,* but local protocol dictated that ladies not wear pants, so when we landed at the Miskito villages, Yvonne and I had to wear skirts. The Indians we visited insisted on giving us several scrawny black chickens which pecked at us during the night.

With such confined quarters and two black crewmen on board, the calls of nature proved a problem. We had a potty and a procedure: a cohort would hold an old raincoat at arm's length as a shield. This worked pretty well until one evening when Yvonne accidentally dropped the potty overboard. As we were anchored near shore at the time, we enlisted an enthusiastic group of native boys who unabashedly removed their shorts before diving in. To our relief, the potty was recovered and the boys rewarded with little packets of M & Ms brought along for just such an exigency. The *Mucus* afforded a lot of laughs if not many comforts.

We sat on the roof of our derelict vessel as we made our way to the Pearl Lagoon through a series of beautiful jungle canals with arching branches of trees forming a canopy overhead. To turn corners the crew often had to reverse the *Muco* several times to ease her around. Brilliantly colored birds darted to and fro and monkeys jumped from tree to tree eying us as we passed. A big baboon appeared transfixed with curiosity. We felt enclosed in a jungle wonderland.

Quite suddenly, we were emptied onto the Pearl Lagoon itself, a large round body of water dotted with Miskito Indian settlements. Although various churches had tried to make inroads in the area, little had changed since time immemorial. The Moravians, the Baptists, the Episcopalians and the Roman Catholics were all competing for favor with the Indians, but I suspected that as soon as the missionary priest or catechist left, the natives reverted to their ancient ways of voodoo and witchcraft. At the primitive hamlet of Orinoco, strange little charms hung around the necks of the natives. They loved to sing, however, and wherever we visited, they belted forth Christian hymns of praise. We were considered oddities because of our clothes, customs and pale faces. Visitors of any sort were a diversion.

At each stop throughout our week–long journey on the Miskito coast, the entire tribe came to the dock, (if there was one), and a selected oarsman would paddle out to the boat in a dugout to bring us to shore. Quite often, neither English nor Spanish was spoken, only the Miskito tongue, but we all enjoyed patting each other on the back while drinking gallons of coconut milk. As we left, the tiny population always gathered to wave good-bye and sing farewell.

One of my treasured memories was at the little hamlet of Raitipura, a desperately poor Miskito Indian fishing village. Before anchoring off shore, Yvonne and I had dutifully changed into frocks. The entire tribe was standing on top of a cliff when we noticed two bare-chested men wading out to the boat. As they approached, one man held up two fingers and patted his shoulder. Our crew explained to us that they wanted to carry the women ashore. We weren't quite sure how this could be done until the first man grabbed me, slung me over his shoulder like a sack of potatoes, and carried me through the water and up the cliff edge as if I were a featherweight and he were a mountain goat. Yvonne was afforded the same treatment.

When we had assembled at the top, the tribe, pointing and giggling, led us to a small square building, painted red, white and blue, which sat precariously on the cliff's edge. On closer inspection we realized that it was an privy, a "two-holer." Through an interpreter, we learned that, not to be outdone by the Roman Catholics who had built a "one-holer" for their bishop, the Episcopalians had built a bigger and better outhouse for theirs, and had painted it the colors of the American flag. This time they thought that Dick, who wore his clerical collar, was the bishop. Our native hosts made it clear that we were to christen their showpiece, and that in "ladies first" style, this rite should be performed by Yvonne and me. So she went in one door and I went in the other. Looking down though the hole, I could see the lagoon waters lapping at the rocks, and wondered about the safety of construction. Yvonne was chuckling quietly in the next compartment and we agreed to exit together. The tribe had formed themselves in a semicircle in front of their masterpiece, and as we emerged smiling our approval, they clapped. Then they burst into song.

♪ ♪ ♪

Lying on a promontory of land between the Caribbean Sea and the Pearl Lagoon was the village of Tasbapauni. As always, we arrived to a warm welcome and much hand shaking. Our lodging was a mission bunkhouse consisting of two rooms, each with a hammock, wash bowl, and pitcher. Two in one hammock, plus the stench of dried shrimp in burlap bags on the dirt floor, led us to wonder how we would get through the night. Had we not been afraid to hurt the feelings of these kind people, we would have opted to return to the discomforts of the Muco. The tribe offered us the usual welcoming coconut drink (which by then I could hardly tolerate), and served us a dinner of fish, plantains, turtle eggs, mangoes, and coconut pie. On several occasions we had been served turtle eggs. They looked like ping–pong balls and no matter how long they were boiled, they never became hard. In April of each year, turtles, some of enormous size, came in droves to lay their eggs in the white sand beaches. Along with other types of fishing, a major cash industry in the area depended on turtle meat, shells, and eggs.

The following day, we ate more turtle eggs for breakfast and attended a service at the mission church. At noon, the church bell rang out and everybody dropped what they were doing and ran into the sea for their daily bath. The adults wore fairly conventional bathing costumes, but little boys stripped and little girls wore only their underpants. We four visitors changed into our bathing suits and joined them; the cool water was a marvelous antidote to the tropical heat. In about fifteen minutes, the bell rang again. Grown-ups went back to work or housekeeping, and children back to school.

On shore in the villages, we were often bothered by flies, especially where fish was drying in the sun. Bill recalled an amusing story about a man from the Administration for International Development (AID), whose mission was to teach the Indians how to take precautionary measures against spreading disease. To help explain that flies often carried germs, he had a picture of a fly enlarged many times to poster size. A young Miskito Indian boy looked skeptically at the enormous fly and held up his hand. The AID man nodded and the little Indian, crooking his thumb and forefinger with almost no space between them, said, "You may have flies like that in the United States, but here they are just tiny little things."

ᴔ   ᴔ   ᴔ

Pearl Lagoon village was quite different from the other missions. At one time it had been a thriving community with well laid-out streets, the center of an active lumber industry. Now the sawmills had disappeared for reasons unknown and the people were attempting to grow pineapples. To us, it seemed that the only thriving industry was an assortment of pigs, chickens, and small children running about on muddy streets. In our travels around the world, Bill and I were constantly amazed to find Chinese in the most unlikely spots, but none seemed more unlikely than Pearl Lagoon Village. But sure enough, Ching Lee was the owner of a little general store where we were able to get a few supplies and patronize his clean outhouse.

჻   ჻   ჻

By the time we arrived back in Bluefields, the heavy rains had become a raging tropical storm. We should have cooled our heels, but Dick and Bill had pressing reasons to get home, so against good judgment, we set out at 6 A.M. for El Recreo in a launch with a native crew. Having already risen twenty-seven feet, the Escondido River was in flood. Furthermore, we were running against the current. Along the shore, only the roofs of little thatched huts were visible. Small animals tried to save themselves by riding atop the floating debris. Twelve hours later we reached El Recreo where we fell into bed exhausted and blissfully unaware that the following day would be worse.

Our dugout for the return trip up the Miko River to Muelle des los Bueyes had a squared off back in order to mount an outboard motor. Like the Escondido, the current was running against us, and again, almost every sizable piece of debris carried a frightened little creature. The rain continued and the outboard motor struggled to buck the strong current. Five times a cotter pin on the propeller broke. Each time we lost power, the dugout was swept up against the river bank where we were forced to hold on for dear life to jungle vines to keep from being propelled downstream. The crew managed to replace the pin the first four times, but on the fifth, they had no more replacements and the dugout was thrust into particularly dense jungle. I saw snakes riding out the crisis on tree branches above my head and what looked to me like man-eating spiders. Scared to death, we hoped that Reverend Dick could say a special prayer of deliverance. The crew finally fabricated a cotter pin out of one of my bobby pins and we made it to Muelle de los Bueyes. Had we had to find our way through the jungle, we might never have been heard of again. I thought of our three near–orphaned children and, for the moment, I wished I had never come.

At Muelle de los Bueyes, we had to climb a steep bank to reach the little hamlet. This proved a comic relief to our harrowing experience. The bank was a slough of brick–red slime and Yvonne and I did not have the strength to master it. Our men, however, reached the top and laughed at our plight. Each time she and I took a step forward, we slid back two or three. Finally ropes were thrown to us from a kind soul at the top, and two weary, muddy travelers were pulled to safety.

The jeep, still where we had left it, finally overcame a reluctance to start and we headed back to Managua arriving close to midnight. I have never been so grateful to see a city, a hotel, a cold shower, and a bed.

అ   అ   అ

In spite of this precarious ending, the trip had been fascinating. We had collected a wealth of tales to tell our children and grandchildren. To prove them Bill had taken a hundred slides and 400 feet of film.

Upon our return, Billy reported a small crisis. Thieves had broken into our house at night through the door of my studio and had taken my typewriter, six bottles of scotch whiskey, and all of our phonograph records. They fortunately did not come upstairs where our two little girls were sleeping, and where they would have found more lucrative items.

Nevertheless, we were overjoyed to return to children and home. After the rigors of the *Muco* and the *Miko,* I vowed, at least temporarily, never to leave home again.

Chapter Ten

PAN-AMERICAN HIGHWAY
February 2 to March 7, 1961

IN DECEMBER OF 1960, WE WERE DUE FOR HOME LEAVE. Officially, this was granted every two years for a duration of two months. We looked forward to seeing family and friends, but two months of carting children here and there, and descending on relatives who didn't always have room or patience for a family of five strays, could present a problem. As a result, we tried to take some of our leave for a family vacation. Fortunately, the government paid transportation costs within limits, whether by ship, plane or car. So we chose a one week cruise on a Panama Line ship, the Cristobal, which sailed from the sub tropical heat of Panama to the sub–zero chill of New York City.

En route, our ship stopped in Haiti for a day. As we were docking at Port of Prince, boys rowed out to the ship in small boats to dive for pennies, apples, oranges, or other objects passengers might throw overboard. We hired a taxi, and drove to the top of a mountain where we enjoyed panoramic views and a luncheon of turtle soup and snails, then visited a rum factory which operated in a bygone castle. Finally, we visited the Episcopal Cathedral and admired the brilliantly colored murals painted by the Haitians. Although the countryside was lush and beautiful, we were appalled by the abject poverty of this most densely populated nation in the Western Hemisphere.

Although Bill's mother met us at the dock in New York City with winter coats, the bitter cold of New York City was a shock to our tropically oriented systems. Almost immediately, Bill flew out to the Rambler factory in Milwaukee, Wisconsin, to pick up a new car, a metallic-bronze compact station wagon. Because we would be exporting it to Costa Rica, his trip, in spite of a one-way air fare, saved us a $200 excise tax plus dealer's fees.

৵   ৵   ৵

We celebrated Christmas in Charlottesville, Virginia, with my family, and Joni's sixth birthday on December 31 in Philadelphia with Bill's. The girls were delighted with new—found uncles, aunts, cousins, and grandmothers. To add to their joy, snow fell almost continuously throughout the holidays, hazardous for drivers, but perfect for the novelty of snowballs and snowmen.

On January 20, 1961, one of the coldest, snow—laden days of the new year, John F. Kennedy was inaugurated President of the United States. While the country said a sentimental farewell to "Ike" and a rousing welcome to "Jack," we were glad to give the children an opportunity to watch this historic bit of Americana on television.

৵   ৵   ৵

In her small book called *This Is Nicaragua,* written in the late 1950s, Maureen Tweedy, wife of the British Ambassador, states, "It is now possible for the motorist, albeit one who is pleased to whet his appetite with the piquant sauce of uncertainty, to motor from New York, via Mexico, to Costa Rica."

She was referring to the Pan American Highway which, at that time, ran for 3,142 miles from the Mexican/American border to San José, Costa Rica. At its peak, it soared as high as two miles above sea level before plunging to the very beaches of the Pacific Ocean.

On February 2,1961, Bill strapped our suitcases and two spare tires on top of the car, and five Rodmans of varied sizes, each with a pioneering spirit, sallied forth on this multifarious trek entailing two-hundred hours of driving time and over 6,000 miles.

The weather could not have been worse, a record breaking sub-zero temperature, and as we tried to set off, the little car balked. I think she was trying to tell us something, but we paid no attention and summoned a mechanic to make her go.

Soon realizing that she was already taking on a personality of her own, we decided to name her. Suggestions came from each member of the family, but none seemed quite right until Channing said, "How about "Maudie?" Maude was a family name on my father's side, and, to the children's horror, I had threatened to use it if ever we had a fourth child. This was unlikely, but the kids felt safer if Mom got the name out of her system, so our new little Rambler was christened "Maudie."

Because of a continuing search to find a college for young Bill for the following year, we did not head south away from the cold and snow, but northwest, right into the predicted blizzards, to look at colleges in Pennsylvania and Ohio. As a musical refrain, we all sang lustily Bill, Jr.'s version of "California, Here I Come" which began:

> *Costa Rica, here we come,*
> *Right back where we started from . . .*

Outside, the temperature was zero, but inside Maudie, it was cozy and warm. Surrounded by luggage, Joni sat like "queenie" upon a sleeping roll in her tiny allotted space in the rear—her own wee nest with playthings around her. She had no conception of distance or time and reasoned that because we had started, Costa Rica and warm weather must be just around the corner. Otherwise, why did we bring our bathing suits? Try to explain to a just-turned six year old that we would be driving for more than a month, and that it would be several days before we were far enough south to open the car windows and discard her bulky snowsuit!

Today, I am appalled by the fact that we were completely unconcerned by the lack of safety features on automobiles. In 1961, there were no air bags, no anti-lock brakes, no front-wheel drive, no reinforced tires, but most of all—no seat belts. We traveled 6,000 happy miles oblivious of those technological advances to come. Perhaps we should have been more apprehensive.

I was in charge of housekeeping. With five in the small car plus assorted, toys, boxes, books, and Christmas gifts, I felt akin to a canned mother sardine. Snacks and water were passed back at intervals, and bits and pieces of paper came forward for the litter bag. Having seen signs telling us that littering could cost us a $250 fine, we were ultra cautious, but we retained a tiny worry that Joni might flutter something out of the rear window toward some state trooper's nose.

I was also in charge of navigation. Maps fascinate me and we had the advantage of detailed strip maps from the triple-A. To pass the time, we agreed to read history aloud and to concentrate on improving our Spanish and English vocabularies. Lots could be learned while driving! Bill, Jr. and I were relief drivers for Bill.

Our daily budget was $30, excluding gasoline (we had a Texaco credit card), but Bill and I hoped that was a generous amount and we could manage on less.

Although it was often difficult to write in the car, I kept diary notes. My scribblings follow.

February 3, Destination: Unknown

Up at 7 A.M., bathed, packed, dressed, and ready to leave at 8:15. Hope to do this in less time as we become more practiced in the fine art of loading Maudie. As it had started to snow, hurried through a doughnut breakfast and went to Dickinson College in Carlisle, Pennsylvania, where young Bill had an appointment with the dean of admissions. Onto the Pennsylvania turnpike at 10:30 A.M. and into the winter's worst snowstorm. Driving hazardous, but we persevered for ninety miles at snail's pace. Bill doesn't complain often, but really let loose when it came to the narrow and poorly lighted tunnels on the turnpike, which bore through mountains with intriguing native American names such as Kittatinny and Tuscarora. Were surprised that Bureau of Public Roads in Pennsylvania hadn't realized that modern science had improved upon Edison's first light bulb. When little brown Maudie started to sputter, we wisely got off the turnpike at Bedford, Pa. Just made it to motel where she choked and quit. Relieved to be safe and warm. Ten minutes later, learned that turnpike had been closed to traffic. Maudie had warned us in the nick of time.

Adjacent to motel was a roller skating rink, which provided entertainment for Channing and Joni during afternoon while the rest of us slept in big comfortable room. According to the two Bills, I snored, but even a few snores were permissible that afternoon. The pressure is off!

Had supper in motel restaurant with lots of stranded truck drivers with whom we exchanged pleasantries and weather experiences. My husband is a paradigm of amiability. We order four dinners and Joni picks selections from everybody's plate. The blizzard continued to roar outside as we went to sleep and fourteen inches of snow piled up. All welcomed thought of being snowbound next day and prayed that Maudie would make it through night. Bill had lovingly wrapped her up in ponchos and blankets like a little brown papoose.

Expenses - $25.95 Distance - 90 miles.

119

Feb. 4, Destination: Unknown

Still snowing this morning. All enjoyed big breakfast of eggs and scrapple except for Channing who turns green at the sight of an egg. She is my picky eater. B and J gobble up anything and everything. Back to room for "Captain Kangaroo" on TV and leisurely morning.

Regrettably, turnpike opened at about 10 A.M. and "boss" decided that the "rugged" Rodmans should push on. There went my day of rest! When top echelon announcement came, I had just washed out a few clothes in the basin and had borrowed ironing board. Upon departure, travel iron so hot that I had to hold it in my hand as we drove, and tuck plastic bag of wet clothes under my feet. Maudie covered with soot, snow and grime, but purring like kitten.

On turnpike, driving conditions abominable. Speed limit is 35 m.p.h. Many trucks and cars stranded along road. Poor souls! Channing has broken out in Spanish and JSR asleep. I have new job—lighting Bill's pipe. The kids get a charge out of this manipulation. "Maudie-made" sandwiches for lunch. Awful.

Finally off turnpike and heading south on Ohio Rte 42. "South" sounds good. Hope it means improved weather soon. Enjoying Ohio countryside, beautiful in the snow, and the neat, typically American towns with tree-lined streets and simple well-kept houses. One feels a strong sense of community. Also enjoying American humor. Sign in used car lot—"BUY NOW - FREE BUSHEL OF SNOW WITH EVERY CAR."

Stopped in small town in Ohio called Medina for night. Only two motels and first full. In desperation took other which was crummy. Lumpy beds. Too tired to unload suitcases from Maudie's roof, so ate stale doughnuts and slept in underwear.

Feb. 5, Destination: Gambier, Ohio

Miserable night. Clearly best to stick to recommended AAA lodging.

In Gambier, stayed at Alumni Hall and Billy visited Kenyon College. Guess I should call him Bill now that he is almost eighteen. Will try to remember to say Bill, Jr. to differentiate from Bill, Sr. Am sure to slip up. Comfortable lodging—two rooms and a bath. Pleasant collegiate atmosphere punctuated by peal of college church bell. Hostess was a windbag, adept at cornering men. Had to rescue our son several times. Delicious Sunday lunch at College Inn.

Feb. 6, Destination: Covington, Kentucky

Channing sick at her tummy during night. In Rodmanesque lingo, this is called "collywobbles in the pontoofle." Fearing appendicitis, took her to doctor. Nothing serious—tummy flu. Didn't get off until 1 P.M. Joni, who doesn't like to be outdone, decided to be sick too, but recovered when cookies appeared, and resettled in her little nest to make valentines.

Today we are averaging twenty-three miles per gallon, or thirty-seven kilometers. Speedometer is in kilometers which means multiplying by .62 to get miles. Nuisance. Took turn at driving—poor road with crown. Maudie sways a lot because of load on top. Not as noticeable on good highways. Looking at map, I'm afraid they are mostly behind us. Goodness only knows what we'll run into in Mexico, Guatemala, etc.

Advised to take the Rte. 50 bypass around Cincinnati. What a bamboozle! Took us one–and–a–half hours and still ended up in middle of city trying to find bridge to cross Ohio River into Kentucky. Obviously navigator screwed up.

Snow getting less all the time which gives us hope that it will soon be warm. Channing still nauseated. Joni amuses us with her commentary. Knows she is American, but as we went to Costa Rica when she was three, her memory of the United States is almost nil.

On the Cincinnati bypass: Joni: "Is this Hong Kong?
Mom: "No dear, this is the United States."

Joni: "Oh boy! We'd better take a good look."

At a gasoline station: "Are we all supposed to get out and try?"

At a restaurant: "OK, I'll eat it, but you won't like what happens next!"

Feb. 7, Destination: Memphis, Tennessee

Breakfasted very early on prune juice, doughnuts, and hot chocolate warmed by little heating coil. Useful gadget. Channing feeling better. Followed Ohio River south. As we could see Indiana on other side of river, she added another state to her collection. Looks up history of each new state in World Almanac. Hope this commendable attitude continues.

Have reached lovely blue grass country near Louisville—rolling hills, white fences, neat farms, and beautiful horses grazing. The children are amazing. No complaining. Entering one little village, a sign read, "Population 100—99 citizens and one old grump."

Long run to Memphis—511 miles. Now and then older kids break out with some teenage hit such as "Fever" while Joni tries to compete with "Row, Row, Row Your Boat." Or, we all sing together, Mom trying to harmonize.

Crossed into Tennessee below Bowling Green, KY—farmland, fair roads, many small towns which slow us down. Beautiful crossing Tennessee River. Now approaching Memphis. Weather cold and foggy. All tired and cranky, but snow has disappeared.

No vacancy at first two motels we tried. Finally found nice room with one double and two single beds for $13. This, as usual, put young Bill on floor on air mattress. While washing up and gathering wits, Joni let off steam by dancing all over the room using the beds as trampolines. Don't allow jumping on beds at home, but when a six year old has been cooped up in a car for 12 hours, we bend the rules.

Average of daily expenses so far - $30.50. Average miles per gallon—26

Feb. 8, Destination: Shreveport, Louisiana

Maudie looks better this morning thanks to rain last night. Cloudy today. Hope to make Shreveport—352 miles. Drove through attractive Memphis suburbs—stately homes, wide tree-lined streets. Crossed long bridge over mighty Mississippi River and found ourselves in Arkansas. Arkansas very flat. Miles of cotton fields. Making less than fifty miles per hour. With this load, dare not drive faster.

"Maudie-made" peanut butter and jelly sandwiches for lunch. Billy has taken over wheel and driving very slowly but well. Sun has come out. Feels almost like spring. Have shed coats and Billy has finally removed his woolly gloves—a Christmas gift. Have teased him a good bit, especially after we caught him sleeping in them one chilly night. Now that she has shed bulky snowsuit, Joni is sure Costa Rica just ahead. Actually, it's Louisiana just ahead.

Arrived Shreveport. Friendly gas station attendant recommended Kickapoo Motel. Two rooms and bed for everyone for $12. Best of all, adjoining garage where Maudie had first bath and vacuuming for a dollar. In preparation, unpacked her completely. When returned to us, she was glowing like shiny new penny—her color listed as "metallic bronze. Will be pleasant to see out of windows again.

Bill decided everyone deserved steak for dinner, but Billy selected frogs' legs. When it comes to culinary tastes, he is as far out as they come.

As usual, Bill engaged waitress in conversation. She looked about twenty-five, so were surprised to learn she had eight children, three born on island of Guam where husband was stationed after World War II. Proudly announced she was pregnant again! Believe Bill and I will be content with three.

Somewhere in bowels of the beds was a machine called a "relax-o-matic" which vibrates when fed a quarter. Supposed to lull you to sleep, but this one akin to electric shock treatment rendering you senseless rather than somnolent. Girls loved it and giggled until we ran out of quarters.

Feb. 9, Destination: San Antonio, Texas

Bill and I and littlest traveler went to diner for breakfast at 7 A.M. leaving Channing and Billy sleeping soundly. Servings of eggs and bacon arrived with "grits" —"Loosiana" style.

Big operation maneuvering family of five, all in one room, one bathroom, and Maudie to reload. Had pair of unconscious teenagers that morning. Didn't get off until well after 9 A.M. To add to frustrations, took every possible wrong turn trying to get through Shreveport. Street signs can be baffling to strangers. They can be nonexistent when needed most.

Crossed border into Texas where countryside flat as pancake and road straight as poker for miles. Fell into spirit by singing cowboy songs and telling Texas jokes.

"Have you heard about the little boy who gave his father a pipe for Christmas?"

"What kind of pipe?"

"The pipe that carries oil from El Paso to Detroit!"

To our delight, gasoline very cheap in Texas—as low as 17 cents a gallon.

Stopped for lunch at little roadside place in Jewett, Texas. Ate cheeseburgers while enjoying newfound luxury—sunshine. In yard was owners' sixty–foot mobile home with pretty garden in front. Obviously proud, they asked if we would like to see inside. Bill and I curious. Had never been in mobile home. Agreed later that it was far from ideal abode. Woman asked where we were going. Let out a huge sigh when we said, "Costa Rica," and gave us each free ice cream cone.

Maudie's showing signs of wear and tear. Gas gauge sticking on empty and horn sounds more like a burp than a blow. Will have her fixed in San Antonio.

This afternoon, Joni taking long nap, snuggling down on her

bedroll. Channing, our shopper, making list of things to buy before leaving U.S., and Billy, our reader, studying Spanish and S.A.T. example book. He does good job entertaining Joni at end of day. I'm beginning to dream of spending two nights in one spot.

Feb. 10, San Antonio, Texas

My dream answered. Big annual rodeo opens tomorrow in San Antonio, so have decided to spend another night.

Channing in seventh heaven—a shopping mall close to motel. Reluctant to part with her money. Must see everything in every store. This, I suppose, is trademark of teenager. Found adorable cowboy outfit for Joni. With pixie haircut, looks like Dennis the Menace. Also bought cowboy hat for Toñito, and dresses for Alberta and María at J. C. Penny's. Incredibly cheap—$3 each, or two for $5.

Went to Alamo. Intrigued by heroic tales of tragic siege in 1836 where 200 Texans defended Spanish mission–fortress against 4,000 Mexicans in struggle for independence. All defenders, including such heroes as Davy Crockett and Jim Bowie, died.

Later, Joni had long nap while I did laundry and hung it over railing on little veranda to dry. Bill and Bill, Jr. sat in sun reading. Channing, under protest, went to beauty shop for haircut. Hair is teenage fetish. Much time spent combing, brushing, setting, unsetting. The two Bills think I'm a pretty good barber, but the girls scream when I come near them with scissors. As big sister is role model, Joni parrots Channing's every move.

Maudie has Wisconsin license plates because Bill picked her up at factory in Milwaukee. This afternoon a big, burly fellow from Wisconsin rapped on door. Wanted to acknowledge state kinship. Somewhat difficult explaining that we originated in Pennsylvania but living in Costa Rica, and had never been to Wisconsin except to buy Maudie.

After dinner, set out for Coliseum. Hawkers peddling circus–type junk, and atmosphere electric with excitement. Spectators decked out in Texas attire—cowboy hats, boots, bluejeans, ornately embroidered shirts. Except for Joni, sporting new outfit, Rodmans noticeably easterners. By the time we found our seats in balcony, the grand parade had just started, and the band blared forth with "The Star Spangled Banner" which never fails to energize butterflies in the core of my being. Saw every kind of rodeo event including border collie demonstration. Hard to fathom why anyone would choose to make living riding bucking broncos or wrestling steers. I get nervous watching football games.

Feb. 11, Destination: Laredo, Texas

Trip from San Antonio to Laredo, Tex-Mex border town, very flat and straight through long expanses of sagebrush and mesquite. Stopped at the Sands Motel on outskirts of Laredo for lunch at adjoining pancake restaurant featuring ten different varieties of pancakes and splendid array of syrups. Kids eyed swimming pool at motel and convinced us we all deserved swim, and afternoon basking in sunshine. Joni so cute in water—no fear. Spends more time under surface than on top. Tail end sinks when she comes up for air.

Feb. 12, Destination: Monterrey, Mexico

Packed and ready to go after more pancakes for breakfast. Crossed Rio Grande at 10 A.M. In spite of name, not much more than big ditch at Laredo crossing. Long, hot delay at immigration filling out forms. Border guards tried to push us through because of diplomatic passports, but Bill insisted we take our turn. He and I disagree. Of course he's right. To push ahead makes very bad impression on fellow American travelers who don't understand why, and complain to State Department.

Hope we are through driving long distances in one day. Only

145 miles to Monterrey over flat, desolate terrain. Have all erupted in Spanish. Amazing how it comes flooding back after crossing border and reading signs. Mexican drivers think they are bullfighters behind wheel of car. Must be careful not to leave Maudie unlocked in this poverty-stricken part of Mexico. A sunny, beautiful day. *Que dicha!*

Mountains loomed up as we approached Monterrey, Mexico's leading industrial city. For $10.50, found best accommodation of trip so far—a suite with beds for all and two bathrooms. Nobody had to yell, "Hurry up." A quick dip in icy pool, dinner, and to bed early after chasing JSR around room trying to get her pajamas on.

Feb. 13, Destination: San Luis Pótosi

Mexican roads dusty and riddled with pot holes. Frequent delays for road work. Flagmen directing one-way traffic. Progress slow and tedious. Approaching Saltillo. Guidebook tells us we have climbed 5000 feet since leaving Monterrey. No complaints from Maudie. Much of scenery along route quite dramatic with stark rugged rock formations in distance, but terrain barren and covered with mesquite and cactus. Stopped at little town of Arteaga for lunch and gas. Only one gasoline company in Mexico, owned by government. Have had to put away Texaco card.

Heading south across forsaken stretch of arid desert-like country with scattered adobe hamlets of four to eight huts. Forlorn, dirty children stand in doorways with little or nothing on. Women seen walking for miles with water jugs on heads. Mountains in distance look made of papier mache. We are fascinated by "dust devils"—cross currents of wind which catch up sand in a swirl like mini tornados and disappear as quickly as they come.

Mexicans use burros for transportation and as beasts of burden. They roam countryside and have affinity for standing smack in the middle of road flicking their ears at oncoming automobiles. Bill pointed out remarkable government irrigation project that stretched for miles, but I didn't see anything growing except cactus, sage, and Mexicans. Joni calls them "Messy-cans."

Stopped for gas in Matehuela, once thriving mining town, but now just hot, dirty place in middle of no-mans-land. As usual, swarm of dirty, runny-nosed boys surrounded us selling wilting flowers, shiny pebbles, and baby armadillos. Whereas we resist overtures, have learned it's better to give out a few centavos, or pay a boy a peso to guard car while in cafe or market. If not, he will wait until you are out of sight and swipe first thing he can get his hands on—gas cap, hub caps, windshield wipers. Even locking car can be dangerous. "Messy-kids" (my word) can pick a lock with ease. If someone comes along, they pull rag out of pocket and pretend they are cleaning car.

At Cactus Motel in San Luis Pótosi (pronounced Poe–toe–see), huge blinking neon sign of Mexican sleeping under cactus—sombrero shading face from sun.

Feb. 14, Destination: Comanjilla, León, Mexico

Next morning, Bill and I greeted with valentines and hugs. Broke out a heart shaped box of chocolates bought in San Antonio, and congratulated each other on surviving two weeks of being cooped up together without any major skirmishes.

Arrived at the Hotel Balnario in Comanjillo near León in early afternoon. Had earmarks of old people's home. Guests appeared septuagenarians and upwards. Hot thermal springs resort. Brochure claimed rejuvenation and miracle cures for aches and pains. Hot, smelly, sulfur springs bubbled out of ground like witch's cauldrons. Went for swim. Temperature of large pool about same as nice hot tub. Old people, bobbing contentedly in thermal water. Amusing to watch. Many so fat they floated upright, their middles acting as inner-tubes. Joni said water felt like "pulling up the covers on a cold night." While everyone else floated around like blubber in the enervating water, she managed to stir things up with six–year–old antics and splashes. Channing looked lovely in bathing suit. Pretty figure!

Joni disappeared before dinner. Found her in kitchen with chef. Had seen dinner menu and gone there for purpose of telling chef not to put carrots on her plate. Also complained about drinking water (smelly because of sulfur in springs). Told him she refused to take her anti-dysentery pill unless he gave her some ginger ale. He must have humored this pint-sized complainer. Before leaving, Joni insisted on going back to kitchen to say good-bye.

After dinner, Billy and Channing had game of ping-pong on long veranda. Guests sat rocking nearby. Whenever ball hit off table, Joni scampered, crawling under chairs and feet to retrieve it. I think the old people quite enjoyed the commotion. No question that during our short stay at Balnario Spa, Joni successfully livened up the geriatric atmosphere.

Feb. 15, Destination: Guanajuato

Built upon ruins of sixteenth century castle, Castle of Santa Cecelia in Guanajuato looked like movie set for Sir Walter Scott novel. About as comfortable as original might have been. Besides being expensive, service and food poor and room cold, dank, dark. Nothing to sit on but wooden bench. Small fireplace—when finally lit, helped take off chill. Plumbing atrocious and smelly. Santa Cecelia highly recommended in Sanborn's guidebook. Fear tourists often hoodwinked by blurb of travelogs. Difficult to look for alternate lodging when you arrive in late afternoon with children. Joni, however, enchanted. Decided to be Sleeping Beauty after Billy assured her that bad fairy Maleficent no longer around.

Guanajuato fascinating. Once the richest mining town in Mexico. Hard to believe outside world knows of its existence. Cobblestone streets wind in jigsaw fashion up, down and around, finally opening onto picturesque little plazas. John Wilcock, in his book, *Mexico On Five Dollars a Day,* gives an apt description:

Guanajuato with its narrow winding streets, so narrow that dogs have to wave their tails up and down, and Moorish architecture, seems like an old Spanish colonial city that has been dumped lock, stock and barrel onto a Mexican hillside.

After wandering through Central Market admiring fresh fruits and vegetables, hired a guide. Arrogant little *vivo* (smart–ass). Drove us to out–of–the–way sites in dilapidated taxi.

Passing churches in and around Guanjuato, noticed signs warning, "Tenga la bondad de no orinarse en este atrio" (Please have the kindness not to urinate in this atrium.) Inside, smaller signs were attached to deeply stained corners.

Church of Valenciana, overlooking the city, considered one of most beautiful colonial churches in Mexico. Has three huge altars of intricate carving and gold leaf, and usual assortment of plaster saints and agonized Jesuses. I am not an aficionada of churches and cathedrals in Latin America. Gaudy and depressing.

Guide drove us to cemetery at top of one of surrounding hills. Entered crypt full of well–dressed mummies in various stages of decay, an unsavory experience that should have been skipped. More agreeable visit to ornate Teatro Juárez, ringed by columns and neoclassic statues.

Feb. 17, Destination: Pátzcuaro
Drove through towns of Irapuato and Salamanca. Strawberry country—vast beds covering miles of luscious berries. Paused to drive around attractive town of Morelia with pink stone buildings and interesting old aqueduct. This forty-mile stretch lovely with tall trees lining road for many miles, gently rolling hills, and clusters of little houses with red tile roofs snuggled into hillsides. Land verdant and productive as compared to stark arid expanses of north. People look happy and well fed. Smile and wave as we pass.

The Posada Don Vasco in Pátzcuaro charmingly decorated with antique Mexican artifacts. One big bedroom for all, but comfortable. Inviting tub in bathroom to delight Mom. Lovely patios and gardens.

Roamed colorful Friday market just off plaza talking to Tarascans. Indian women wore high–necked blouses tucked into long dark skirts of heavy homespun wool held up by bright sash wound around waist. Dark-golden skin, black eyes, and long black braids pulled back to show ornate earrings—handsome and proud. Tarrascans industrious and skilled at crafts—wool and basket weaving, wood carving, pottery, embroidery, jewelry making, and figures made out of corn dough. Dogs and children slept or played in shade of stalls. Although Maudie already bulging at seams, I bought six pottery plates of primitive design for 20 cents each, and Billy bought old wood mask for 80 cents. Joni always thirsty and Channing always hungry—stopped at shabby little kiosk for cokes and *pan dulce* (sweet rolls).

Hotel on shore of great lake studded with green islands. Early next morning, hired boat to take us to island of Jinotega. Watched fishermen carry on their unique way of fishing with huge butterfly nets. Kids loved freedom of being released from car. When we reached island, they ran uphill to highest point where colossal statue of José Maria Morelos, Tarrascan hero-martyr in Mexico's fight for independence from Spain, overlooked lake. Island children realized that being photogenic monetarily rewarding—extended hands, palms up, while calling out "Take a pic, take a pic." Some local color diminished by this pecuniary resourcefulness.

Feb. 19, Tuxpan

En route to Mexico City, stopped at a roadside motel, Mitzie's, in Tuxpan, run by American whose Mexican husband raised cattle. When he learned that Bill was agricultural attache, begged assistance with cow having difficulty calving. After laboring for several hours over poor creature, Bill delivered healthy calf to joy of hosts.

Feb, 20,21,22, Mexico City, Saturday

Lodging in Mexico City called Hotel Gin. Engaged taxi with friendly driver named Miguel. Drove us about sprawling city and into suburbs to see Chapultepec Park, and Museum of Anthropology, wonderful monumental masterpiece dedicated to Mexican people.

Our pleasant driver informed us that famous matador would be fighting that afternoon at Plaza de Toros. Young Bill, well informed on art and drama of bullfighting, especially thrilled. Bought tickets for shady side of arena, including one for Miguel. (Didn't want to lose him in traffic jam after corrida.) As matadors paraded in, atmosphere sparkled with excitement and five Rodmans roared "olé," along with 5,000 Mexicans. Admired stately ballet of bulls and toreros, and courage of both, but our "olés" faded at end of each bout when crazed and bleeding bull was speared, killed and dragged out of ring by yoked oxen. Channing, lover of animals, especially upset.

Channing and Billy went off on own to explore city, she to shops, he to nose out bookstores, one of his finely-tuned talents. Bill to embassy. Mom did laundry in bathroom, and all met for lunch before strolling through Zona Rosa (Pink Zone). Abundance of flowers and fruit stands added to visual pleasure of city. Bought heavy box of yellow and blue ceramic tiles for use someday, and charming, gilded, antique door panel depicting a griffin in bold relief. Poor Maudie!

Feb. 23,24, Destination: Taxco

Much of road to Taxco winding with sheer cliffs on one side and rock walls on other. Goats and burros wander on and off roadway. Fields of prickly cactus shaped like candelabra stretch as far as eye can see. Boys hold up iguanas for sale. Indian farmers, trying to scratch living out of rocky soil, appear as statues, impassive and isolated on precipitous hillsides. Although drive seemed endless, finally arrived at motel, series of attractive bungalows perched on edge of canyon just outside of town. From balcony, watched the changing colors of beautiful sunset. Threw coins and candy to group of Indian boys who crawled cliff ledge to beg with up-stretched arms.

Taxco, an ancient cobbled silver mining town cupped in mountainous terrain. Overrun with tourists and cars, overflowing with hundreds of small silver shops up and down steep and winding streets. Paused to watch artisans at work. Cathedral is centerpiece of town. Billy, bored with silver shops, wandered off. Found native woman selling medicinal herbs—fascinated by commentary on cures, poultices, and pain relief.

Feb. 25, 26, Destination: Oaxaca

Back on road again. Spanish improving. Have become captivated by Mexico—people, countryside, villages and towns all blending together in colorful rhythm. Traveled across waste land on which only cactus seemed to thrive. Here and there small patches of green where native farmers, in white clothing and straw hats labored to cultivate scant soil. Awed by isolation of these Indians. Crude dwellings tucked into eroded hillsides; lives so unrelated to civilization as we know it. How fortunate we are!

Marvelled at name Oaxaca, pronounced "Wah-hah-ka." Settled into bungalow at Victoria Hotel—name unimaginative in comparison.

Oaxaca potpourri of Mexican local color—women wrapped in *rebozos* balancing bundles on heads, hustle–bustle of central plaza, men selling serapes, marimba band, torrents of flowers in market place, interesting aromas, scruffy shoeshine boys begging for business—"Please Meester, shine shoes, very chip," Like Tarrascans, Zapotec Indians skilled craftsmen. Ply wares with good-natured persistence. Know to start out far too high to make tourists think they have *ganga* (bargain) when final price reached. Surprised that we spoke Spanish and were such tough customers.

Made interesting excursion to Coyotepec, small village noted for shiny black pottery. Had good fortune to find Doña Rosa, a legend renowned for skill, working in yard of shabby hut. Wore black from head to foot, including rebozo wound around head. Row of black pots recently baked in outside kiln being given her touch of magic. Bought large shapely pot with three birds adorning rim. Poor Maudie!

Drove south from Coyotepec to ancient ruins of Monte Albán, a Zapotec city 2,000 years old. Zapotec kings, priests and nobles buried there amidst splendor of earthly goods. Tombs like low pyramids with flat tops. Walls decorated with fine, geometric mosaics of carefully cut stone. Difficult to see where stones join. Ancient Zapotecs invented calendar and writing system. Highly developed society. A puzzle how they built such a monumental site without benefit of metal tools, horses, mules, oxen, or the wheel. Where did immense stones come from? How were they hauled to site from distant quarries?

No other tourists at Monte Albán. Ch and J, like freed butterflies from cocoon, ran up terraced steps to explore tombs and eerie passageways. Young man sold us small clay pot from Indian grave. Suspect it had been buried during last decade to age it. Channing, trip photographer, took many pictures with small camera.

Feb. 27, Destination: Tehuantepec

Left Oaxaca in mid-morning after buying embroidered skirts and blouses for Ch and J at 22 pesos each ($1.76 US). Hard to resist beautiful filigree jewelry.

Stopped few miles south of Oaxaca to see famous Tree of Tule, said to be oldest living thing in Americas. Onto another Zapotec ruin at Mitla. Fascinating, but Indian women and children selling beads and trinkets pushy and pesky. Ruins very well preserved. Date from 1,000 AD. Long hall of columns. Beautiful mosaic patterns more intricate and dramatic than at Monte Albán. Unlike Aztecs who sacrificed humans, Zapotecs sacrificed animals.

In dusty town nearby, Bill bought squat little bottle of mezcal, the local joy juice, made from type of cactus.

On to Tehuantepec maneuvering corkscrew curves and rugged mountainous terrain. Now beyond the range of tourists. Long stretches without seeing another car, or even a living soul. Passed under ominous looking rock cliffs. Saw signs of recently cleared rock slides. Many objects to dodge—rocks, burros, cattle, goats. Have been warned that this is *bandido* (bandit) country. Counting on Maudie not to break down! Lunched on doughnuts and Pepsi in locked car. Average speed only twenty-nine miles per hour.

Gratefully descended to sea level and tropical town of Tehuantepec at 6 P.M. Hotel Tehuantepec run–down and filthy— first lodging disaster. Nothing worked—drains, toilets, lamps, locks. Infested with roaches and other crawly creatures. After tough day, we were as disheveled as hotel. Joni and I took first shower to discover drain in the middle of bathroom floor clogged. Water not only flooded bathroom but gushed under door into bedroom. No hot water. Looking forward to good dinner.

Tehuantepec only ten miles from ocean. Assumed seafood would be fresh. Bill, Jr., ever adventurous, ordered *calamaries* (squid) in own *tinta* (ink) which looked revolting, and *callos* as appetizer, which looked even more revolting. None of us knew what callos were. A likely guess—cow's intestines. Iguana stew also on menu. Rest of us had safer carne asada, a thin broiled filet of beef surrounded by tortillas and beans. Girl in native Tehuana costume our waitress. Wore *huipile* (blouse) over long graceful skirt thickly embroidered with roses, and edged with ruffles. Stiff ruffled headdress crowned her head, and around her neck a thick gold chain. At end of chain dangled a twenty dollar gold piece.

Didn't trust miserable place. Screens cut and locks broken. Before going to bed, propped big chairs against doors. Two rooms—150 pesos (about $6 US). No other lodging in town.

Feb. 28, Destination: San Cristobal de las Casas

From under window, singing and cheery little band woke us up with jolt at 6 A.M. Told later it was customary for young man to hire musicians to serenade sweetheart on her birthday. In spite of hour, this Tehuanan reveille struck our funny bones and we all got up in good humor.

For sake of safety, completely unloaded Maudie in Tehuantepec which delayed departure in morning. After unappetizing breakfast (three flies in water pitcher), left at 8 A.M. Our twenty-seventh day en route. Beginning to get impatient to get to San José and home.

Long, sultry drive along southernmost stretch of tropical Mexico to cool mountainous altitude of 7,000 feet at destination, San Cristobal de las Casas. Winding through mountains breathtakingly beautiful. Occasional primitive village. Hoping for centavos, clusters of children extend their palms and wave. Very few cars.

Las Casas (for short) a pretty town unspoiled by tourists and progress. The people, of Mayan descent, wear native dress. Men immaculate in loose white clothing, high backed sandals and ribboned straw hats. Women, hung with babies and bundles, less colorful in dark shapeless folds of wool. Bill, Jr. commented that the women are like covey of little pea hens trotting behind lustrous peacocks.

Comfortable rooms at Hotel Español surrounded pretty courtyard with columned arcade. Cost $6 per night per person including three meals. No charge for Joni. During afternoon, Bill, Jr. felt increasingly ill, no doubt from squid of previous night. Upon reaching hotel, had full blown case of ptomaine poisoning.

March 1, Destination: Quetzaltenango, Guatemala

Bill, Jr. feeling worse. Doctored him up and decided to push on.

Stopped at police checkpoint a few miles from Las Casas. Hearts sank when told that because of recent rock slides, section of Pan Am Highway called El Tapon, (the cork or stopper), officially closed—road crew working on it. Alternative was to drive forty miles to town of Arriaga to put ourselves and Maudie on railroad flatcar for twelve–hour trek to Tapachula in Guatemala. No schedule. Wait could be several days. Coincidentally, another American arrived at checkpoint and faced same dilemma. He and Bill discussed problem with Mexican policeman who finally allowed us to proceed at own risk if both cars went in tandem in case of breakdown or accident. With trepidation, decided to give it a try. Feel sure policeman fully expected to see us again with tail between legs.

Upon reaching rock slide area, found that workmen had filled portion of road with large rocks that had broken away, but no cement or other binding to hold rocks together. Bill and fellow traveler walked across repair appraising situation. On left was sheer drop to valley below, and on right mountain rose almost vertically. Men flipped coin to see who would go first. Bill won toss. Children and I got out of Maudie and watched nervously as Bill, following hand signals from road crew, inched Maudie over bed of rocks until he'd reached comparative safety.

Guatemalan side of border almost worse than Mexican. Again all out of car except Bill. This time because steep gravelly incline necessitated starting well back from problem to gain momentum, then zooming up and over hump. At site of recent landslide, two boards had been laid across cavity. Again there was 1,000 foot drop on one side and mountain wall on other. All limp, dirty and relieved when we reached safety of paved road.

Bless Maudie—she was dauntless.

During this long day, young Bill's condition worsened. Fever rose to 103 degrees. Must have been wretched bouncing over rough roads. Except when we had to get out of Maudie so that she and Bill could overcome another hurdle, Bill, Jr.'s head on Channing's lap. At Guatemalan border, roused him to sit up tall and straight. Major effort on his part. Didn't want border guards to think we were bringing in dread disease. Billy's illness changed plans to visit picturesque Indian towns of Chichicastenango and Atitlán. Instead, made beeline for larger city of Quetzaltenango to find doctor.

The group, including Maudie, looked a sorry sight as we straggled into Quetzaltenango in late afternoon. Spotted two young men in gray business suits, and felt hats. Recognized them as Mormons doing volunteer year of missionary work. They were as glad to see fellow North Americans, however disheveled, as we were to see them. After explaining our predicament, they led us to simple but clean Hotel Bonifáz and called doctor.

Doctor came almost immediately. Prescribed medicine. Next day, Billy much improved, but decided to spend another night before traveling on. Our Salt Lake City friends returned to see if all was well. Enjoyed their company over cup of hot chocolate. As representatives of their faith, they won our respect and gratitude.

March 3, Destination: Guatemala City, Guatemala

Traveling across Guatemala, admired beauty of lakes, and cone–shaped mountains in distance. Paused in villages. Each Indian community appeared to have own native dress of colorful homespun material. Women's attire skillfully embroidered with significant amount of red, setting off dark eyes and long black braids. Shy little girls and boys, clones of parents, followed behind mothers.

In Guatemala City, unanimously voted to stay at four-star

hotel, the Biltmore. To heck with budget! Two Bills longed for good shower, and we girls needed shampoo and bathtub of hot water. Craved American food. Didn't have to worry about safety of water. Good mattresses and pillows for long night's sleep. Paradise!

March 4, Destination: San Salvador, El Salvador

Refreshed and rested. Greedily consumed waffles and maple syrup for breakfast. Our one thought—to get home. We are ventured out. School starts March 10. Bill, Jr. and Joni each at end of spectrum—one a senior and other a first grader. Channing will enter high school, eighth grade.

Reached outskirts of San Salvador. Found pleasant motel, El Patio. Last night for young Bill on air mattress. Tomorrow night expect to reach the Gran Hotel in Managua. Old favorite. El Patio needed our patronage. We were the only guests. Temperature a sizzling 100 degrees! Maudie not air-conditioned! During night, someone tried to force open door of room. Bill jumped out of bed, landing on poor Billy who let out such a whoop that would-be intruder fled.

March 5, Destination: Managua, Nicaragua

Today's run long through bleak and barren section of Honduras. On into Nicaragua. Finally arrived at Gran Hotel in Managua, our own dominion again. Greeted as old friends. Still beastly hot. Kids in pool in record time. Exotic birds with brilliant plumage strutted about.

March 6, Destination: San José, Costa Rica

Crossed border into beautiful little Costa Rica singing loudly, "Costa Rica here we come, right back where we started from."

Maudie not feeling well. Sputtered and died at village of Libéria, only 100 miles from San José. Mechanic at gas station diagnosed problem in differential gear. Parts needed only attainable in San José. Had to spend the night in small hotel.

Following morning, Bill returned to gas station. Recognized limousine of Nicaraguan ambassador who kindly offered me and children ride to San Jose. Bill stayed with Maudie. Four out of five of us arrived home to rousing welcome from Alberta, Maria and little Toñito on March 7. House bedecked with flowers. Savory aromas from kitchen. Handmade gifts from Alberta and Maria— embroidered pillowcases and place mats. Home never looked so wonderful.

Called Rambler agency. Replacement parts flown to Libéria same afternoon. Sad that brave little Maudie couldn't journey on a few more miles—she had simply swallowed too much dust and grime.

Bill returned next day. Trip from Philadelphia to San José had taken thirty-five days.

Bill, Jr., Channing and Joni in San Antonio

140

Chapter Eleven

COSTA RICA
The Final Months

COSTA RICA was a popular "junket" getaway from Washington. The country was not only safe, but warm during the winter months when Washington was freezing, and pleasant during the summer months when Washington was sweltering. Generally, our visitors were businesslike, gracious, and dignified and it was a pleasure to act as their hosts. If a man was accompanied by his wife, I would be pressed into service to meet them at the airport along with Bill, and bid them farewell. In between, I acted as escort for the wife. She might want to see the countryside, tourist attractions, shops, or go to the hairdresser.

But there were a few exceptions to the norm. Every so often, our visitors expected their federal representatives abroad to do cartwheels to accommodate their whims and fancies, and sometimes they became an embarrassment. One senator, who will go unnamed, descended the ramp of his jet and announced pompously to the press, "This is a nice little country—I think I'll buy it for my son." Another was so drunk when he disembarked that his mission aborted completely.

☙ ☙ ☙

Beautiful, peaceful little Costa Rica was churned into a swirling cauldron for two weeks in August of 1960 when San José became the site of an important meeting of the Organization of American States. The meeting was prompted by a formal complaint by Cuba alleging that the recent reduction in the import quota for Cuban sugar represented economic pressure forbidden under the OAS charter. Altogether, an influx of about 400 delegates from all Latin American countries descended on San José. The U.S. contingent alone, headed by Secretary of State Christian Herter, numbered forty. A recent Summit Conference in Paris had turned into a fiasco when the communists, directed by Moscow, managed to capture the attention of the world with angry demonstrations. Rumors were rampant that similar problems would develop in San José, but the Costa Ricans had the situation well in hand, and the conference went forward peacefully.

The charming Teatro Nacionál, built around the turn of the century in baroque style, was the site of the meetings. Bill had a pass, and once, he was able to wangle one for myself and Bill, Jr. Almost magically, the theater had been transformed into a conference center; the original design allowed the floor to be raised level with the stage. Flags from each of the twenty-one countries were arranged in a huge fan at the far end. The foreign ministers' desks and chairs were in a circle under the central chandeliers. Everything was polished to the nth degree inside and out.

To relieve the tiny Costa Rican police force, boy scouts helped to direct traffic, and many local people, including British and Americans, acted as security guards, leaving their own shops and businesses. Others volunteered as typists and interpreters. The "esprit de corps" was magnificent.

For the United States, the outcome of the conference was a success. At ten o'clock on the last night, the OAS countries voted down the Cuban allegation by a large majority, and in a dramatic moment, the Cuban delegation, led by Raul Castro, brother of Fidel, stormed out of the theater singing the Cuban national anthem and

142

shouting, "Death to the Yankee Imperialists." At that moment, a Cuban flag was raised in the balcony by a group of exiles shouting down the fleeing delegation.

Secretary and Mrs. Herter were charming aristocrats. In spite of crippling arthritis, the secretary was tireless in his effort to bring about a successful conclusion to the proceedings. I learned that during such a conference, just as much work goes on at night as during the daytime.

ꝏ   ꝏ   ꝏ

One morning during the conference, Mrs. Willauer, our ambassador's wife, asked me to take Mrs. Herter shopping and sight-seeing in our car. I quickly hosed down Maudie, brushed out the mud and cracker crumbs, and removed toys and candy wrappers. Tailed by security men, we walked through the colorful Mercado Central, then drove twenty miles to Cartago to visit the Basilica, a church built on the site where, in 1620, a little Indian slave girl had found a doll in the image of Costa Rica's patron saint, The Virgin Lady of the Angels. The very ragged doll, encased in glass, could still be seen on the altar.

On the return trip, we made the long ascent to the top of Irazu Volcano which rose two miles above sea level. Because of low cloud cover, people appeared as ghosts—farmers tending their fields or walking along the road, women and girls doing the family wash in fast flowing streams. At the top, where it was bitingly cold, a few white crosses marked spots where suicides or accidents had taken place. We approached the edge of the crater with care and looked down. At the bottom of this enormous cavity in the earth's crust, there was an iron red lake, the result of mineral deposits dissolved by the last eruption in 1910.

ꝏ   ꝏ   ꝏ

About this time, the Washington scene was cranking up for the presidential election in November. John F. Kennedy was running against Richard M. Nixon, the incumbent vice-president under Dwight D. Eisenhower. This was the first time that presidential nominees had debated on television, still a black and white luxury item in the United States. It was not available to homeowners in San José, but our U.S. Embassy had a set. Bill and I went to the embassy for each of the two debates to hear this miracle machine produce the images and words of the two nominees. The appealing JFK entered the stage first—handsome, smiling, poised, well–dressed, and confident. Nixon followed. He looked like an escaped convict on a WANTED poster—unshaven, rumpled suit, and dark circles under his eyes. How did his staff let such a thing happen? Where were the make-up people? It was almost a no-contest situation. Kennedy went on to win the election and we had The New Frontier until an assassin's bullet killed the young president in Dallas, Texas, on November 23, 1963.

৵ ৵ ৵

One night in May of 1961, the gentle rhythm of Costa Rica was jarred by an earthquake. When a quake strikes, electricity is immediately turned off at a central switchboard, so darkness is added to the awful roar and vibration. Four consecutive quakes followed in quick succession, the third reaching number six on the Richter scale. With the walls pulsating in and out like an accordion, balance was as difficult to maintain as standing in a rowboat on a rough sea. Seconds seemed a lifetime. Bill was in Panama, Alberta was out for the evening, and I was at a meeting across town. Fortunately, Bill, Jr. was home with Channing and Joni.

When I believed the worst was over, I drove home with a warning from friends to drive on the same side of the road as the telegraph poles. In case of aftershocks, they reasoned, falling poles would cause less damage if the car was on their near side. People were running in the streets screaming (the Latin temperament can be triggered by much less than an earthquake) and my leg was shaking so violently on the accelerator that I stalled three times.

Reaching home safely and thankfully, I found our three children, plus Maria and Toñito, sitting in a circle in the downstairs recreation room where Bill, Jr. was calmly passing out jelly beans and telling stories by flashlight. When the quake struck, he had dashed upstairs in the dark to get the girls out of bed and had herded everyone under the archway of the front entrance which he knew was the safest place to stand.

ॐ   ॐ   ॐ

In 1961, we continued to pursue our interests in fine arts. Channing's talent at drawing seemed to blossom. Joni continued to love ballet, and Billy was active in both high school dramatics and the Little Theater Group of Costa Rica. I had begun to make a little money doing pastel portraits of children while continuing my correspondence course with the Famous Artists' School.

Much to everybody's surprise, big Bill joined this happy throng by accepting a role in *My Sister Eileen,* put on by San José's Little Theater Group at the Teatro Nacionál. He was excellent as "the Wreck," a big, kindly, dumb football player who was making the most of life with the "bottle" before the pro football season started. His costume was a pair of white satin basketball shorts, a Georgia Tech undershirt, size 36" (he took a 42"), and a very hairy chest which grew in profusion all the way up to his neck. It looked so real that Channing spent a lot of time explaining that, "It wasn't really her Daddy's hair."

ॐ   ॐ   ॐ

Our production was only a prelude to what was to come. Under the auspices of John F. Kennedy's Cultural Exchange

Program, and the Little Theater Group of Costa Rica, the Theater Guild American Repertory Company descended on San José for one week: sixty-one people and twenty–one tons of equipment arrived at the airport on October 9, 1961. Heading the list of principal actors was no less than Helen Hayes, known as the "First Lady of the American Theater." Because I was connected with the U.S. Embassy and active in theater work, the ambassador asked me to be the liaison between the Costa Ricans and the company, and to be in charge of recruiting back-stage workers before and during the plays. The latter involved hiring Costa Rican wardrobe women for ironing, mending, unpacking, and packing over 100 costumes, stagehands for setting up and striking the three sets, interpreters, electricians, guards, and cleaning women. I also handled the payroll for this group of thirty individuals. The plays included, *The Glass Menagerie, The Skin of Our Teeth,* and *The Miracle Worker.* No one dreamed what a thespian cyclone the week would become.

The drama started at the airport when immigration authorities discovered Fatima, a toy poodle, in actress June Havoc's handbag. Smuggling an animal into any country is against the law, and she had gotten away with it in twenty others, but little Costa Rica was particularly sensitive, having recently spent thousands of dollars to wipe out rabies. June was quite definite that if Fatima had to leave the country, she would depart with her, and this would throw the play in which she starred, *The Skin of Our Teeth,* into a cocked hat. When the government said that the dog could stay if impounded, June created more embarrassment by insisting on living with Fatima at the pound. Finally, June simmered down after meeting Costa Rica's official veterinarian, a forceful woman, and relinquished Fatima into her private custody. I must add that, in spite of the above complication, June Havoc, sister of Gypsy Rose Lee, was a charming person and a fine actress. Even Dr. Vargas, the Minister of Health, who had been red hot under the collar upon June's arrival, sent, "Best wishes to June and Fatima" upon her departure.

An even more explosive incident occurred regarding another actress who will remain unnamed. She and her lover, a lesser light in the company, decided to return to nature in the swimming pool at the country club. She started out in a bikini, (banned at our very decorous club), and ended up strutting around the pool twirling the bra section of her scanty attire in the air. The life guard, who was teaching proper little Costa Ricans how to swim, quickly reported the incident to the manager, who had the pair abruptly removed from the premises. All the while our American "good will" star was responding with verbal damnation.

This, too, would probably have been forgotten in time had she not committed an unforgivable sin in theater ethics after her performance as Annie in *The Miracle Worker.* Seething over the pool episode, she had built up a head of steam against the Costa Ricans whom she claimed had ruined her reputation as a "lady." As a result, during the curtain call, when a society matron presented her with flowers, she banged them down on the floor scattering petals, tossed them over her shoulder, and stomped off the stage in a rage. This little scene was enacted before an audience of 1,800. Feathers flew in all directions. The Costa Ricans were shocked. Her fellow actors, refusing to continue with her, dispatched a cable to Actors' Equity in New York asking to have her withdrawn from the repertory company. Back in her dressing room, she went berserk, throwing make-up bottles and jars at the mirror. I tried to calm her down with gentle admonitions, but the situation was beyond control.

On the brighter side, other members of the company conducted themselves with decorum. Especially charming and gracious were the two notable actors, Helen Hayes and Leif Erickson, both of whom became our life-long friends.

Bill drove Helen Hayes to and from El Coco Airport and I had the privilege of escorting her on shopping tours and various excursions outside of San José. One afternoon she and another actress, Nancy Coleman, kindly agreed to go to the little Arlequin

Theater where Costa Rican actors held workshops and put on plays. It was a noteworthy "good will" effort in that actors of both nationalities spontaneously mixed on stage and acted out spur-of-the-moment skits. How proud the Costa Ricans were to have Helen Hayes on their tiny stage! Helen held a symposium at the University of Costa Rica, and, in all her glory, did passages from her New York triumph, *Victoria Regina.*

The most special memory of all occurred in our own home. The occasion was the great actress's sixty-first birthday. We invited twenty–four guests in all—twelve principals from the company, six Costa Rican actors, and four Americans from the Little Theater Group to a buffet supper. Singing "Happy Birthday," Joni and Toñito carried in the birthday cake, whereupon Miss Hayes gave them each a hug and invited them to go to the movies with her on Saturday afternoon to see *The Swiss Family Robinson* in which her son, James MacArthur, had a leading role.

When Saturday arrived, Joni and Toñito, each holding one of Helen's hands, plus two other children from the company, walked to the movie house from the Balmoral Hotel where she

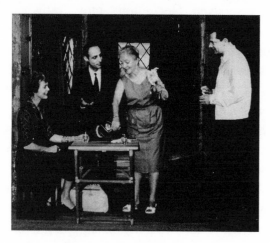

*Helen Hayes with Costa Rican actors
at Arlequin Theater, San José*

148

was staying. Channing was the official guide. When her son's name appeared on the screen, Helen and her little brood clapped so loudly that the excitement spread throughout the Rex Theater, and, not knowing why, the entire audience joined in.

Young Bill was not only an interpreter on my backstage crew, he was also Miss Hayes' official escort to and from the Teatro Nacionál. Although he had an embassy car and chauffeur ready and waiting, she preferred to walk, and off they would go arm in arm. When he took her back to the hotel at night, they would stop at the bar for a ginger ale. To our great good fortune, each member of our family became well acquainted with this wonderful lady during that one week.

Each of the six principal actors wrote notes to Bill and me thanking us for our efforts on their behalf and apologizing for the behavior of two of their fellow players. Helen Hayes graciously invited us to her home in Cuernavaca, Mexico. We were unable to accept at that time, but in the years to come, we would visit her many times.

ﾞ   ﾞ   ﾞ

In November of 1961, Bill received a cable from F.A.S in Washington stating, "Transfer to Australia approved for beginning of new year—letter follows." During Bill's thirty-year career in the foreign service, the U.S. government, we found, was full of surprises, and this was certainly a big one. We had expected to be in San José for another year.

This sudden move half way around the world came about because of a growing problem with Australian meat imports to the United States. The trouble was exacerbated by the absence there of both an American ambassador and an agricultural attache over an extended period of time. As a result, the Australian Meat Board was upset, and something had to be done to rectify the situation and appease ill will. Officials in Washington knew that

Bill could handle the ticklish problem diplomatically and intelligently.

᭝   ᭝   ᭝

For his outstanding performance in Central America, Bill was nominated and approved for a superior service award by the U.S. Department of Agriculture. The citation reads as follows: "For skill in developing and maintaining relationships and representing U.S. Agriculture abroad, and for superior initiative in promoting the sale of U.S. Agricultural products." Later, Bill returned to Washington from Australia for the Honor Awards Ceremony. Secretary of Agriculture Orville Freeman presented the award at the Sylvan Theater on the grounds of the Washington Monument. This ceremony was a part of an important conference which brought together attaches posted abroad and their colleagues in Washington to celebrate the 100th anniversary of U.S.D.A. Sometime during the conference the assembled attaches met with President Kennedy in the Rose Garden at the White House, Bill's first step into the enchanted realm of the New Frontier.

᭝   ᭝   ᭝

Bill, Jr. graduated with honors from high school on November 24. That evening, a graduation dance was held at the country club. Along with other parents, we gazed proudly upon our son as we celebrated the occasion. The girls wore white evening gowns and the boys white dinner jackets. At 10 P.M., mothers and sons, and fathers and daughters marched arm–in–arm in grand parade around the swimming pool to a fitting orchestral refrain.

The pending move to Australia changed the complexion of Bill, Jr.'s application to colleges in the United States, and we began to think in terms of an Australian university. Education at all levels in Australia was excellent.

Our last month in San José was a whirlwind of commotion. There was the sorting and packing to attend to along with Christmas preparations and parties. Of the many sad farewells, the hardest was saying good-bye to Alberta, Maria, and Toñito. Alberta, who had come into our family during those first difficult days of relocation, had become a close friend with whom we would keep in touch over the years to follow. Bill went to Washington for briefings the day after Christmas and, on Friday, January 5, the children and I flew to Los Angeles where he met us the following Sunday at a Disneyland motel.

���

I look back with nostalgia on those years in San José, where life flowed smoothly and happily. Bill loved his job and his travels into the more remote parts of his three assigned countries. I turned forty and felt fulfilled and contented with home and children. I loved the lush green country, the Costa Rican people, and the language. I was gratified to observe my children becoming fluent in Spanish. Holidays were spent in convenient and beautiful places. We enjoyed the county club, our comfortable home, our many friends, the perpetual springtime weather, and especially each other. The beautiful little Church of the Good Shepherd remained a focal point in our lives. For more than three years we had a good life in this small Central American country. Now it was time to move on to another hemisphere, and we looked forward to the next chapter.

���

I have often been asked which overseas assignment was my favorite, a question almost impossible to answer as each of our six countries had its own distinctive flavor and charm. Yet, if a ballot had to be taken, Costa Rica would be a contender for the top spot.

· —— Chapter Twelve —— ·

AUSTRALIA
January 1962 to June 1966

WE ARRIVED AT THE LOS ANGELES AIRPORT ON FRIDAY, JANUARY 5, 1962 and made the short hop to Disneyland by helicopter.

Two days at Disneyland proved a whirlwind of excitement—roller coaster rides, parades, shows, and an introduction to Mickey Mouse himself. Joni was thrilled. She sat on Mickey's lap while Channing snapped a picture. This magic kingdom was well established in early 1962, but still in its infancy as compared to the expansion that was to come.

Bill flew in from Washington and joined us on Sunday evening. The following day we drove to Los Angeles in a rental car and booked into a motel. June Havoc, a member of the repertory theater group that had come to San José in October of 1961, had procured passes for us to Warner Brother Studios where we walked down the unpaved street of an early western town. On closer inspection we discovered that the buildings were nothing more than facades. We saw bubble machines, rain and snow machines and other tricks of the trade for use on the set of a musical extravaganza; finally, we watched television episodes of *Hawaiian Eye* and *Maverick* being filmed. Signs were everywhere warning us not to make any noise, and, being a cigarette smoker at the time, I was scared to death that I would cough.

Foreign service officers and their families flew first-class in early 1962. On the flight to Honolulu, a battery of stewards treated us like royalty, plying us with delectable tidbits, cards, magazines, and toys for Joni. An elegant champagne dinner was served and we wallowed in culinary happiness.

In Honolulu, we had reserved a family suite at the Moana Hotel on Waikiki Beach. Our two small rooms were affordable because they were in the rear of the hotel overlooking the parking lot. By maneuvering miles of corridors and numerous elevators, we could emerge onto the famous beach only to be disappointed by both its insignificant size and indolent surf. I had imagined Waikiki to be a broad stretch of golden sand with billowing waves carrying bronzed young surfers to shore.

A poignant memory was our visit to Pearl Harbor and the monument over the sunken ship, Arizona, where 1,103 bodies still remained undisturbed in the depths of Pacific waters.

That afternoon, we flew to the island of Maui where we rented a little pink vehicle called a "mote" with a fringed canopy like Rodgers and Hammerstein's *Surrey*. The girls and I were wearing colorful Hawaiian "muu-muus" and the two Bills had equally flamboyant Hawaiian shirts. We must have made quite a splash of color bouncing along the dusty roads. Maui was just beginning to be developed as a resort. Here and there, bulldozers were clearing land for golf courses, buildings, and roads to come, but the island was still resplendent in primordial beauty.

The hotel on Maui was still under construction. As the dining room was not yet open, we bought native foods which father and son cooked in the only available cooking pan—a wok, and ate sitting Chinese style on straw mats on the floor. For four glorious days, we explored hidden beaches, climbed the rocky shore, and lazed in brilliant sunshine. On January 17, we returned by small plane to the airport in Honolulu where we departed for Australia at some ungodly hour of the morning. Somewhere in the sky, we crossed the international date line, completely losing January 18, and arrived on a hot midsummer Friday in Sydney, January 19,1962. We were halfway around the world from home.

ℬ   ℬ   ℬ

Although the traffic can be chaotic, Sydney will always remain one of my favorite cities. It is not only Australia's swinging town, but offers generous portions of theater, music and art. The people are easygoing, lighthearted, and friendly, and the streets are studded with small islands of flowers, fountains, and blooming shrubs. People enjoy outdoor amusements—yachting, surfing, swimming, picnicking, and tennis—all favored year–around by a mild climate and innumerable bays and sandy beaches. At night the graceful Harbor Bridge spans the magnificent harbor like a enormous diamond tiara.

We checked into the Chevron–Hilton at an early hour. Too excited for jet–lag, we wandered through botanical gardens along the harbor's edge and visited the Sydney Zoo where, along with familiar wild animals, we saw our first kangaroos, platypuses, and koala bears. We were told that these sleepy, fat little bears remain perpetually doped due to the soporific effect of the eucalyptus leaf on which they feed. Lamb cutlets were as common in Australia as hot dogs in the U.S. They were on the menu for breakfast, lunch and dinner and quickly became Joni's favorite food. From then on we teasingly called her "lamb chop."

From our first taxi driver, we learned that tipping was an insult. After the palms-up routine in Latin America, this commendable trait came as a pleasant jolt. We also learned that single passengers rode up front with the driver in taxis. The Aussies were a proud lot.

On Saturday, we visited the campus of the University of Sydney. Sending Bill, Jr. to the other end of the world to an American university was a heart–wrenching thought. We talked to the admissions office and found that his scholastic record was such that he would be accepted. On first view, the university was impressive and we began to seriously consider this course. A favorable consideration was that classes began in early March rather than September as in the States.

That evening, Bill and I left our offspring at the hotel and went out for dinner and theater. We saw a play called *The Sentimental Bloke* and might as well have been listening to Hungarian. Our ears had not yet become attuned to the unique Australian accent.

In order for foreigners to fully understand Australian English, it is necessary to learn about a hundred words and phrases in the Aussie vernacular, a language called "Strine," whereby the letter 'i' sounds as in "stike" for steak, and "die" for day. There is a little anecdote about an Aussie who was asked,

"Did you come here to–die?"

"No," came the reply. "I came here yester–die."

As an agricultural attache is attached to an embassy, his home is always in the capital city of the country to which he, or she, is assigned. We therefore would be living in Canberra, Australia's capital.

My first recollection of Canberra was of intense heat and bush flies. These pesky little insects were so profuse that they could cover a man's white shirt to the point of making it appear black. Whacking away flies was a summer occupation, sometimes referred to as "the Australian salute." This infestation disappeared later in the year with cooler weather.

We were met planeside by the economic counselor, Eddie Schodt, and his wife, Margy, who informed us that a female reporter and a photographer were awaiting Bill's arrival inside the terminal. The recent problem with meat exports had caused tension between Australia and the United States, and Bill's first assignment was to try to smooth the furrowed brows. An interview took place inside the airport and, as reporters are sometimes wont to do, the article that appeared in *The Canberra Times* the following morning was full of misquotes. The caption under a poor photo of Bill was, "U.S. EXPERT'S WARNING TO AUSTRALIA," followed by:

"Mr. Rodman sees little future for Australian beef in the United States other than of manufacturing quality. Our consumers, he said, do not like the taste of your grass–fed meat . . ."

The next day, Bill called Jack Shute, chairman of the Australian Meat Board in Sydney. Shute said a meeting was scheduled for that afternoon and that the members would very much welcome the American attache's attendance. Poor Bill! Before his bags were unpacked, he flew back to Sydney and took a cab to the offices of the board. The meeting was already in session and, as he entered the room, the members riveted my husband to the spot with cold stares. Then, suddenly, they exploded into laughter, banging their hands on the table and extending emphatic Aussie handshakes along with a warm welcome. It took Bill several moments to realize that this scene had been staged. They then put him further at ease by telling him to forget *The Canberra Times* article. Misquotation in newspapers was common practice, especially in *The Canberra Times,* they said. Bill thanked them for their unusual welcome adding that it beat being run out of town as he had expected.

At 5 P.M., as was the custom in Australia, Bill and his new friends filed out of the building, crossed the street, and lined up at the bar of a pub for a cold beer. Contrary to the British, who drink their beer at room temperature, Australians like to keep their schooners in the freezer.

☞   ☞   ☞

Going back to our arrival in Canberra, after Bill's press interview at the airport, Margy and Eddie kindly took us to their home for lunch. They briefed us on various facets of life in Canberra and introduced us to their two teenage sons and a pet kangaroo. At that time, if a kangaroo mother was killed, her offspring, called a "joey," could become a household pet. Joni was thrilled to pat a joey on her first day in Canberra.

Later that day, the Schodts took us to the Hotel Wellington, our home for the next three weeks. We each felt a little lost, but knew it would not be difficult to settle into life in this friendly country where we could converse in our own language, and where the concepts of life, liberty and the pursuit of happiness matched our own.

I believe Australia and the United States are bonded in a special kinship. Common ancestry with England is likely a part of the reason. When England could no longer dump her undesirables on us after the American Revolution, she shipped them off to Australia and both nations remain today favored havens for the restless and persecuted of the world. Between 1788 and 1868, 160,000 convicts, many of them mere boys and girls, were transported to Australia for no worse crime than stealing a loaf of bread. During the eight–month journey, they were crammed into the dark holds of ships where scores died of dysentery, brutal treatment, and starvation. Those that survived were set free after serving out their sentences and became instrumental in forging a new nation. When we were in Australia, it was very fashionable to claim convict ancestry.

The bond between Australia and the United States was further strengthened in 1942 during World War II. The Japanese were on their way to invade northern Australia when they were intercepted and defeated by U.S naval forces in the Battle of the Coral Sea, a victory still celebrated annually in May.

In spite of shared values, however, we soon learned that various verbal expressions were interpreted quite differently in Australia. For instance, we were still residing at the motel when Bill called one morning from Sydney. An employee answered the phone at the reception desk. When Bill asked for Mrs. Rodman in room 7, the man answered, "She's not in her room, sir. I knocked her up at 7 o'clock this morning." My startled husband quickly learned that "to knock up" meant "to awaken" in Australia.

℘ ℘ ℘

At the turn of the twentieth century, a tremendous rivalry existed between Melbourne and Sydney for urban supremacy. Each, having reached a population of half a million, sought vigorously to become the nation's capital. Government offices were divided between them, an unwieldy arrangement as they were 700 miles apart. In 1901, a constitutional convention agreed on a compromise—an entirely new capital city would be built between the two feuding cities and the site chosen would become the Australian Capital Territory (ACT). Canberra, the Aboriginal name for "a woman's breasts," existed inside of the chosen ground and was nothing more than a small agricultural center. But because Melbourne and Sydney continued to feud and wrangle, it wasn't until 1927 that the new Parliament House was completed and the fledgling city of Canberra ready to become the new seat of government.

Canberra, a planned city, lying in a valley in the southern tablelands, boasted a lovely setting and lots of open space. A worldwide contest, ordered by the government, to design an impressive capital within the ACT, had been won by Walter Burley-Griffin, a U.S. citizen and junior colleague of the famous architect, Frank Lloyd Wright. Burley–Griffin's vision was of a geometrically designed city of spacious parks, wide tree-lined avenues lined with golden wattle, gray-green eucalyptus, oaks and elms, and a sparkling man-made lake crossed by a stately bridge connecting two distinct residential and civic areas.

The residential areas Burley–Griffin created incorporated a series of planned neighborhoods. The larger had their own shopping center, school, tennis courts, swimming pool, cricket ground, and greens for bowling and croquet. Every new property owner was offered gratis twenty young trees and fifteen shrubs by the ACT Parks and Gardens Commission. Birds were in abundance—parakeets, flaming lories, rose-crested cockatoos, laughing kookaburras, and chattering magpies. Australians were convinced that life on earth was to be enjoyed and lived outdoors. They worked hard during the week, but on Friday at 5 o'clock sharp, business came to an abrupt halt, and the glorious weekend ahead was for family picnics and outings, sports, and other recreational endeavors. Even shops and markets closed down at 12 noon on Saturday. In summer, the Aussies were off to the beaches, and in winter, to the Snowy Mountains to ski. It is no wonder that Australians excel at many sports.

ॐ   ॐ   ॐ

In 1962, it was extremely difficult to find a house to rent in Canberra. As government offices were moved one by one to the ACT over a period of years, the capital burgeoned with employees transferred from Sydney and Melbourne. Small business, shops, and markets followed, and a major problem became one of housing. In Burley–Griffin's plan there were no apartment buildings nor multiple housing projects to absorb the influx. During the week, parliamentarians, who had chosen to stay in their constituencies rather than move their families to the infant city, occupied the two hotels. In addition, Australia was having an upsurge of immigrants from Europe. (The White Australian Policy was in effect restricting people from Asia and Africa.)

Many were attracted to Canberra by the ever-increasing demand for laborers, and many of those skilled in construction became "spec" builders. They knew that once a house was completed, it would sell immediately. The 1962 population of about 50,000 was expected to double by 1970.

As well as the U.S. Chancery and Embassy Residence, the U.S. State Department owned a number of houses for officers and staff in Canberra. Other personnel, which included the agricultural attache, were taken care of by their own departments on a housing–allowance basis. Therefore, our first priority was to find a place to live. Real estate agencies were nonexistent because there were no rental or sale properties. It began to appear that our best bet was to buy a "spec" house already under construction.

After three weeks in the Motel Wellington, we rented a small house in the suburb of Narrabundah on a four-month lease while the owners were on holiday in England. This suburb was close to the area where we hoped to settle, and four months would give us time to search for a place of our own.

Just after we arrived, we heard that one of the Marines at the embassy was being transferred and had a 1951 Volkswagen for sale. Like houses, cars were in short supply, so Bill bought it— a funny little two-toned brown and tan Beetle, which we affectionately dubbed, "the Doodlebug." The little car served us well for two years before finally giving up. An embassy joke was that the Rodmans liked to park their shabby little car beside a big, flashy Cadillac at diplomatic functions hoping the two would mate in the moonlight.

As Australia was my first experience of driving on the left–hand side of the road, it was fortuitous that there was little traffic in Canberra. After a few hairy practice sessions, I felt enough at ease to set off in the Doodlebug to cruise the streets in search of a permanent home. One day, I drove up a stately, tree–lined street called Mugga Way admiring the large homes and embassy residences. Beyond a certain point, however, in the suburb of Red Hill, Mugga Way continued on through what appeared to be undeveloped territory except for three houses in various stages of construction.

I stopped to speak to a man who was working on the foundation of one of the houses. In broken English he said his name was Hans, a "spec" builder, originally from Switzerland, now a naturalized Australian. Unlike the other two houses, this one had not been sold. He showed me blueprints of the Swiss–style ranch house he was planning to build, and I knew immediately that this would be my dream home. Because of the scarcity of housing, I also knew I had to act quickly and raced to the embassy to fetch Bill.

Back at the site, my husband studied the blueprints and became equally enthusiastic about the house as both a home and an investment. We then asked Hans to give us a few days to arrange financing. First we received permission from the Foreign Agricultural Service to assign our monthly housing allowance toward a mortgage, obtained from a local bank. We then cabled my brother, Channing Daniel, our trust officer at the National Bank in Charlottesville, Virginia, to extend us a small bank loan, and transfer savings to our bank in Canberra as a down payment. The contract was quickly drawn up, and we were the proud owners of 87 Mugga Way. Houses were still relatively inexpensive. If I remember correctly the total cost was about $25,000.

ॐ   ॐ   ॐ

In early March, Bill, Jr. entered St. Paul's Anglican College, a time-honored institution at the University of Sydney. St. Paul's, with its attractively sinister Gothic architecture, would give him the advantage of a small college within a big university. Several anachronistic customs were still in effect such as saying grace in Latin before meals and wearing academic gowns to chapel and the dining hall. I think he quite enjoyed being the only Yank at his college. As with hazing the world over, the "fresher" system, according to Bill, Jr., reduced first year students to the "lowest form of existence known to man." The new boys were gofers for the upperclassmen. Identification signs had to be worn around the neck and the name written in small letters. No fresher had a first name so Bill became "fresher rodman."

"How is your name written, fresher?"

"With the smallest letters possible, sir."

The most dreaded antics involved what were called "turnouts" and "summons." Turnouts were mass rallies where the freshers became the performing animals.

"You're an American, aren't you, rodman?"

"Yes, sir."

"Well, if you're an American you know how to do the 'twist.' GET UP ON THAT TABLE AND DO IT."

A "summons" entailed going to the room of one of the seniors, four freshers at a time, where a group of seniors lounged about in easy chairs while the freshers stood at attention answering all manner of stupid questions.

"What is your name?"

"Fresher rodman, sir."

"Your name is not fresher rodman. It is 'Telephone.' Now, if you are a telephone, what do you do?"

"Ring, I guess."

"Well then, start ringing."

"Ring-ring . . . ring-ring . . . . ring . . . . ring."

"DON'T JUST STAND THERE, FRESHERS, ANSWER THE PHONE!"

One fresher grabbed Bill's right arm and held his fist to his ear while Bill continued to go "ring...ring..."

"Hello, St. Paul's College."

By this time, the seniors, in fits of laughter had ordered another new boy to do handstands on the floor and one to twirl a hula-hoop. This ridiculous scenario continued for a half-hour or so. When it was over, Bill and his three classmates went outside and laughed like hell. He wrote, "It really was painless and served to tie a closer bond between the four of us."

We felt extremely fortunate to be in a country where the educational system was excellent at all levels. Literacy was virtually 100 percent. Channing, now fourteen, entered the ninth grade at The Church of England Girls' Grammar School (CEGGS). The academic standard at the Lincoln School in San José was not up to this scholastically superior private school; she needed outside tutoring to catch up.

Joni and Channing in Church of England
Girl's Grammar School winter uniform.

All children wore uniforms to school, and dating was discouraged until girls were about sixteen years old. Australia seemed a wholesome place to grow up—a place where a child could enjoy the rhapsody of childhood just a little longer.

ᘓ   ᘓ   ᘓ

An advantage of living in Canberra was the absence of crime. We rarely locked our house or car doors, and bicycles could be safely left in the front yard. Children roamed about at will. A lost wallet or watch would invariably be returned to the owner, or turned in at the police station.

Whereas Channing made friends easily, Joni was more reserved. Most of her dolls and toys were still with our effects in storage somewhere in Canberra. She missed Alberta, Maria, Toñito, her friends, pets, and room in San José. Nevertheless, she put on a brave front. I knew a breakthrough had come, however, when she came home from school one afternoon holding another little girl's hand and announced, "This is Jillian—my best friend," And Joni and Jillian were inseparable from then on.

One day, the students of Joni's class were asked to tell what their fathers did to earn a living. Her teacher later reported to us that Joni stood up and answered proudly, "My daddy is an agricultural out–of–shape. She of course meant "attache." That remark followed Bill around for years to come. In time, Joni's accent became pure Australian, but for awhile, it was an amusing mixture of Spanish, English, and "Strine."

About a year after we settled in Canberra, Australia went through a change of currency from pounds sterling to the decimal system. This resulted in throwing an entire nation into a cocked hat! Shopkeepers and merchants were befuddled for months as to how to tender the proper change, school children were utterly baffled, and old folks traumatized. Having struggled myself with learning pounds, shillings, and pence, I must have been one of the few housewives delighted to return to my native nickel and dime system.

Our telephone was used for local calls, never long distance. Letter writing was still the norm of communication with friends and family in faraway places. Only once in our four and a half years in Australia did we call the United States. That was an appointment call to my mother on her seventy-fifth birthday. And I must admit, without copies of letters, this journal would have been infinitely more difficult to write.

As far as housework was concerned, I was spoiled by Alberta and Maria in San José. In Canberra, where there was no unemployment, only chiefs of mission had household help. I therefore resumed the task of cook and cleaning woman, and quite liked having the house to myself during the daytime when the kids were at school. I also thought the time had come for Channing and Joni to learn to keep tidy their own rooms, make their beds, and help with household chores. As with most teenagers, Channing had an increasing messy–room problem, and she and I crossed a number of swords on that subject.

When the lease was up on the Narrabundah house in June, we still had almost three months before ours would be completed. Fortunately, Bill learned that an Australian cabinet minister was being sent abroad for a few months and would rent his house. This fit in perfectly with our schedule and again we moved. In the foreign service, moving, though never easy, became a part of life.

The three months before finally moving into our own house at 87 Mugga Way were memorable for three things: our new ambassador, William C. Battle, arrived with his family; we acquired our beloved Casey, a short-haired dachshund puppy; and next door to us, a staff member of the Russian Embassy hung herself on an outdoor clothes line. This last event was hushed up so quickly that it hardly caused more than a ripple in the diplomatic corps. I was glad that the children were at school when it happened.

ॐ   ॐ   ॐ

Bill Battle was appointed ambassador to Australia by John F. Kennedy in July 1962. He and the president were close personal friends, having served together as Navy P.T. boat captains in the South Pacific during World War II. Coincidentally, the Battles lived in Charlottesville, Virginia. When my husband was in Washington for a few weeks in May of that year to attend meetings, he had gone to Charlottesville to see my mother and was introduced to Barry, Bill Battle's wife. The role of ambassador's wife was to be a very new experience for this young and beautiful Virginian. She was only twenty-nine years old, the mother of three children. It didn't take her long, however, to fit into the role with grace and distinction, but at that time, she was awed by the prospect of moving her family to Australia, and uncertain as to the life and style of an ambassador's wife. Barry asked my husband many questions. One, about which we teased her later, was, "Do I need to bring a refrigerator?" Little did she realize that the ambassador's residence would not only be equipped with ample refrigeration, but also with two cooks, a butler, and a majordomo.

After a few months in Australia, a leading newspaper printed the following excerpt.

> Although she is playing the role of Ambassador's wife for the first time, Mrs. Battle is handling it with great diplomacy, charm, and dignity, and brings to it as well the light touch of youth and gaiety.

When the Battles arrived in July, I was unsure as to how I should greet the new ambassador's wife. Protocol dictated a formal call at the proper time, but my intuition told me differently. I had known Bill Battle slightly when he was a student at the University of Virginia, and we had many mutual friends. I felt strongly that Barry needed a friend rather than another white-gloved caller, so I roared over to the residence the day after they arrived. Huang, the Chinese majordomo, who let me into the marbled hall, said that Mrs. Battle was upstairs. I'm sure he was greatly surprised when I climbed halfway up the stairs and shouted, "Bar–reeee!" She came tearing down to greet me and we embraced like old friends. Sometimes, even in the diplomatic service, it is best to let your heart rule your head.

Joni came to look upon six-year-old Janie Battle as a surrogate little sister. A particularly telling experience, about a year after the Battle's arrival, was when our charming deputy chief of mission's wife, Jody Lydman, via an engraved invitation, invited Joni and Janie to her residence for tea. On the appointed day, the two little girls put on their prettiest frocks and white gloves, and were called for by the ambassador's chauffeur–driven limousine with small American flags flying on the front fenders. The tea party was very formal. A silver service was placed before the hostess and a uniformed maid served tiny cakes and finger sandwiches. Jody told the children tales about tea parties that she had held for her dolls when she was a little girl. She was quite intentionally introducing our daughters to diplomatic protocol and party manners at an early age.

A few days later, I observed Joni and Janie hostessing a doll's tea party in our back yard. Their venue was a renovated packing crate saved from our move. With the help of our neighbor, Bill had built a foundation, cut out windows and a door, added some blue paint, and so turned the crate into a playhouse.

ॐ   ॐ   ॐ

During this period, with a feeling of pride and accomplishment, I watched our house grow brick by brick until it was ready for occupancy by mid–September. We were thankful that the long, unsettled period of temporary lodging was over. Channing and Joni were delighted to at last occupy their own rooms where they could have their own belongings, especially their menageries of stuffed animals. I was blissfully happy. I loved Bill Rodman even more than I had loved him when we were sweethearts. Our life was just right: just enough earned wealth, just enough position, just enough social life, just enough time for the tenderness of home.

Because we had bought the house at 87 Mugga Way at its inception, we were able to modify the plans to suit our needs and preferences. We added extra cabinets and a dinette alcove in the kitchen, lined the den with oak paneling and, at one end, covered the wall with built-in bookcases. The living room was spacious with a circular sandstone fireplace in one corner; the hearth was raised, a favorite spot to sit. Double doors opened onto a wide flagstone terrace. Off of a long hallway were four bedrooms and two baths. At each end of the house was an under–floor oil heater, primitive contraptions by American standards, but "state of the art" in Australia. Few Aussies heated their homes. When the weather turned to freezing in the winter, they just stuck out their chests and put on an extra "woolly."

A quirk, required by antiquated building codes, were the six-inch, square openings in bathroom walls designed to let in fresh air at all times including the dead of winter. We Americans called them "pneumonia holes," which we covered over with tape to keep out the cold in winter and the flies in summer, and hoped not to be caught by the health inspector.

Our house was light and sunny with wide picture windows framing beautiful views. The outside walls were made of brick covered over with white plaster left rough rather than smooth. As a highlight, we painted the front door, a bright coral. The front faced a typical Australian landscape of sheep grazing under eucalyptus trees on the rising hills; the back overlooked the valley of the growing city of Canberra.

ℛ   ℛ   ℛ

Australians are a physically hardy lot—informal, good-humored, kind, open, and always honest. With appealing candor and directness, they say what they think, no matter the subject. The men can be verbally or physically aggressive at one moment and gentle the next. If a man knocks another down in a pub brawl, he picks him up and "shouts" him a beer. Aussies are dedicated to their work, their families, and their country. The following verse from a poem by Dorothea Mackellar well expresses their love of country:

> I love a sunburnt country,
> A land of sweeping plains,
> Of ragged mountain ranges,
> Of droughts and flooding rains.
> I love her far horizons,
> I love her jewel–sea,
> Her beauty and her terror—
> The wide brown land for me!

Perhaps the Australian's finest trait of all is the gift of receiving and bestowing friendship. No immigrant nor visitor to Australia is a stranger in a strange land for very long.

ॐ　ॐ　ॐ

One of our joys of living in the capitol city was the friendships formed through business contact with government ministries, especially with a group of young parliamentarians from the Country party which formed a coalition with the Conservative party led by Prime Minister Sir Robert Menzies. One of these able young men was Doug Anthony. Still in his early thirties, Doug possessed an easy charm and strikingly handsome good looks. Doug was named Minister of the Interior when he was thirty-four years old. On the morning that he was told of the appointment, our front door bell rang, and there was Doug asking if he could come in for a cup of coffee. The complete surprise of being appointed a cabinet minister had left him stunned. He had tried to call his wife, Margo, but had not been able to reach her, and he simply needed reassurance from a friend. Doug went on to occupy various ministerial posts including deputy prime minister.

At the invitation of Peter Nixon, another young parliamentarian, and his wife Sally, Bill, Joni and I drove to Orbost, an agricultural and logging center in the state of Victoria, to spend a weekend on their dairy farm. On Saturday morning, Bill was to officially open the Annual Agricultural Show and Fair, and I had been asked to judge the district Beauty Contest. I had no idea when I accepted this offer what a delicate job it would be. The first contest for young ladies went off fairly smoothly. Each contestant had made her own outfit, and the group ranged from quite pretty to downright homely. Obviously, there had been no pre-contest screening. After the older girls had been judged, however, problems arose. In a second contest for little girls, twenty poisonous cherubs were decked out in exaggerated finery with bonnets, furbelows, and nosegays. Each had a proud and domineering mother in tow who made it clear to the judges that her child was the only possible choice for first prize. I felt thoroughly intimidated, and thought, "Uh oh! Here's where I become The Ugly American." Fortunately I was saved from being run out of town by one of Australia's summer plagues, a raging bush fire.

Shortly before noon, standing in the middle of the show ring, Bill was just coming to the end of a short speech officially opening the show. I was to follow with the announcement of the winners of the two beauty contests. Suddenly, the microphone went dead, and the booming voice of the fire marshal came over the loud speaker: "All able-bodied men report to the main gate for transport to the bush fire area now less than three miles distant. Snap to it."

While the men rushed off, the ladies and children hastily

dismantled tents and booths, loaded animals onto lorries and raced away from the approaching inferno. In twenty minutes the showgrounds were reduced to fields of dust, and I was spared being lynched by a brigade of outraged mums.

ॐ   ॐ   ॐ

We became close friends of Paul and Ruth Siple, the American Science Attache and his wife. Many years before, as an eagle scout, Paul had won a contest to accompany Admiral Byrd on his first expedition to the South Pole. He went on to become a noted scientist and Antarctic explorer, returning many times to its icy wastes. In addition to his explorations, Paul was noted for his design of arctic clothing, which was adopted for army use in World War II.

The Siples and our family spent each Christmas together, either at home or at the beach. Even at the beach, in stifling weather, "Uncle" Paul insisted on a big Christmas tree decorated with homemade garlands and ribbons of popcorn. In spite of his brilliant mind, he was a child at heart. He loved to fly kites, play games, tell stories, and explore beaches and streams for interesting flora and fauna. He and I spent hours battling over Scrabble games. Lying on a gigantic polar bear hide on the living room floor of the Siple's house in Canberra, our daughters would become transfixed by fascinating tales of the Antarctic. They adored him.

They also adored "Auntie" Ruth, a tall, handsome woman with gorgeous white hair. As their own three daughters were grown and gone, the Siples took pleasure in fostering ours. If I could not be home when Channing and Joni returned from school, I would know where to find them.

ॐ   ॐ   ॐ

In early 1963, Australia was graced with a royal visit from Queen Elizabeth II of England, and His Highness Prince Philip.

In spite of a rather uncharitable attitude toward the English on occasion, the Australians went all out to welcome the monarch and her duke. In Canberra, the schools dismissed the students to line the streets were the royal motorcade would pass, and each child was given two little flags, one Australian and one British, to wave to the smiling couple. There is a delightful story about one such procession when Queen Elizabeth had a momentary lapse in her smiling demeanor. In the crowd lining the street was a deaf woman, a lip reader, who, watching closely, saw Philip turn to the queen and say, "Smile, Sausage!"

చ   చ   చ

Each year we attended the Royal Easter Show in Sydney with our dear friends Alister and Dorothy Paul. He was a handsome doctor and she a distinguished horsewoman. While Bill was on one of his trips, Joni and I met the Pauls on a ski weekend at Perisher Valley in the Snowy Mountains, some three hours from Canberra. I was a shaky skier, and Joni, at age seven, a rank beginner. When Joni fell and sprained her wrist, Alister was kind enough to tape it up. The following day, Joni was feeling somewhat sorry for herself when Alister came along and asked her to ride the T–Bar with him up the mountain. He placed her on his skis just in front of his boots, and, while holding the bar with one hand, held her tightly with the other.

"How are you ever going to get her down?" I asked.

"Not to worry," replied Alister.

A short time later, I was amazed to see Alister expertly skiing down the mountain with Joni on his shoulders!

We visited Alister and Dorothy many times at their small farm near Gosford, New South Wales, and loved their informal lifestyle. The Pauls had a collection of animals, some as pets and others making a contribution to the daily fare. The most unique of the latter was the family cow. Her placid nature and skeletal contours had earned her the name "Hatrack."

৶   ৶   ৶

As two and a half years had passed since our last home-leave, Bill, Joni and I departed Canberra in May 1963, just as winter was setting in and returned in August, in time to enjoy the first signs of spring. Bill, Jr. and Channing stayed behind as it was the middle of the school year. They would get their turn during the summer vacation. Janet, a teacher at CEGGS, came to live at the house with Channing. Before leaving, we enrolled Joni at CEGGS for the semester after our return. The third grade teacher there was willing to outline the work to be covered, and give her the necessary books to study on the trip. She also said she would give Joni extra help upon her return. At Red Hill School, the attitude was "Oh, a world trip is education in itself. Tell Joni to enjoy it and forget about work!" Her mother did not agree. Traveling around the globe didn't cover math, science, spelling, and grammar.

৶   ৶   ৶

Our first stop was Hong Kong, strikingly beautiful in its mountainous setting. A hodge-podge of color and bustle, we loved its myriad of little shops, narrow streets and mixture of ancient eastern and modern western architecture. We rode in rickshaws, experimented with chopsticks, scaled the mountain on the Peak tram, and hired a small river boat to watch the people who lived on sampans going about their daily routines.

On to Bangkok, where we were awed by ornate temples, gilded Buddhas, and glittering spires. Most interesting was the network of *klongs,* the site of the "floating markets," where the people went to and fro in an endless parade of small boats selling their wares and produce. Shanty dwellings lined the klongs, and children, like frogs, jumped in and out of the dirty water. We saw a beautiful demonstration of Thai dancing and a brutal match of Thai boxing, where the boxers, after a silent prayer to Buddha, whacked each other, not only with their hands, but also with feet, knees, head and elbows. One evening, friends invited us to dinner and we engaged a three-wheel "taxi" called a *tuk-tuk*. After initial greetings, Joni suddenly realized that she had left her teddy bear in the tuk-tuk. Our little girl was shattered, but miracle of miracles, the driver returned about a half hour later with her treasured pet.

New and Old Delhi were incredibly hot. Even at 2 A.M. when our plane landed, it was like walking into a blast furnace. In spite of the heat, I am quite convinced that the most beautiful sight I have ever seen was the Taj Mahal in Agra in the moonlight. Its marble mosaic glittered like sparkling gem stones, the beauty enhanced by the soft light. On the road to and from Agra, we saw all the storybook sights of India—the snake charmer, a dancing bear, camels drawing water from a well, elephants hauling blocks of stone, monkeys, holy men, and people by the droves, dirty, often in rags, and inevitably suffering from malnutrition. In spite of poverty, they are a beautiful people with smooth olive-brown complexions, pitch black hair, and large soulful eyes. Along the way, we also stopped at a little village where Joni became an instant curiosity because of her blond hair and blue eyes. She was not amused when the women and children tried to stroke her hair and touch her skin with dirty hands.

ॐ   ॐ   ॐ

Because it was so cool and clean in comparison, our next stop, Beirut, was literally a breath of fresh air. We stayed with friends, a professor and his wife at the American University of

Beirut, and drove with them into the countryside to see the Cedars of Lebanon and the Roman ruins of Baalbek. At that time Beirut was a beautiful and peaceful city, and I went off alone to explore. One of my valued possessions is a silver crusader cross and chain that I bought in a small silver shop.

Then came Rome, where we stayed at a charming *pensióne.* Bob and Alice Tetro, old friends from Argentina, entertained us, and directed us to the compulsory tourist attractions. Disappointingly, St. Peter's Cathedral and the Sistine Chapel were closed to the public due the recent death of the popular Pope, John XXIII.

Paris and London followed. At our hotel in Paris, a vivid memory was the ritual of the bath. In our private bathroom was a bidet, but no tub. A small sign told me to ring three times for a "bathtub" maid who dutifully arrived in a crisp blue and white striped uniform. Over her arm was a terry cloth robe and assorted towels. She and I then marched to the cage-like elevator and rose two stories to what I guessed was the bathtub floor. When we entered one of the little cubicles, she drew the bath water while I sat on a white stool. When the tub was full, my little French mademoiselle handed me a small bar of soap and exited the tiny room. After bathing for seven or eight minutes, I heard a discreet rap on the door. Enter my smiling *aide de bain,* ready to escort madam back to her boudoir two floors below.

A highlight of our stay in London was the "Changing of the Guard" at Buckingham Palace with the extra added attraction of four-year-old Prince Andrew peeking out of an upstairs window and waving the paw of his teddy bear to the crowd before a nanny snatched him away.

At each stop along the way, we had friends to greet us. Joni collected masses of treasures, postcards, and brochures to put into a memory book when she returned to Canberra. She never complained about being dragged to just one more old tomb, temple, or cathedral, but when we finally arrived at her grandmother's house in Philadelphia, she was more than happy to plunk herself down in front of television for a change of pace.

We spent our time in the states yo–yo–ing between Bill's family in Pennsylvania and my family in Virginia amidst a plethora of grandmothers, aunts, uncles, cousins, and friends. The fact that my three brothers and I had each produced a child within a twelve–month period meant instant playmates for Joni. Bill made his obligatory ten–day visit to Washington, D.C., for briefings and debriefings. For a few days of that time, Joni and I joined him and visited the important landmarks of our capital.

The return trip to Australia was pure enchantment. After a stop in San Francisco, we crossed the Pacific on the S. S. *Monterey,* a Matson Line ship, where we could vegetate in the sunshine of the South Seas. The island of Bora Bora was our favorite port of call. Its unspoiled beauty blended the aquamarine sea, golden sands and swaying palm trees into a glimpse of paradise.

While anchored at Tahiti, we went by launch to Moorea, the beautiful tropical island filmed as Bali Hai in the musical, *South Pacific.* Our shipboard tenor was along and, as the sunset burst upon the western horizon, he sang "Some Enchanted Evening." At dark, the Moreans sang and danced by torchlight after serving up the native feast called the "tamaaraa." The food, from red bananas to suckling pig, had been cooked all day long in a great pit of hot coals covered with banana leaves. When the "feast" emerged, each item had lost its identity, and the resulting gooey mass was consumed with one's fingers, then sloshed down with coconut milk laced with rum. Bill, who can eat anything, managed pretty well, but for Joni and me, this "delectable Polynesian meal" was a disaster. She and I survived on little slices of coconut meat.

I was not thrilled by the black volcanic sand of Tahiti. After a swim, one emerged from the beach looking like the tar baby in *Uncle Remus.* We enjoyed, however, walking the streets of Papeete, and having a drink at Quinns. This notorious bar, frequented by tourists and native customers of doubtful character, had not been swept out in years. A briefly clad Tahitian girl came along and emptied the ashtrays by throwing the contents under the table. And while I was sitting in a booth, a man's arm came around the corner of the next booth and pinched my bottom!

Life on shipboard was slow and easy—twenty-one days in all. Most of the passengers were wealthy retirees, a generation older than we. Joni, the only child on board, took part in all activities and became what might be termed the ship's mascot.

Perhaps the greatest thrill of the entire trip was entering beautiful Sydney Harbor at sunrise, then arriving home in Canberra to be greeted by Bill, Jr., Channing and our little dog, Casey, who did flip-flops and pinwheel circles in ecstatic greeting.

჻   ჻   ჻

Less than three months later, at 4 A.M. on November 23, the telephone awakened us with the startling news of the assassination of John F. Kennedy. (The time in Australia is fourteen hours earlier than the United States.) As Bill was duty officer at the time, he immediately rushed to the U.S. Chancery to receive follow up cables and inform embassy personnel. It was a moment in history that is indelibly imprinted in the minds and hearts of millions of people across the globe. Even those who become forgetful in later life can remember where they were and what they were doing when this thunderous news struck. Not only our nation but the world was thrust into a period of mourning. Incredibly, the life of this vital young president with his dreams of "A New Frontier" had been snuffed out in an instant by a sniper's bullet.

჻   ჻   ჻

One of the attractions of Canberra in the summertime was the nearness of coastal beaches just three hours from home. With a makeshift rack for luggage on top, we would pile into the Doodlebug, Casey included, and off we'd go winding up and up along the cliff edge of mountains, then down and down to the resorts of Mirimbula or Mollymook where we rented a cottage on the ocean. One time, we carried with us an important Washington official who had come to evaluate the Rodmans' diplomatic performance in Australia. Suddenly, the load atop the Doodlebug came unhinged and slid off onto the road on a particularly steep incline causing a traffic jam. For about fifteen or twenty minutes, a gaggle of embarrassed Rodmans scooped up the mess, saturated with the unmistakable stench of a broken bottle of bourbon, and tried to stuff it all into an already overstuffed VW. Our distinguished guest was a bourbon drinker whom we were trying to impress.

꧁ ꧁ ꧁

Bill travelled continually, meeting with agricultural groups and making speeches. Many of his talks were in town halls and sheep sheds in remote outback areas with intriguing names— Gundagai, Warrumbungle, Humpty Doo, Tangmalangaloo, and Cocklebiddy—where he would draw a crowd of about thirty or so rugged and proud men who owned their own soil. Later, he and his audience would all repair to the local Returned Serviceman's Club for a schooner of ice-cold beer and the Australian rite of "matehood." Australia in the 1960s was still a man's world. With Bill's winning personality, and his self-appointed crusade to become acquainted with every inch of the country in which he worked, he made many friends far and wide for America. He could put on a homespun manner in distant country settings in order to establish rapport with the local people, or be a polished gentleman at elegant embassy functions. Whatever was called for, he was always the ultimate diplomat.

·——— Chapter Thirteen ———·

THE OUTBACK AND BEYOND

I HAVE NEVER KNOWN just where the *Beyond* started, but every Australian knows that "back of Beyond" means the outback. I went along on one such excursion. We had been told by city dwellers that venturing along the "Wallaby Track" was sheer madness, just miles and miles of parched emptiness, red dust, and blowflies. There were lurid tales of abandoned cars whose occupants were never found. But, in spite of these admonitions, we drove north from Melbourne across Victoria into New South Wales on the route established by Burke and Wills' explorations of 1860. Although the miles stretched along forever, the jeep did not break down, and we finally reached Broken Hill, the site of the richest mine deposits of silver, lead and zinc in the world. This desolate outback city was also the center of two of Australia's greatest institutions—the Flying Doctor Service, which carries medical attention and supplies across the vast distances by aircraft, and the School of the Air, which conducts classes by two–way radio for children on remote properties.

Next we drove along the "Dingo Fence." Some years ago, the Australian government built an impenetrable, heavy gauge wire fence that stretched from South Australia into Queensland. It was sunk about five feet into the ground and rose ten feet above. The purpose was to keep marauding dingoes, the wild dog descendents of the wolf, from devastating large flocks of sheep that grazed vast areas of the outback. As we drove the dirt track along the fence, we came across a typical touch of Australian humor. Firmly attached to a wide sturdy gate was a sign which read, "Close the gate. It keeps out the bloody blow flies."

Windmills along the track pumped water from artesian wells into large metal reservoirs, which in turn fed into troughs. In these vast areas of sparse rainfall, the distance between windmills was based on the maximum radius sheep and cattle could graze, yet always be in the proximity of water. An interesting note was that camels were used by the early settlers and explorers to traverse the four Australian deserts and other wilderness regions. They were better able than horses to withstand the intense heat and lack of water. In the 1960s, a few still remained, running wild.

Outback hospitality was legion. No doors were locked and the traveler, known or unknown, was always welcome for a meal and lodging. Cattle and sheep stations could be as much as 4,000 or more square miles in size, and the owners often used small planes to oversee their properties. If a station house was not in sight at dusk, the traveler could seek out one of the scattered wooden structures called "out-camps." These simple buildings with wide verandas, tin roofs, sheep pens, and small corrals were used by the "jackaroos" (station hands) when working on fences or rounding up livestock.

A highlight of our trip was a two–night visit at Comanche Station owned by Dinie and Eustace King, an engaging couple with four lively children. I could not get over the remoteness of their existence—not another soul within fifty miles or more. One might think that loneliness would drive them crazy, but Bill and I observed a happy family, hard working to be sure, and not unlike the pioneers of the western plains in America. The children made up their own rowdy games. Bill and I worried about the baby, Sasha, age two, whom the older siblings treated like a plaything. They carried her about in rag doll fashion, and pushed her at great speed in her stroller, sometimes right off the veranda. Her only reaction to this rough treatment was a wide grin and bubbles of laughter.

A strict schedule was maintained, however, in the morning hours. The School of the Air started up at 8 A.M. and each child except the baby took his or her turn for half an hour on the short wave radio with a teacher located hundreds of miles distant. At first the teacher carried on a friendly chat with her student, then asked questions about homework. After each answer the child gave the wireless command, "Over." When his or her session was finished, the child went to a table, where a young governess helped with lessons until noon. To me it seemed very sad that these kids would be sent to boarding school when they were eight or nine. Little Bruce, the oldest child, was to go off the following year and he could hardly wait.

While Bill and Eustie went off in the private plane to see different parts of the huge property, I watched with awe as Dinie went about her daily chores. She not only did the housekeeping and watched over four young children, but tended the garden, fed the chickens and pony, and prepared meals for her family, guests, and four or five jackaroos who lived in the jackaroo barracks. Drought was a continual worry and water was a problem. None was wasted. Dinie pointed out four thriving young trees in her fenced–in yard. Each was named after one of her children, Bruce, Angus, Anna, and Sasha. This was because the water in which she washed that child's diapers had been used to fertilize a seedling.

The day ended sitting on the veranda watching the sunset emblazoned across the sky. Darkness came swift and sudden, followed by a night of brilliant starlight.

ふ   ふ   ふ

In August of 1964, Bill was called back to Washington for four months. Cattlemen in the United States had wrongly accredited a drastic decline in cattle prices to meat imports, and the administrator of the Foreign Agricultural Service felt that Bill could help solve the problem. This appointment may have been a feather in his cap, but it was a difficult one for our family. He hated being alone in Washington, and we hated being without him for such a long period.

I made the decision to cross Australia alone by train while he was gone and again asked our friend, Janet, to stay with the girls. It took four nights, three different trains and three time zones to chase the sun to the west across the continent. At 9 P.M. on a Saturday night, I boarded in Sydney and cozily settled down in the soporific luxury of my little roomette. The following morning I was in Melbourne, where I had a day to wander before reboarding. Compared to Sydney, Melbourne was a calmer, more sedate and carefully groomed city, known for its cultural initiative in art and theater. Unlike Sydney, it was not founded as a penal colony. Instead of convicts and their keepers, the early settlers were free men with visions of building a new and prosperous existence of conservative lifestyles and refined tastes.

The second lap of my journey was another night trip—to Adelaide, South Australia, about one-third of the way. There I was met by the U.S. consul who had received a cable from Bill in Washington to present "his bride" with a large bouquet of flowers. When I boarded the next train an hour or so later, I was highly conspicuous with my prodigious bouquet. Later that afternoon, we chugged through mountainous country to Port Pirie where three different railroads, each a different gauge, came together. This was a hangover from the days before federation when each state was a separate Crown Colony. After an interminable wait for another train on a dusty platform, we set out on a thirty-eight hour span of emptiness across the Nullabor Plain (Latin for "no tree"), the longest straight stretch of track in the world. Nothing existed on this vast plain—said to be the dried-up bed of an inland sea—except reddish-brown scrub, blue sky, telegraph poles, and insufferable heat. Every hundred miles or so, a pathetic group of *fettler's* cottages could be seen along the tracks. In these lived the people who tended and mended the rails. A few straggly children waved as we passed. Their only lifeline to the rest of the world was this train which slowed down to throw them supplies and water. I was told that the fettlers were rotated back to civilization every few months to keep them from going bonkers.

The nicest train so far, several of the cars were ornate period pieces which had been built in 1922 for H.R.H. Edward, Prince of Wales, when he came to Australia on an official visit. The lounge car was "posh," as the Aussies would say, with shiny wood paneling, easy chairs upholstered in red velvet, a brass-railed bar, and a gilt piano. At the tail of the train was a spacious observation platform. The dining car was equally elegant and the food bordered on gourmet. Whereas on other legs of the trip, especially at night in my roomette, I had felt very far from home and alone, the atmosphere on this lap of the trip was gala and friendly. Other passengers asked me to dine, and afterwards we congregated in the lounge car where we spent a rousing evening of camaraderie and song.

The last leg of the trip to Perth was from Kalgoorlie, a town where gold was discovered in the 1890s. In the 1960s, one still felt the hard-living frontier atmosphere where a continuing trade in prostitution, beer, and gold reflected the town's earlier intrigue. An interesting side note was that President Herbert Hoover had lived and worked in Kalgoorlie as a young mining engineer at the turn of the century.

I was intrigued by a story of how water came to Kalgoorlie.

A young Australian engineer had built a dam which, when opened, would pour water into a pipe line that stretched all the way from Perth, a distance of about 350 miles. Excitement mounted as the grueling years of construction came to an end, and the anticipated day arrived. The young engineer pulled the device that opened the flood gates, then waited for the first water to reach Kalgoorlie. Day followed day. When no water appeared, hopes and dreams of success faded. Tragically, the young man, thinking he had failed—a disgrace to his profession and country—killed himself, and the very next day water gushed magnificently into Kalgoorlie's empty reservoir.

When news of the discovery of gold to the east of Perth reached the outside world, that city's tiny population rocketed into the thousands. But once the rush for gold had subsided, the new inhabitants came to appreciate the area for its climate, vegetation, and natural beauty. For several days I stayed with the American consul and his wife at their home on the Swan River, and had a chance to tour this impressively gracious "City of Light." Perth earned this moniker after discovering the city was directly below the flight path of John Glenn's world orbit in February 1962. Every light in the city was switched on to show support for the astronaut.

In 1935 another national precedent was set when Russian ballerina Anna Pavlova visited Perth. A hotel chef expressed his love for the ballerina by creating a billowing desert based on egg whites, sugar, and fruit, including passion fruit as garnish. The chef named his creation *pavlova*—always the crowning glory of a sumptuous meal in Australia.

Shortly before my arrival in Perth, the wreck of a sunken bullion ship named the *Gilt Dragon* had been discovered by amateur divers. Before the Australian government had a chance to interfere, about half of the 6,500 coins found in the old hulk had been sold. Many had been bastardized by being turned into brooches and pendants by local jewelers, and sold to the public.

Thrilled with such a unique memento of my trip, I bought a brooch with two mounted "pieces of eight" coins. Some days later, newspapers were full of the story of the *Gilt Dragon*. A Museum Act Wrecks Amendment bill was quickly introduced in the Legislative Assembly making it an offense to interfere with an underwater wreck, and, in the future, anyone possessing relics would have to declare them to the government. Some time later the bill was passed. Each time I look at my treasure, I suffer very small pangs of guilt.

My journey home was by sea on the S.S. *Canberra,* a new P & O Orient Line ship. I still feel giddy when I think of boarding that huge ocean liner alone for the five–day trip to Sydney. Under glorious sunny skies and a calm sea the ship crossed the Great Australian Bight, the Bass Strait, and the Tasman Sea. Other passengers asked me to dine and dance on several occasions, but I felt far removed from a *femme fatale* as portrayed in a Hollywood movie. In fact, I missed Bill and the children terribly and my one thought was to get home. A cruise is not much fun without your firstmate.

༄   ༄   ༄

Bill, Jr. turned twenty-one on October 16, 1964. A very big to-do is made in Australia over this coming-of-age birthday. As his friends were in Sydney rather than Canberra, his girlfriend's parents kindly held a festive celebration in their home to which Joni, Channing, and I were invited. Bill, Sr. was still in Washington.

One reason we loved to go to Sydney was to lodge at our favorite hotel, the old Belvedere at Kings Cross. Iron gates and an impressive driveway led to the large veranda of a stately mansion where guests were met by two great danes. The interior retained a gracious Edwardian charm, and the hosts, after extending a warm welcome, offered tea and biscuits. Our favorite room looked onto the garden. No doors were locked. In the morning, an unheralded Mary Poppins entered our bedroom at 7 A.M. with a cheery "good-die," and placed tea and a newspaper on the tea table. She then opened the blinds with a flourish to welcome the dawning of a new day. For those who wanted to sleep late—too bad! This was a Belvedere observance, not to be questioned.

The evening after Bill, Jr.'s birthday party, I took my three offspring to a stunning premiere performance of *Camelot.* Joni wore a party dress and the rest of us were in evening clothes. Whoever thought the Aussies were an informal lot was mistaken. They could swing from one end of the spectrum to the other with great agility—the bare–chested bloke mowing his lawn in the morning was just as comfortable as an elegant gentleman in evening dress at night.

Peter, Paul and Mary, the Beatles, and the Twist were all at their peak of popularity in the mid–sixties. Everywhere were the impassioned cries of "We love you, yeah, yeah, yeah," moderated by the more gentle strains of "The Lemon Tree." I now realize how conservative these entertainers were compared to today's minstrels with long hair, beards, anguished expressions, and sledgehammer music.

ॐ   ॐ   ॐ

After his third year at the university, Bill, Jr. was invited to go on an anthropological dig in the wilds of Tasmania during his summer vacation. From a career standpoint, this offer would decide the course his life would take. The expedition was sponsored by Cambridge University, in conjunction with the Australian Institute of Aboriginal Studies, and headed by Dr. Rhys Jones, a Welshman. A group of anthropology, zoology and archeology students, both male and female, were Jones' henchmen. In early December, a red-bearded Rhys, driving a

Land Rover stacked to the roof with equipment, pulled into our driveway to collect our son.

From Bill, Jr.'s letters, we learned that the work of setting up camp sites was strenuous and the digging tedious in the God-forsaken scrub country on the northwestern tip of the island of Tasmania. After a seven by seven foot trench was dug with a trowel, all dirt had to be sifted while the workers looked for aboriginal implements, artifacts, and bones dating back about 8,000 years—before pyramids, Babylon, or even civilization itself. Rhys himself did the final sorting and classifying before the pieces, some microscopic, were carefully put into plastic bags and mailed to Sydney for further examination.

The weather was erratic but generally cold, damp, and muddy. Swimming in the icy sea was the only way to bathe, and constant nose colds plagued the workers. Christmas must have been dreary, but Bill described a welcome day off from digging, and a party of eggnog, lobster, and caroling on the beach. According to his letters, spirits were so high and enthusiasm so great that one might assume they were discovering gold instead of old bones. Someone had brought a guitar and in the evening, the group would talk, sing, and compose songs around a fire. Bill wrote, "I'm a scrungy, sorry sight but fit and happy. If you could see me, you'd disinherit me."

I worried about our son's safety. From time to time, sudden hailstorms and gale force winds whipped through the camp, and in the high scrub were poisonous tiger snakes. Another worry were cave-ins in the deep pits where they worked, and on two occasions there were bush fires. One of these, lasting three days and nights threatened to overtake their campsite. The team managed to evacuate their archeological equipment and materials to the beach and transfer the most valuable finds to a town a safe distance away. Yet in their frantic attempts to keep the flames at bay, hair and eyebrows were singed, and tents, air mattresses, beds and clothes damaged or ruined.

Bill, Jr. returned home in early March for the start of his final year at the university. Even with a neatly trimmed beard that disappeared after a few days, he looked wonderful. The expedition had been a scientific success.

ॐ   ॐ   ॐ

On a Saturday afternoon some weeks later, two mini-vans pulled up to the curb in front of our house, and a handsome group of twenty young men spilled out onto our lawn. They were the University of Sydney's track team, scheduled for a meet with Duntroon Military College. The captain explained that our son, Bill, had asked him to pick up a pair of shoes for him, and had suggested they might enjoy having tea with his folks after the meet. I don't think young Bill realized how many were in the group. Nevertheless, in my husband's inimitable style, he invited them all back for supper. By this time, Channing, now seventeen, had emerged from the house full of golden smiles and nodding approval.

After the team left for their meet, tooting horns, she bubbled off to invite several friends to this serendipitous occasion, and Bill, Sr. and I dashed off to get supplies. Fortunately, there were a few small Greek-owned grocery stores that stayed open on Saturday afternoon in Canberra, and we went from one to the next buying them out of baked beans, hot dogs, potato chips, salad fixings, and soft drinks.

As promised, the team returned aglow with victory and the ensuing party, an unqualified success, filled the house with youth, laughter and song. When time to depart, the young athletes thanked us profusely, hugged the ecstatic girls, and presented Bill with a university tie.

Two other young Australians became special friends, Lin Tinkler and Peter Fox. Lin worked for the local TV station and Peter was a newscaster. On Sunday evenings, sometimes bringing friends, they would come to our house to enjoy a home-cooked meal, a family poker session, and general merriment. Peter had a baritone voice of professional quality. He would hold a make-believe microphone and entertain us with "What Kind of Fool Am I" and other current hits. Then everyone would get up and do their vaudeville routine or dance in chorus-line fashion, except for Mom, who, as sole spectator, applauded loudly.

I believe it was these evenings that helped Joni over her shyness. She was very serious about her ballet lessons and started to blossom as a dancer. Together with brother Bill playing the guitar, they formed a duo which they called Mister and Sister. The words and music of most of the songs were Bill, Jr.'s original compositions, with tuneful melodies and charming words. Two that bring back happy memories were "Peaches and Apples," a little folk ballad about a vendor who meets a pretty girl, and "The Paradise Tree," a magical quest to an enchanted land. A crowning moment came when they were asked to perform on a television program called *Focus on Folk.* Joni, then eleven years, was completely at ease, her voice as clear as a bell. Bill, twenty-two, the adoring big brother, was handsome and poised. The film was run several times after that, and one of my great regrets is that we never acquired a copy.

♪   ♪   ♪

In September 1965, Bill, Joni, and I drove north to Queensland, stopping at various small agricultural centers on route. These were much like Hollywood images of our early western towns with a wide central street for droving cattle and sheep. At Gladstone we took a launch to Heron Island on the Great Barrier Reef, a dreamlike undersea forest of marine life. We stayed in a small bungalow and ate a steady diet of fish in a common dining hall. When the tide was right we ventured out onto the reef collecting shells, and snorkeling in crystal clear

Bill, Helen and Joni at a bird sanctuary in Queensland.

pools where a colorful display of tropical fish was dazzling to the eye. Tennis shoes were mandatory because of poisonous shells and sharp coral. A wooden staff was provided to help with balance.

On our way south, we drove along Australia's Sunshine Coast. The familiar gray-green color identified with Australia turned to lush green along the rocky highway. A favorite stop was the Currumbin Bird Sanctuary where overwhelming flocks of bright green lorikeets (a type of parrot) came swarming in at feeding time. They had no fear of humans and unabashedly landed on heads, arms, and shoulders to peck at the little plates of seed given out for the price of a ticket.

ॐ   ॐ   ॐ

After spending two Christmases at the beach, we decided to stay home in 1965 as the older children had various plans and engagements. As usual, Ruth and Paul Siple were with us for the festivities. While we were trimming the tree on Christmas Eve, the phone rang. It was a young man named Doug from Connecticut who had taken a year off from his studies at Princeton University to go around the world on a motorcycle. A friend had given him our name. When he arrived at our door, he was a sorry sight—cold, wet, and miserable. But a shower and some Christmas cheer soon transformed him back to his normal, kinetic self.

On Christmas morning the Siples were back at our house bright and early for the opening of stockings and presents. Ruth and I rushed about "stealing" from other's piles to find gifts for our unexpected guest.

Doug stayed with us for two weeks. He and Channing welcomed the New Year at Templemore, a purebred cattle station some three hours distant from Canberra. This large property was owned by friends, Bruce and Pip Walker. During our years in Australia we spent many happy weekends at Templemore, where we observed the jackaroos rounding up cattle for branding, and the shearers deftly shearing away the wool from large numbers of sheep. The Walker's youngest son, Sandy, taught Joni how to herd cattle and set traps for rabbits. She was aghast, however, when he skinned a rabbit and presented her with the hide. A lover of animals, she could not accept this token of his esteem. Nevertheless, the Walker home was a pinnacle of gracious country living and Australian hospitality.

🙠   🙠   🙠

Each year thousands of young Australians left home on a Grand Tour of Europe seeking excitement and a mind-broadening experience. Generally they were gone for a year or more and financed themselves with odd jobs along the way. As Bill, Jr. knew several of these travelers, thoughts of returning to the states via Asia and Europe began to germinate in his mind. Gradually these thoughts grew to include Channing. Each had finished important stages of their education in December 1965, he at the University of Sydney and she at high school. As Australia is roughly halfway around the world from Washington, D. C., there was little difference in cost between heading east or west to return home, and the Foreign Agricultural Service paid the basic fare. So, with our blessing and a little guidance, Bill, Jr. set about making plans for a six–month trip with his sister. There was lots to do—working out an itinerary, shots, visas, costs, currencies, flight schedules, travel books, and youth-hostel listings to study. And how to squeeze their travel gear into two backpacks. Among his collection of travel books, he had a copy of *Europe on $5.00 a Day*. He read it thoroughly, then remarked, "I bet we can do it on less."

In order to earn money for the trip, Channing took a job for the month of January on a sheep station near Canberra as a nanny to four children. She claimed she was worn to a frazzle, not because of the children, but because the lady of the house expected her to cook, clean, and iron as well. As Channing had never been domestically inclined, the account of her travail was of considerable amusement to her parents. She came home once during that time to get her cholera and typhoid shots for the trip. This proved a good thing as she was battered and bruised from a fall from a horse, and needed a little TLC.

As a precaution, my husband had the brilliant idea of buying Channing a wedding ring. He reasoned that if it appeared that she and her brother were married, she would be safer from the hue and cry of lascivious males. Together Channing and her father went to a local jewelry store where Bill asked to see something inexpensive in wedding bands. With a knowing look at this middle-aged gentleman and his teenage companion, the dignified salesman removed a tray from underneath the counter and placed it on top. Bill picked out a ring and tried to stammer an explanation, but obviously didn't erase the clerk's suspicions that he was dealing with a dirty old man. Channing could hardly contain her giggles.

On the Saturday night before our children departed on their "Grand Tour," we gave them a farewell, out-of-doors barbecue with dancing inside. It was a heart-wrenching time for me; my two oldest chicks were not only leaving the nest but going off into the wild blue yonder for six or more months. Realizing that I had no choice, I tried not to show my anxiety. Many friends gathered at the airport to say farewell, and little Joni was completely dissolved. Except for short periods, she had never been separated from Channing, and she worshipped her big brother. Thank goodness we had her! To think that we debated whether to have a third!

Both Channing and Bill were exhausted by the time they departed Sydney for Bangkok. Emotionally, they must have felt stirred with a spoon. They had loved their four years in Australia, and Bill had left a sweetheart behind.

ℑ   ℑ   ℑ

The first letters we received were from Istanbul, where our adventurers managed to find a "clean cut young Turk who offered us his little flat for free." From the tone of his letter, I ventured a guess that Bill was recovering rapidly from his departure blues over leaving Marilyn. From Turkey, they proceeded on to Greece, Italy, Switzerland, Germany, Spain, Portugal, Morocco, France, Holland, England, Scotland, and Ireland. Pan American Airlines offered a deal whereby air travelers could visit up to a dozen capital cities on the same ticket, providing the stops were within a certain radius. Their schedule was flexible, the only restricting feature being money. Both had small savings accounts which they had turned into traveller's checks, and we gave them $500 each, plus the small extra amount their fare had cost over the government allowance. Bill, Jr. was right—daily expenses often came to less than $5 a day. Lodging was generally in youth hostels that cost 50 to 75 cents a night. Hostel meals, which they prepared themselves, were equally inexpensive—pasta in Italy, olives and sardines in Spain, cheese and snails in France, knockwurst and beer in Germany, cous-cous in Morocco, bangers and mash in the United Kingdom, and cheap wine when the drinking water was questionable.

At night, in hostels, young travelers exchanged experiences, shared books, wrote letters, guided each other as to where to go, places to eat and stay, what not to miss, and equally, what to miss. Often, someone had a guitar and a group would join together in song until the appointed time for lights out. Most hostels had very strict rules about when to get up and when to go to bed.

Luggage was limited to a backpack each. Except for long hops, most travel was by road—hitchhiking! Had I known this before our kids left, I would have had a fit, so they kept me blissfully ignorant for a long time. When I finally found out, I was told that hitchhiking in Europe in the 1960s was an accepted practice and relatively safe. Yet, in spite of their reassuring letters, I continued to have niggling worries until I saw them safely home.

Generally, Channing and Bill travelled with other students whom they met at hostels. Calling themselves "the Moles," two or three would hitchhike together, and six or seven would meet at a prearranged destination. Channing was the only girl until Spain, where they added two French Canadian girls to their entourage. Bill said that the young men among their traveling companions, often Australians, treated his sister like a princess and she "fell in love" with each in turn. Occasionally, with her wedding ring displayed on the fourth finger of her left hand, Channing and Bill would sometimes rent a room, then surreptitiously admit the other "moles" through a window where they would shower and sleep on the floor. Bedbugs were a problem, often making the floor preferable.

Letters from our adventurers were frequent—instead of keeping diaries, they wrote home. When I showed several letters to a friend who happened to be an editor of *The Canberra Times,* he asked permission to publish them in serial form on a weekly basis. Payment would be $40 an issue. I agreed, but did not tell the kids as I was afraid their spontaneous and spirited missiles would become self–conscious and stilted. Also published were Channing's amusing and descriptive illustrations of their journey. Many readers wrote complimentary letters to *The Times*. I quote an example: "One of the most appealing aspects of these letters home is the natural and unaffected manner in which they are written, due, I believe, to the fact that the two young people concerned are unaware of the fact that they are appearing in *The Canberra Times*." Upon their return home in August 1966, they were somewhat appalled that their letters had been published without their consent, but glad to receive well-earned checks.

ॐ   ॐ   ॐ

Back in Canberra as summer drifted into fall, we fell into a routine as a family of three, and waited anxiously for news from our nomads. Lyndon Johnson had become president of the United States upon the death of John Kennedy, and the world mourned the death of Winston Churchill. Australia had a new American ambassador, Edward Clark, and Joni entered the sixth grade. After a welcome summer break, the diplomatic social whirl started up again.

ॐ   ॐ   ॐ

Our new ambassador was an influential lawyer from Austin, Texas, where he had known Lyndon Johnson. When Clark and his partner decided to establish congressional representation in Washington, they successfully promoted and backed Johnson, then a school teacher, as a Democratic party candidate for Congress. By midyear 1965 Australia had been without an American ambassador for a year, and Prime Minister Menzies, on an official visit to Washington, asked Johnson to fill the vacancy. Menzies added, "Send us a friend. Send us a Texan." Johnson had not forgotten past kindnesses and Edward Clark was duly appointed.

Edward Clark was a wealthy and flamboyant Texan with a tremendous liking for people from all walks of life. He felt strongly that the beautiful embassy residence was not his private domain, but should be open for all to enjoy. He had been known to flag down a bus load of tourists or boy scouts in front of the chancery, and invite them to the residence for tea. Open House was the norm, and many charitable institutions, plus thousands of visitors, were recipients of this bountiful hospitality. No door was locked. Sadly, in later years, security measures would have intervened.

Anne Clark had become accustomed to her husband's cornucopian generosity, and the household staff soon learned to be prepared for an abundance of unexpected guests. She was a gracious hostess with an eye for detail and a well-tuned sense of humor. I'm sure she was often worn to a nub by a formidable amount of entertaining, official functions, and the running of a large household, but she somehow found the stamina to endure, and keep pace with her energetic husband.

I sometimes hosted affairs at the residence when Anne Clark could not be present, and in time we became good friends. One day I told her about my after-dinner coffee cup collection and asked if there was any possible way of securing a cup and saucer with the gold seal from the U.S. Embassy. She explained that the china at the residence was carefully inventoried on a monthly basis by someone from the embassy's administrative section. But, she added, with a mischievous gleam in her eye, if I would call the following morning at the residence, there would be a package on the hall table. And there it was, wrapped in Happy Birthday paper with a big yellow bow! Later, when we were alone, Anne told me she had done a little night prowling on my behalf.

Another addition to my demitasse collection was from Parliament House. Bill and I were dining there with Jeff Bate, a member of the Liberal Party, when I happened again to mention my collection. Jeff told me that he would love to give me a cup and saucer but dared not because all parliamentary china was zealously guarded and counted by the dining steward. Chipped china was smashed. After the dinner, Jeff courteously escorted Bill and me to our car. As he bade us good night, he ceremoniously withdrew his unwashed cup and saucer from his inside pocket, and presented them with a wink.

A memorable visit was that of Vice President Hubert H. Humphrey. Before his departure from Canberra, a ceremonial farewell was held at the ambassador's residence for the children of embassy personnel, a thoughtful gesture on the part of Ambassador and Mrs. Clark. The VP was to stand on the white columned portico facing the lawn where the children were gathered. One of the marine guards had loaned his pet kangaroo for Aussie flavor. Unfortunately, this plan was thwarted because of an unseasonable cold drizzle, and the occasion had to be moved inside. Mrs. Clark called me to come early to help with the arrangements. With Joni in tow, I parked in the garage area and we came in through the kitchen. When we reached the living room, we beheld a most amazing sight. There before us was the Veep of the United States of America hopping about after a gray kangaroo. No one else was in evidence. Greatly amused, Joni and I watched for a minute or two until Humphrey, realizing others were in the room, stopped hopping and came to greet us. He gave Joni a hug and asked about her school. Then he took a felt tipped pen and a U.S. Senate pass out of his pocket, wrote her name on it, signed it, and said, "When you come to Washington, come to see me at the Capitol." This was the first of several encounters the Rodman family would have with this gregarious and likable politician.

Later, about thirty-five embassy children with muddy feet gathered in the large marble foyer while HHH stood on the stairs where he made a pleasant little kid-directed speech and handed out his monogrammed pens. When he met Bill at a reception that evening, he remarked, "Oh yes, I enjoyed talking to your wife and Joni this morning. I understand you live in Virginia." His astonishing memory was surely a political asset.

❧ ❧ ❧

By March, we knew that our delightful years in Australia were coming to an end. Bill had been appointed to attend the Senior Seminar in Foreign Policy in Washington, D.C., a coveted assignment. We put 87 Mugga Way on the market and sold it almost immediately, making the profit we had hoped for. Luckily, we could stay in the house until May 5. (Our departure date for the United States by ship was May 14.)

Knowing that there would be a long period of unsettlement before finding a home somewhere near Washington, we decided not to take Casey. The parting was very difficult, but he went off quite happily with our friends, the Taylors. He had already visited their small farm several times where he had played with his friend, Blaze, a golden retriever. Joni was parceled out to stay with schoolmates, and Bill and I spent the last nine days at the Commonwealth Club, a brilliant move that relieved some of the frenzy of departure. Between packing and farewell parties, the last month at a post was always hectic. Even Joni became the center of attention with her own round of parties.

A notable occasion was a dinner dance given in our honor by Ambassador and Mrs. Clark at the embassy residence. Sixty of our friends came from near and far. I arranged the seating at eight round tables adorned with flowers, crystal, and the handsome gold–rimmed china with the U.S. seal. The ladies had elegant hairdos and wore exquisite evening dresses. Mine was a new green satin creation adorned with swirls of iridescent sequins. It just happened that Bob Crosby, brother of Bing, was in Sydney doing a TV program, and he and his lovely redheaded wife came to Canberra for the occasion. Other distinguished guests, invited by the Clarks, were the new prime minister, Harold Holt, and his wife, Zara. I felt like a bride all evening, but one of my most vivid memories was my two dances with the charming PM. I had never danced with a prime minister before and was swept off of my feet. When we parted, he gave me a hug and said, "This is the start of a beautiful friendship. Will you and your husband come for cocktails at the Lodge tomorrow at 6:30?" Of course we did! Three years later, Harold Holt drowned in a scuba diving accident. His body was never found.

Just before the end of the party, our friends linked arms and sang "Auld Lang Syne" followed by "For They Are Jolly Good Fellows" while Bill and I danced alone in the middle of the large circle. Then two of my favorite parliamentarians, Doug and Peter, picked me up and carried me out of the room. And guess what? I felt as light as a feather—all 130 pounds of me!

Our last view of Canberra was of our friends waving good-bye from the balcony of the airport. Many had brought gifts. One gift in particular was very unusual—a fur-trimmed, academic hood from the University of Sydney. Don Alexander, manager of David Jones, Canberra's finest department store, wrote on the accompanying note, "You will not be able to find this in the States and young Bill will need it when he receives his master's degree and doctorate."

Peter Fox met us in Sydney and drove us to the *Mariposa,* sister ship of the Matson Line vessel on which we had crossed the Pacific after home-leave in 1963. Our stateroom was overflowing with flowers and gifts and telegrams. Aussie friends, the Pauls and the Tinklers, joined us for dinner aboard the ship, and the following day at sailing time, they and several younger friends gathered for a lively champagne party in our stateroom and a rousing send-off from the pier. As the ship left the dock to the strains of "Waltzing Matilda" punctuated by several blasts of the foghorn, Joni, Bill and I leaned over the railing waving and throwing streamers at our friends, and the younger members of our farewell party ran all the way down the length of the pier so that our last glimpse was of them, still waving frantically. I remained on deck until I could no longer see Australia. Then a tremendous melancholy overcame me, and I let the tears flow.

Chapter Fourteen

ALEXANDRIA, VIRGINIA
June 1966 to September 1967

THE TWENTY-ONE DAY VOYAGE ACROSS THE
PACIFIC ON THE S. S. *MARIPOSA* was a relaxing antidote to
the whirlwind activity of our last weeks in Canberra when everyone
was killing us with kindness.

Our first port-of-call was Fiji. As we docked at Suva, the capital,
the Royal Fijian Band marched along the quay playing rousing
music. The musicians were dressed in dark blue tunics, white lava-
lavas fringed at the hem, and magnificent red turbans. Their leader,
a man of majestic height and stature, wore a sash of fringed scarlet
and carried a silver mace. A rickety sight-seeing bus was waiting to
take us into the interior for a day's trip on a river launch. The boat
moved slowly in the sultry heat as it passed thatched villages nestled
in clearings in the lush jungle vegetation, fields of sugar cane, and
groups of little brown children playing and splashing in the water.

Two episodes aboard ship are indelibly etched on my memory.
The first was when the *Mariposa* paused in mid-Pacific to drop
overboard a rectangular box called the "Tin Can Mail," the tiny
isolated island of Rarotonga's only link with the outside world.
Strong armed natives paddled out to retrieve it in a dugout canoe.
The second occurred one night when the loud speaker announced

that the ship was steaming off course to enact a rescue at sea. Joni, Bill, and I dressed quickly and went up on deck to watch a small boat from a freighter pull alongside the *Mariposa* to transfer a crewman with acute appendicitis. As the sea was rough, it was a precarious maneuver to load him into a sling-type contraption and haul him to safety aboard our ship where he could receive medical attention.

About halfway to San Francisco, as we approached Pago Pago in the island group of American Samoa, boys manning a fleet of small craft swarmed our ship, a ritual every cruise ship encounters. Making diving motions with their hands, they called to us on deck in broken English to throw coins into the crystal clear water. We laughed as we watched their lithe bodies dive into the water squirming like fishes to retrieve a coin, then surface to hold it up triumphantly shouting, "More, more!" Ashore we took a mile long ride to the top of a mountain in a suspension cable car which swayed back and forth like a pendulum gone berserk. Since I hate heights, this was a daunting experience. I sat scrunched in a corner and prayed for deliverance.

To the strains of "I Left My Heart—in San Fran-cis-co," we arrived in that beautiful city on the last day of May 1966. A new red Rambler station wagon, which Bill had ordered in advance, was awaiting us dockside, and the three Rodmans set out on a three-week motor trip to see America from coast to coast. I look back on that trip as a lovely memory with our youngest daughter. We traveled south to the Redwood Forest and Yosemite Valley, then east to Las Vegas, the Hoover Dam, the Grand Canyon, Rocky Mountain National Park, Arches National Park, and on and on until we reached Niagara Falls. Joni at last had a chance to see her own country.

જ્જ   જ્જ   જ્જ

Before we left Australia, we had arranged for Joni, now eleven years old, to attend Mont Shenandoah Camp in Milboro

Springs, Virginia, for six weeks during the summer. We knew that she would be happier at camp than in the midst of the hustle-bustle of getting settled in a new home. In mid-August, Bill would attend the Senior Seminar in Foreign Policy, a ten-month assignment, at the Foreign Service Institute in Roslyn, Virginia, so it made sense to settle in Northern Virginia. We chose Alexandria.

After driving Joni to camp, we booked into the George Mason Hotel in Alexandria, where we settled down to serious house-hunting and quickly purchased a large, attractive home on a shaded street. Bill's assignment to the Senior Seminar ended the following June, and F.A.S. had assured us that Bill would then be given a Washington assignment. Had we known that he would be posted to Mexico in a little over a year's time, we would have been better off renting.

During the latter years of the 1960s, the Vietnam War raged on. Outwardly, life continued in America with little change, but inwardly there was a constant sense of heartbreak. The tragedy and suffering was brought cruelly home when word reached us of the death of Erskine Wilde, nineteen-year-old son of my dear friend, Mary Cam.

Joni returned from summer camp at the end of July and soon after, our two itinerants returned from their great adventure. I cannot begin to express the relief and joy Bill and I felt when Bill, Jr. and Channing stepped off the plane on a Friday evening in mid-August at Dulles International Airport. They had been traveling for six months and had spanned the girth of the globe. In September, our eldest would begin a master's degree course in anthropology at the University of Chicago, and Channing would start her undergraduate studies at Briarcliff College in Tarrytown, New York.

꠸   ꠸   ꠸

The Senior Seminar in Foreign Policy was the most advanced program in international relations and foreign policy offered by the United States government. Each session was limited to a group of twenty-five senior officials at the height of their careers. Half of these were from the State Department; the other half were officers in the Army, Navy, Air Force, Marine Corps, and other U.S. departments and agencies in Washington. The program was designed to give the members an opportunity to recharge their batteries in an atmosphere of learning, research and creative thinking. Relieved of their normal duties, they would have the opportunity to hold discussions with their peers, talk to people in all walks of life, read extensively, travel, and study American foreign policy and the contemporary American scene. Membership was awarded on the basis of "excellence of past performance, demonstrated leadership, and potential for the assumption of greater responsibilities."

In Washington, the seminar's schedule included a series of lectures by prominent persons including such notables as President Lyndon B. Johnson, Vice President Hubert Humphrey, Cabinet secretaries, House and Senate committee chairmen, and members of the Joint Chiefs of Staff. Field trips were planned to many parts of the United States where the members could talk to presidents of universities, CEOs of large corporations, leaders of labor unions, municipal government, law enforcement and urban renewal. They visited a nuclear-powered submarine in Charleston Harbor and the scene of the Watts riots in Los Angeles; they walked the streets of Harlem in New York City and roller-coastered in Disneyland.

So while Bill was becoming Americanized, Joni and I were also getting accustomed to life in American suburbia. During our years abroad, a great deal had changed—supermarkets had become colossal and television had added color. Prices had doubled, traffic had tripled.

Joni's public school was very different from the all-girls' school she had attended in Canberra. Boys in class! No uniforms! One day when she returned from school, there was a small red ribbon pinned to her blouse, but she seemed a trifle upset. I learned the problem when she said they had had a field day at school and that she had run in the hundred-yard dash, but only came in second. I, of course, said, "Joni, that's great—good for you. Who won?" And she answered simply, "A boy."

There was no doubt that Joni was very athletic and tremendously well-coordinated. Soon after we arrived, she joined the Virginia Ballet Company and continued her drive toward a career in dance. At the Christmas production of the *Nutcracker Suite,* she lost out on the part of Clara, but demonstrated her ability in two smaller roles. She also took guitar lessons.

Joni, age 10, showed talent early in life.

Whenever Bill, Jr. was home, they continued to practice and expand on their Mister and Sister routine.

Although life was falling into place nicely, something was missing, a hollowness in the gut, undefinable, until one day in mid-September when Joni piped up with, "Gosh, I miss Casey!" Bill and I looked at each other with that understanding born of many years of marital clairvoyance. He went immediately to the telephone and called Casey's caretaker, Jack Taylor, in Australia. The conversation was brief. Jack would put the little dog on a plane for Washington as soon as arrangements could be made. He would cable time of arrival. We three breathed a sigh of relief. We knew that the missing link in our lives would soon be filled. Waiting for Casey's arrival was like waiting for the prodigal son. We bought a new doggie bed, squeaky playthings, and gourmet dog food.

The cable soon arrived and we went to the airport to welcome our beloved little animal. He had flown from Canberra to Sydney where he had been loaded onto a Quantas plane for Los Angeles. From there he had made the final leg of the trip to Dulles Airport on a cargo plane, a two-day trip in a wire cage about three feet square. As instructed, we went to the building where freight was off-loaded. As his cage was lowered onto a cart, we called "Casey, Casey" from quite a distance. He answered with a bark and proceeded to spin around in circles in the space allowed by his tiny cage. His recognition was instant. Obviously, he had been watered and fed on the long journey and seemed none the worse for wear. Joni's joy reminded me of Freddie Bartholomew in the film *Lassie Come Home.* Our family was again complete.

ᔕ   ᔕ   ᔕ

In the spring, each member of the Senior Seminar was given the opportunity to travel abroad individually for about six weeks to gather material for case studies to be later presented to the

Seminar. As they were encouraged to visit an unfamiliar area of the world, Bill chose Ethiopia and Kenya in Africa, where he did a comparative study on land use.

Bill, Jr., having completed the first year of his studies at the University of Chicago, was asked to teach cultural anthropology at an enrichment program during the summer of 1967 at Chatham Hall in Chatham, Virginia, my old school. In late June, I drove him to the school. When I helped him settle into his dormitory room, my thoughts went back thirty-one years to the time I had entered these halls as an awkward teenager. Little did I know then that, as a result of his summer job, our family would be enriched by the introduction of Margy.

One evening I called Bill, Jr. who said he had met a certain girl named Margy Critchlow, whom he planned to visit in Maryland the following weekend.

"Where in Maryland?" I asked.

"Just a minute." And I heard him say, "Where do you live in Maryland?"

"Oxford—on the Eastern Shore."

This was clearly a coincidence as Bill and I had planned a sailing weekend with an old friend in tiny Oxford on the very same weekend.

So, we met our future daughter-in-law for the first time at her home in Oxford. Margy was a fellow alumna of Chatham Hall. She had just finished her sophomore year at Goucher College in Baltimore and had been asked back to her old school as an intern for the purpose of stimulating conversation in advanced English classes. She was a tall slender brunette with classic features and a winning smile; especially beautiful were her dark eyes. There was little question that she and Bill had fallen in love.

Bill took a few weeks' leave after the Senior Seminar finished in mid-June. He still had not been advised of his future Washington assignment. One evening we invited an old friend, the economic counselor at the Australian Embassy, and his wife to dinner. His initial greeting was, "Congratulations, Bill, I hear you are being sent to Mexico as agricultural attache."

Bill's response was a startled, "What?"

"I can't believe you didn't know," said our dinner guest. "I heard about it at a reception at the Australian Embassy last night."

♪　　♪　　♪

The next morning, Bill called the administrator of F.A.S. and learned that it was indeed true that he had been assigned to Mexico, and, that after a refresher course in Spanish, he would be departing in September.

Mexico! We had just settled back in the States!

♪　　♪　　♪

Bill left for Mexico in early September and I was left in another tailspin—sell the house, sort out the junk, pack up and move. Mexico would be post number five, so I should have been a change-of-scenery expert by then, but it didn't work that way. Each move became more difficult. The flexibility of youth had been left somewhere in the past.

This time, however, we would not have to search for a home as the embassy rented and furnished a house in the Mexico City suburb of Polanco for the agricultural attache. Except for lamps, pictures, and a few small pieces, our furniture was put into storage.

In winding up business affairs, I was surprised by a bill from Sears. The first item was for 5,000 baby chicks. In 1967, computers, just coming on the national scene, were still a mystery to most. Sears at Landmark Shopping Mall was one of the first stores to install this inscrutable item. Obviously, once it made a mistake, nobody knew how to correct it, and the baby chicks remained steadfast. Even a personal visit to the business office did not eliminate the chicks from future bills, and the service charge mounted. Some months after we arrived in Mexico, the chicks suddenly disappeared from our account.

Bill returned home in time to make final preparations to drive to Mexico City. Along our planned route were Vicksburg and Natchez in Mississippi. In Vicksburg we visited the National Military Park in a small van driven by a large cheery woman who expounded on stories about the Civil War. Our fellow passengers were a mother, father and two teenage children on an extended journey down the Mississippi River in a small sailboat. The father was gathering material to write a book. His wife was sweet, but his teenage children were far from pleased with the ordeal, and moped in the backseat of the van complaining about the injustice of being cooped up in a small sailboat day after day.

The monuments to the soldiers who had fought on the battlefield were worthy of the beautiful river setting, perhaps the most impressive being the Illinois State Monument. Inside, sunlight streamed through an opening in its marbled dome, casting a dramatic stillness and illuminating the engraved names of those who had died. And suddenly our guide, in a magnificent contralto voice, burst into a medley of Civil War songs—a poignant moment in time.

We followed the trace to Natchez where we toured the stately antebellum homes, enchanted . . .

> *To look with reverent eyes upon*
> *The treasures of a people gone.*

On and on we went—west, then southwest, until we finally crossed the border and turned due south in the direction of Mexico City.

・——— Chapter Fifteen ——— ・

MEXICO
October 1967 to January 1972

W HEN WE ARRIVED AT OUR GOVERNMENT-
LEASED HOUSE IN THE SUBURB OF POLANCO, just a
few miles from Mexico City, six or seven lovely flower
arrangements, and a delicious dinner provided by an embassy
wives' committee, awaited us. We were overawed by the size of
our dwelling, which we quickly dubbed the Cow Palace. On the
good side, the furniture was comfortable and well-chosen, and
one never had to stand in line for a bathroom since there were
six. On the bad side, to reach the top floor, we had to ascend
forty-eight steps of a spiraling, marble staircase with an
elaborately scrolled wrought-iron bannister. On the extremely
bad side, there was no central heating and we nearly froze in the
cold weather.

By car, the Cow Palace was ten minutes from the American
Embassy in the heart of the city, and only one block from the
beautiful tree-lined Avenida de la Reforma with its stately statues
and splendid parks. Just a block away was little Lincoln Park,
with a big chiming clock at one end and a statue of Abraham at
the other—I found it quite a comfort to have him there as it
bespoke of good Mexican/American relations. Just beyond this

park was an outdoor market and shopping center where we could buy meat, groceries and other necessities. I could also have my hair done in a place that looked like Fernando's Hideaway for a dollar. For the first week or so, due to the high altitude (7,600 feet), I felt like a pea in a ten-gallon pod—sleepy, listless and forever cold.

We were fortunate to inherit a cook, Lupe, and an upstairs maid, Consuelo. Lupe was a taciturn little Mexican about four feet tall and almost as wide. Once in a while, a reluctant smile crept across her face, but, for the most part, she kept her feelings to herself. She was skilled at Mexican cuisine, but had a lot to learn about American fare. I bought her a Spanish/English cookbook, which she could barely read, but with this bolster and my help, she learned quickly. In fact, she stayed with us for four years and became an excellent all-around *cocinera.* Consuelo was lazy at times, but pleasant. We also had a government car and Mexican driver named Davíd, a luxury I'd never had before and one which I appreciated. The traffic in Mexico City was diabolic. However, this grandeur didn't last very long as Bill felt a chauffeur was an unnecessary government expense. He saw no reason not to drive our own car or use public transport. So within weeks, I summoned courage to drive in the suburbs, then in Mexico City, a feat deserving, in my opinion, of an award for valor.

Lupe and Consuelo made it clear that they alone could not handle the work of keeping up with such a enormous house, plus the necessary representational entertaining. They pointed out that when we had visitors, suitcases would have to be lugged up those forty-eight marble steps. Obviously we needed a house boy, so the final addition to our staff was Antonio.

From an embassy acquaintance, I heard about a poor boy who was looking for odd jobs and tracked him down through a policeman on the beat in our neighborhood. The policeman, a kindly man, told me that he had found the boy asleep in

Chapultepec Park, but, because of the cold, had permitted him to sleep in the tiny red-and-white striped structure which housed the controls for the *barrera* at a railroad crossing. He would find the boy and send him to our house.

That afternoon, Antonio entered my life. He didn't look a very promising prospect as a house boy. He was small, shy, and bedraggled, with a dark Aztec complexion, handsome features and unruly black hair. In one hand he clutched a small paper bag containing all of his worldly belongings. This he placed on the floor at his feet and proceeded to crack his knuckles nervously. He explained that he had grown up in the country, the last child in a large family. His father was disabled and his older brothers chided him because he was so small, the runt of the litter. Having had but three years of schooling, he decided to leave home and had walked and hitchhiked two hundred miles from Vera Cruz to Mexico City in search of an education. He thought he was fifteen years old and his goal was to get through the sixth grade. (A *sexto grado* certificate is all important to a Mexican boy or girl; without it he or she can hardly get a license to sell balloons.) Aware that so many kids in Mexico were dirty little urchins and beggars, I was touched by Antonio's drive to improve himself, and decided to give him a try. Lupe and Consuelo were horrified. They were certain he would rob us blind, rape Joni, and run off with the family jewels, but some unseen Tinkerbell told me that this would not happen. I installed him in the laundry room over the garage.

The next day, greatly transformed from the benefits of soap and water and a visit to the *peluquería* for a haircut, Antonio and I went shopping to purchase a basic wardrobe, plus a white jacket for waiting on table. In his mind, this badge of distinction ranked the same as a star on a general's uniform. But, best of all, I bought him a bicycle, so that he could ride back and forth to school.

The afternoon session ran from 1:30 to 6:30 P.M. each weekday. This meant he could work in the house in the morning, be off to school in the afternoon, and back in time to serve dinner. With his security and ambition now established, he pulled himself up to his full five feet four inches and showed interest and intelligence in learning the role of Number One House Boy. I paraded him around the dining room table teaching him how to tread softly and pass the food from the left side, how to clean silver and brass, dust, vacuum the downstairs area without damaging the furniture, and how to tend bar. In regard to bartending, a few mistakes were made until he learned the art of mixing drinks and into which to drop the olive or the cherry. In time Lupe and Consuelo accepted Antonio as irrevocable and the wheels of the household began to run smoothly.

The social life in Mexico City was strenuous, a constant whirl of receptions, cocktail parties, dinners, luncheons, teas, and bridge. Also, an unrelenting stream of official visitors arrived at the National Airport at an hour when you longed to be home in bed—somewhere between 9 P.M. and midnight. For Mexicans, 9 P.M. was just the shank of the evening, and the normal dinner hour was somewhere between 9:30 and 11:30. This made it pretty hard on American tummies which started growling at about seven. And it was particularly deleterious to a good night's sleep for Bill who got up early in the morning in order to be at the office by 8 A.M.

As for me, I very quickly became spoiled. Antonio brought my breakfast to my room every morning at eight. After a second cup of coffee and a shower, I studied a bit of Spanish and got dressed for the day ahead. Often, I longed for the days when I could sweep out the garage and plant pansies in rumpled slacks and an old sweater, and not worry about my hair. I had to remind myself of my present status-quo as "la Señora de la casa." In fact, I couldn't even wash out my own panty-hose or carry the groceries to the car. As soon as I stepped out of a shop or market, even with one little bag containing two apples, I would be encircled by a half-dozen dirty little boys offering their services for a few centavos; the problem was to choose one and kindly swat the others away.

My chief complaint, however, was the coldness of our house—a bone-chilling cold such as one would expect to find in a mausoleum. I was tempted to buy a fifty-yard extension cord, wrap my pink electric blanket around me, and walk about the house like an Indian squaw. We tried to solve this problem with an assortment of gas, kerosene, oil, and electric heaters, but they hardly made a dent in the high-ceilinged rooms. It could be a beautiful, warm day outside, but forever cold inside. Our house had the wrong exposure and was squashed in between two other large houses which cut off the sunlight.

There was no garden or patio at the Cow Palace. The only patch of green was a tiny spot in front in which had been planted about twenty straggly rose bushes, not a very inviting spot in which to enjoy a bit of sunshine. And, if the rose bushes were eliminated, the view would be of a great wall and wrought iron gate which had to be opened and closed upon entry and departure. But this was Mexico, where the norm was to barricade.

Another concern was that the servants' quarters over the detached garage might as well have been three blocks away as far as Joni was concerned. When Bill and I were out at night, one of them had to sit up in the big house until our return. Even with someone sitting downstairs, it must have been very lonely for Joni. For the first few weeks before our effects arrived, she did not have the comfort of familiar objects such as the piano, her record player, her dolls, and her beloved stuffed animals. Her little-girl Spanish from Costa Rica had all but disappeared so that she could not converse easily with the servants. Thinking back, I realize what a little trooper she was! This new and strange existence in the barricaded Cow Palace was so different from the freedom she had known. Thank goodness for Casey. He quickly forgot the squirrels and woods in Alexandria, and became Joni's constant companion and nexus with the past.

Joni entered the seventh grade at the Lomas Grade School, a small private school in an old converted house with no play yard.

There were other Americans there and in time she adjusted and made friends. During those first weeks, I believe that what kept Joni going was looking forward to the arrival of Channing, Bill, Margy, and Granny Rodman for the Christmas holidays. Bill and Margy's summer romance had blossomed into full-blown devotion.

To fill our mausoleum, we purchased the biggest Christmas tree this side of Rockefeller Center and set it up in the atrium, where its branches rose two stories and we could trim the top from the second floor landing. Since those we had brought with us were inadequate, Joni and I enjoyed buying quantities of inexpensive but charming ornaments to adorn it. Then, to make the hallowed halls look less forbidding, we spread about masses of greenery accented with glistening decorations. Antonio was out of his mind with excitement over the Christmas preparations. He kept a log fire ablaze in the fireplace and the record player busy with a steady stream of Christmas music, while helping with the decorations. We gave a rousing Christmas party for Bill's embassy staff, and Joni danced to the theme song of *Mame,* making a grand entrance down the wide staircase with a boa draped around her neck. Soon after we arrived in Mexico, she had switched from ballet to modern dance classes and her style and talent delighted everyone.

Over New Year's we spent several days in Acapulco where, on a balmy starlit night on the balcony outside our room, Bill and Margy announced that they were engaged to be married. It was December 31, Joni's thirteenth birthday.

Now that Joni was thirteen, a true teenager, she decided that it was time to grow her hair. I loved her short bob and neatly trimmed bangs, but she had made up her mind. Finally, I struck a deal with her—if she would agree to have a formal picture taken after one more haircut, I would get off her back. She agreed, reluctantly. She and I had few altercations, but this was one. We went to "Fernando's Hideaway" where a very grim-faced little girl grimaced at every snip of the scissors. The photograph turned out quite well although the expression affirms Joni's displeasure with both the ordeal and mother.

ダ   ダ   ダ

My favorite colonial town, San Miguel de Allende, about a two-hour drive north of Mexico City, was a place of sharp contrasts and shadows when the sun pierced its narrow, cobbled streets. I loved its baronial doorways, fountains, niches, and wrought-iron adornments on ancient walls. Joni spent a good part of two summers there, living with local families and attending the Academia Hispano Americano, where she studied Spanish and jewelry making. She also took riding lessons at the famous Escuela Equestre de San Miguel. One day, while Bill and I watched her ride the show-jumping course, she had a bad spill. My heart stopped for a few seconds until she raised her helmet and waved.

Our preferred inn was the Villa Santa Monica, but, on one occasion, Bill and I were unable to get a reservation and stayed at a third-rate *posada* on the central square. Having eaten hot Mexican food for dinner, I became thirsty in the middle of the night. We had already consumed our jug of *aqua puro* provided by the posada, and, when I could no longer stand it, I foolishly drank water from the bathroom tap. The result was a case of typhoid fever. Had I not had typhoid shots and a lot of tender loving care, I might not have survived. I was very sick for over six weeks.

ダ   ダ   ダ

Early in the year, Mexico's Minister of agriculture had strongly hinted to Bill that the country would welcome U.S. participation in the biannual Livestock Exposition to be held in April. Consequently, Bill sent a memo to F.A.S. suggesting that a real bonanza could be achieved if President Johnson would send a bull from the LBJ Ranch in Texas to Mexican President Diaz Ordaz for the cattlemen of Mexico. This goodwill gesture, he believed, would be both an excellent political move and a boost to U.S./Mexican relations.

Some time later, Bill was called to Washington. He planned his trip so as to see his mother in Philadelphia over the weekend prior to official business. When he returned to his hotel on Sunday evening, there was an urgent message from the administrator of F.A.S. to call Marvin Watson, special assistant to the president, at the White House. He dutifully called on Monday morning and was told to come to the Southwest Security Gate at 6 P.M. that evening. There was no explanation why.

At the appointed hour, Bill arrived at the designated gate and was escorted to the West Wing where Watson was waiting for him. Outside of the Oval Office, three secretaries, still working at their desks, rose to greet Bill by name.

"Good evening, Mr. Rodman."

The two men walked past the Rose Garden and down the covered walkway to the White House itself. At this point, Watson said, "The president is waiting for you in his private quarters."

Bill tried to assimilate this bit of information as he and Watson entered a small elevator operated by a massive guard and rose to the third floor. Emerging from the elevator, Bill could see the president in a room at the end of a hallway. He was sitting in a chair with a towel draped around him having his hair cut. Just then, the first lady appeared from another room and called,

"Bye, Lyndon."

Having come from a long day of meetings, Bill was a bit rumpled and still had a *Time* magazine under his arm. Lady Bird spotted this and cried out to Bill as she brushed past,

"Oh, hello—I see you have the new *Time*. May I borrow it? I'm on my way to the ranch and haven't a thing to read." Bill handed her his magazine, and she evaporated into the elevator.

In the meantime, Watson had disappeared to have a word with LBJ. Bill heard the president shout, "Hell no." He later surmised that Watson had asked him if he wanted to see Mr. Rodman while his hair was being cut.

In a few minutes, putting on his suit coat, the president came into the hallway, shook hands with Bill, and invited him back into the living room. He indicated a small sofa where Bill should sit, and placed himself in a large armchair with a telephone hanging over a toggle switch.

"Tell me about yourself, son." began the president.

Bill still didn't know why he was there, but dutifully gave him a short profile. Then the president got to the point, "I understand Mexico is putting on a big livestock show, and you'd like a bull from the LBJ Ranch."

It suddenly dawned on Bill that somehow the contents of his memo had reached presidential ears, and he replied with a resounding, "Yes, sir."

LBJ then picked up the telephone and was immediately talking to his farm manager at the ranch—no operator, no dialing—a direct line. He asked if there was a bull good enough to give to the president of Mexico. A moment later, he put his hand over the receiver and whispered, "Bill, if I give you one, will you sell five for me?"

"Yes, sir." His answer was less emphatic this time, but one doesn't say "no" to the president of the United States of America.

When my husband left the White House, he walked to a little park, sat on a bench, and wondered if he had been dreaming. No, the episode was real enough. He then went to his hotel to call the head of the Hereford Cattle Association to tell him about the presidential gift, and to inform him that he had five bulls to sell. The two men were old friends and the Johnson bulls were duly sold.

The exposition opened with great fanfare and the cutting of the ceremonial ribbon by a team of VIPs including, the U.S.

Secretary of Agriculture, Orville Freeman, who represented the president of the United States. The Mexican Minister of Agriculture then proudly announced that the LBJ bull could be viewed at the U.S. pavilion, and that his semen would be available free of charge to cattle breeders throughout the country.

NNNN NNNN NNNN

During my bout with typhoid fever, the doctor had discovered lumps in my left breast. Just before leaving for Mexico, on a routine State Department medical exam, the surgeon had found a bunch of fibroid tumors in my right breast and had operated on them at the Doctor's Hospital in Washington, D.C. Now I needed a second operation, and, in my weakened condition from typhoid, it seemed wise to return to the same surgeon. U.S. Secretary of Agriculture, Orville Freeman, was in Mexico City at that time to present the LBJ bull to the president of Mexico, and offered to take me to Washington in the presidential jet, which featured a bed. Some five hours later, the Secretary gently awakened me to say we had landed at Andrews Air Force Base where we were met by an official limousine and I was escorted to the hospital. I had slept the entire flight.

After the operation, I regained my strength while visiting my mother in Virginia and mother-in-law in Philadelphia. Bill, meanwhile, celebrated his fiftieth birthday on May 13, 1968. Ambassador and Mrs. Fulton (Tony) Freeman graciously gave him a party at their residence. Several embassy officers, including the ambassador, a trombonist, had formed a small musical jazz band and on this occasion, Bill was initiated into the group with the presentation of a "gut-bucket." A "gut-bucket" is an upside-down galvanized tub with a string stretched from the bucket to a broomstick handle. When the string is plucked, a heavy base tone emerges. To further entertain the guests, Joni danced to the tunes of *Georgie Girl* and *The Spanish Flea.* I missed a good party.

About a week before my scheduled departure from Philadelphia, I was alarmed to hear Dr. Smyth's voice calling from Mexico. He said that Bill had suffered a mild heart attack and was in the hospital. A few quick calls, and I was on my way back to Mexico City. We believe that a combination of events had triggered this attack: Bill had been extremely worried about me for weeks. He had not only deplored having to send me home without him for an operation, but had pressing work at the embassy. He had also been upset about the world in general—the Vietnam War, the riots and killings on U.S. campuses, racial tensions, and unspeakably, the third assassination of the decade—the murder of Robert F. Kennedy on June 4, 1968.

Added to this, the preceding months for Bill had been laden with tension, leading up to the aforementioned Agricultural Livestock Exposition in Mexico City. He stayed in the hospital for three weeks, then curtailed his activities for the remainder of the summer. By late August, he was well enough to travel to the States where he was best man at Bill, Jr. and Margy's wedding on September 7, 1968, at Christ Church in Easton, Maryland.

ჯ   ჯ   ჯ

In October, Mexico set a beautiful stage for the 1968 Olympic Games, the first ever held in Latin America. We were fortunate to be there.

Before the Opening Ceremonies, many were skeptical that Mexico, still an economically developing country, beset at the time by student riots, communist infiltration in the universities, and general unrest, could pull off the occasion. Ticket computers were all fouled up, sports areas appeared unfinished, traffic would prove an insoluble problem, and the altitude of 7,437 feet would drain the energy of the athletes, keeping them from achieving their best results.

The skeptics were wrong. Through a concerted and

courageous effort, hundreds of hands took over the ailing computers, athletic installations were finished in the nick of time, and traffic was admirably controlled by the police with the help of hundreds of volunteer auxiliaries. New sparkling-white Olympic buses traveled back and forth from key points at no cost every few minutes, and the altitude seemed to pose no problem as both Olympic and world records were broken. The Dove of Peace reigned supreme, from the little dove stickers on cars to the magnificent array of lights depicting doves along every major thoroughfare. Even the huge billboards were covered entirely by a large white dove on a vivid blue background—no words. Each event had its special color, so that traffic was led to the right stadium by streamers hung from street-light poles, with the symbolic dove flying on the designated color. The almost 8,000 athletes and the million or so visitors became caught up in a feeling that something could be proved in Mexico '68—that 108 different nationalities could live side-by-side in one compound called the Olympic Village, and that neither war, riots, politics, nor differences of race and creed could mar the moment.

And Mexico added another dimension to its stage by promoting the ancient Greek tradition of combining cultural achievement with physical prowess. Performers from many nations entertained throughout the city, poets gathered in Alameda Park to recite their works; sculpture, dance, drama and music were provided by scores of countries. In Chapultepec Park, children of every color, in traditional costumes, stood in front of huge canvases painting their own thoughts in brilliant colors. There was just about as much paint on the kids as on the canvases which later lined Avenida de la Reforma for ten blocks.

The Cow Palace was a beehive of activity. Our guests for three weeks included friends from Australia, Alister and Dorothy Paul; two disappointed volleyball players, Beth and Mary, who had failed to make the Olympic team; and a public relations man named Ian who had driven the two girls down from the tryouts at Lake Tahoe. I happened to meet this trio in front of the security desk at the American Embassy asking for information on lodging. As this was impossible to find, I must have taken pity on them and invited them to stay at the Cow Palace. The two girls were sweet, and Ian had a car which was useful. Best of all, he managed the miracle of getting Joni a pass to all of the gymnastic events.

Before leaving Australia in 1966, Bill and I had made a pact with our friends, Alister and Dorothy Paul, that our next reunion would be at the 1968 Olympics, wherever they were held. Little did we dream that the site would be Mexico City and that we would be living there. When news of our assignment came, we were delighted to send them an invitation to be our guests. As a doctor, Alister secured a position as medical advisor to the members of the Australian field hockey team, and he and Dorothy accompanied the team on their flight to Mexico. As she was an accomplished horsewoman, we didn't miss a single equestrian event. We even went to Avándaro, a hundred miles distant, where the "three-day-event," (cross-country, jumping and dressage), took place on a foul and muddy day. Prince Philip, Duke of Edinburgh, was one of the judges. In testimony of the dangers of the course, two horses were killed in the cross-country race, one a Russian mount and one Irish. The Russian horse jumped into a stream swollen by rain and drowned.

Had it not been for the Pauls, the XIX Olympiad might not have been as much fun. Alister knew everyone on the Australian swimming and field hockey teams, and Dorothy knew everyone on the equestrian team. Ray Evans, a hockey player, became a special friend. On several occasions he and others invited us to the Olympic Village for luncheon where we met Prince Philip. Joni had a pocketful of Australian and American pins which she traded with athletes for pins from other countries, including the most coveted of all—Russia. When Australia made the final in field hockey, we were all thrilled and shouted ourselves hoarse. The Aussies lost to Pakistan, two to one, but Joni had her own homemade gold medal for Ray which she ceremoniously hung around his neck after the match.

The Olympic Village comprised a series of buildings housing 3,000 athletes. There was also a theater, cinemas, stores, practice fields, gymnasiums, and a row of restaurants which catered to the culinary tastes of each participating country. What made it even more interesting was that many Aztec ruins were unearthed during excavation, lending contrast between the old world and the new. Thank goodness for diplomatic license plates; without them, the area was strictly off limits.

The only sour note of the two-week period was the shameful performance of U.S. track men Smith and Carlos. When they mounted the victory pedestal to receive their medals for the 200-meter dash, they proceeded to bow their heads and raise their black-gloved fists in defiance of the American flag and national anthem. Although bad timing for a "black power" demonstration, they achieved their purpose if it was to embarrass and anger their countrymen. Except for this rebellious act, we Americans in Mexico were thrilled by the outstanding showing of our athletes. The U.S. won one-hundred and eight medals, including forty-six gold, well ahead of Russia for the first time in twelve years.

Most impressive of all was the closing ceremony. When the lights went out for the lowering of the Olympic flame, a fabulous display of fireworks exploded noisily in the sky in a great abstract field of color, and thousands of athletes and young people poured onto the field. A thrilling kind of bedlam followed in a melee of blazers, Nehru jackets, Bermuda shorts, turbans, fezzes, fedoras, and flowing robes—brown people, yellow people, black and white people. Each seemed to forget both nationality and race as they embraced, kissed, pranced and strutted, some in conga lines, others with arms linked. They exchanged hats and blazers and carried their medalists on their shoulders. At the same time, over 1,000 mariachi paraded onto the field, their normally stentorian sounds almost drowned out by the boom of fireworks overhead and the roar of the crowd waving sombreros and shouting, "Méjico, Méjico, Méjico." When the fireworks stopped, the mariachi played the traditional farewell song, "Las Golondrinas," while everyone sang, and the huge lighted MEXICO '68 on the scoreboard changed to MUNICH '72. The Games had come to an end with the grand finale of the biggest fiesta in the history of Mexico, and Mexico could be justly proud.

ᴣ   ᴣ   ᴣ

After the excitement and happy confusion of the Olympics, it took time to come down from cloud nine and return to normal. We didn't, however, have long to be normal as Secretary of Agriculture and Mrs. Freeman arrived unofficially in mid-November, and Bill and I escorted them on part of their ten-day vacation. The Freemans had been campaigning tirelessly for Hubert Humphrey who had just lost a close race for the presidency against Richard Nixon. Both were exhausted and needed to distance themselves from the pressures of Washington.

We four retreated to Taxco, a national treasure of cobbled, corkscrew streets spilling over with flowers and silver shops. On the outskirts was an enchanting colonial inn called the Hacienda del Chorrillo, run by our friends, the Sullivans. There we had reserved La Flora bungalow, a cozy retreat with a big open fireplace and bougainvillea cascading over the tiled roof. Orville was not only exhausted from the presidential campaign, but had finally come to the end of a very turbulent eight-year stint in Washington. He had first become Secretary of Agriculture in 1960 under John F. Kennedy. In order to unwind, he found the serene setting a place to pour out the trials, errors, disappointments and frustrations of his tenure to sympathetic ears.

Bill and I were fascinated listening to his descriptive word pictures of JFK and Jackie, LBJ and Lady Bird, Humphrey, Nixon, the election, Vietnam, the racial crisis, and the recent

Poor Peoples' March on Washington, led by Ralph Abernathy. The latter backfired miserably because the marchers had no organization nor real purpose in mind except to arouse sympathy—the same type of sympathy, he said, sought by a drunken blonde in a New York discotheque because she has just lost her fifth husband. Orville was the main target of their anger, and they blockaded the Department of Agriculture so that he couldn't get to his office by the main entrance and had to use a secret passage and stairway. He referred to Martin Luther King as "a very good man—sensitive, soft spoken, articulate," and his assassination as a terrible loss to both black and white Americans.

It was a rare privilege to relax with Orville and his lovely wife, Jane. In the evening hours, we sat peacefully in front of an open fire discussing the problems of America and the world. During the day, however, Orville was sometimes pestered by publicity hounds. With a huge scar on his left jaw from a World War II wound, his face was easily recognizable.

※　　※　　※

For three of our more than four years in Mexico, I was chairman of the Scholarship Committee of the Embassy Wives Group. The students we helped were invariably very poor and very bright. We found them in cities and towns within a radius of about 200 miles of the capital. The selection system was very painstaking, requiring a personal interview, medical certificate, security check, and a handwritten essay describing goals and interests. After entering university, a student was required to maintain a B average and send a transcript of grades to our committee on a regular basis. The work was gratifying and I grew to love my "becados." I shared both their problems and successes. When they received their degrees, I was as proud as if they were my own. At one time, we had four medical, two engineering, three architectural, and one music student at six

Mexican universities, as well as four nursing students at the Anglo-American Hospital.

↜   ↜   ↜

I had expected Christmas of 1968 would be calm and serene, but it didn't turn out that way as Bill and I were house-hunting. This came as a shock as we never dreamed our present landlord would sell out from under us. In spite of its many steps and deep-freeze temperature in winter, we had grown fond of the old Cow Palace. Perhaps it was for the best, however, as we found a large ground-floor apartment, immediately dubbed the "Calf Palace," on Calle Esplanada, a wide street with palm trees running down the median strip, in the quieter and more attractive neighborhood of Las Lomas. Although it was spacious with wall-to-wall carpeting, well-chosen wall paper, and built-in electric heaters in every room, we downsized when it came to bedrooms—only three, each with a bath. The living room, however, was forty-

Taxco, Mexico

three feet long, and the dining room eighteen feet, plus a separate breakfast room, so we had plenty of space for entertaining, always an important consideration in diplomatic life. The master bedroom was also commodious with an adjoining dressing room, and an enormous sunken bathtub which her ladyship entered down a series of steps.

We did not move until mid-January. Granny Rodman and Channing both arrived for the Christmas holiday, and we all went to our beloved San Miguel de Allende over New Year's.

જ   જ   જ

Channing and I left the others in San Miguel and set off on a fascinating trip to the state of Michoacán where she did a study of the Tarascan Indians for her senior art portfolio at Briarcliff College. The Tarascans, one of the oldest surviving cultures in the western hemisphere, still spoke their own language and practiced their ancient arts and crafts, some of the most beautiful in the world.

Our first stop, however, was in Morelia, an aristocrat among Mexican cities. Our large room at the friendly old Spanish Colonial Hotel held the graciousness of the past—a beamed ceiling twenty feet high, and a bay window traditionally draped in red velvet and lace curtains. A little balcony overlooked the central plaza. When we returned from dinner, we found our beds turned down and a pristine white linen mat between them. I claimed that it must be there to place our dainty feet upon so as not to dirty them. Channing claimed otherwise—she thought it was there so that our dainty feet wouldn't dirty the beautiful oriental rug.

We spent the next day roaming the streets of Morelia, a lovely old town of winding arcades, graceful arches, scattered parks, and a beautiful cathedral, elegant in its simplicity and architectural balance.

But as glorious as it was, walking through streets teeming with antiquity, it was the people who intrigued us most: the small woman, cloaked in black, huddled into a dark corner selling beans from a blackened crock; the old man wrapped in his serape, his face lined with the tale of centuries; the young starry-eyed lovers holding hands on the cathedral steps; a group of teenagers chattering on a street corner eating tacos cooked over a coal-fired brazier; the little girl carrying a baby whose tiny foot protruded from under her shawl; happy children darting to and fro; unkempt urchins begging for centavos.

In spite of poverty, Mexicans are an amiable and gracious people with a well-tuned capacity to enjoy life, "gozando la vida." A national characteristic is *machismo,* the unremitting desire to prove oneself a man. The male ego seems to invent a bigger life, a bigger frame, a bigger sex appeal than that with which his body is endowed. Right or wrong, the macho Mexican will always have an answer.

When we reached Patzcuaro and checked into the Posada Don Vasco where we had stayed on our Pan American trip in 1961, Channing was feeling poorly. She was running a temperature and I thought it best to call a doctor. A plump little gentleman soon arrived, gave her some pills, charged us twenty-five pesos ($2 U.S.), and the following day she was shaky but ready to carry on. Ever since, whenever I have had the flu, I have wondered about those magical Mexican pills.

We followed a southbound road through the hilly Tarascan countryside to Paracho, where we had a letter of introduction to a missionary couple named Lathrop. Their organization called Light of Life originated in Philadelphia, and they were spending seven years in Michoacán translating the New Testament into the Tarascan language. Their own printing press was housed in a small outbuilding. Elizabeth's husband was not there, but she, standing tall and handsome, welcomed us into the bareness of her modest home. She wore the clothes of an American pioneer woman, a long checked gingham dress and bonnet, and her thick white hair was braided to her waist.

Elizabeth explained that the distribution of the Bible to the Tarascans would be a problem. A large majority of the local Indians were afraid of the gospel. Some called it the devil's work. Others realized that it was a good book, but feared it because they knew it would change their lives, and they were content to continue on in the centuries-old traditions of their forefathers.

The special craft of the Indians of Paracho was guitar making. Everywhere were sundry guitars in various stages of completion—dozens of them were drying in the sun. In one small shop we watched the artisans putting finishing touches on the beautiful instruments and bought one for Joni.

Channing and I continued on to Uruapan, an agreeable, pretty town, proud of its tropical gardens and waterfalls. We were welcomed at a small posada by an amiable landlady who decided these two scraggly Americans needed mothering. She couldn't do enough for us: fresh flowers in our room, beds turned down, and a breakfast fit for a queen and princess. The following day, she packed us a picnic lunch for our trek to the extinct volcano of Paricutín. The volcano had suddenly burst through a quiet cornfield some twenty years before covering towns and surrounding countryside with black ash and rock. To get there, we drove to a tiny village of thatched huts where we hired two old plug horses and a guide named Pedro, a pitiful little Indian with a dirty white bandage covering an eye socket—his eye had been gouged out in a drunken brawl. Pedro ran behind the sluggish horses swatting them with a switch. When we reached the volcano we were stunned by the sight of utter desolation that had once been a town surrounded by fertile fields. For two or more miles, only a church spire was visible.

Channing sketched and took hundreds of photos, indelible reminders of a unique trip.

ॐ ॐ ॐ

During the winter of 1969, Bill and I set off on a 2,500-mile trip by car to Mexico's Yucatan Peninsula, a vast area jutting into the Gulf of Mexico like a hitchhiker's thumb. Its isolation is due in part to the peninsula's geographical position, but also to the fact that when the Spanish came, the Mayans stubbornly held onto their language and customs.

Yucatan heat hit us like an blast furnace. Little hamlets of thatched white adobe huts sizzled in the sun. Older women wore white rather than the usual black of central Mexico, their hair pulled back into a club-like knot which had been the fashion for centuries. Younger women, especially in Mérida, the provincial capital, also wore white, but glittered with gold chains and earrings, a flower in their hair. The men wore white as well—usually an embroidered shirt called a *guayabera,* white pants and the prevailing straw hat. In the country, the men rode burros, often shaded by an umbrella, while the women walked behind, sometimes as laden as the burro.

The ancient city ruins of the Mayans appeared to achieve new beauty in decay. Chichén Itzá was awe-inspiring, but gray, jagged and forbidding. Impressive were the temples, carvings, and pyramid-like structures with narrow steps to the top, impossible to climb. One pyramid about 200 feet high, its sides set at sixty degree angles, had a chain draped down the steps to aid venturesome climbers, but as we heard tales of tourists breaking bones, Bill and I decided to remain on the ground. Uxmal was more refined, with walls of open work and geometric patterns of stone mosaic, a subtle pink glow over all.

The Mayan culture was one of wide class distinctions with priests, nobles and warriors at the top, slaves at the bottom, and artisans and merchants somewhere in between—a vast population bedeviled by gods who could blow hot or cold according to their own arcane reasons. A favored method of appeasing them was to throw virgins into sacred wells, Yucatan's only source of fresh water. A well, the Indians reasoned, would be the abode of powerful and greedy spirits.

Bill and I were glad to escape the ruins as well as mile upon mile of barren scrub growth to reach the peaceful island of Isla Mujeres, a boat ride across a stretch of the Yucatan Channel joining the Gulf and the Caribbean. In 1969, the island was still unspoiled with only one recommended hotel called Posada del Mar. We hired a boat and guide who amused us by diving for abalone as we explored the coast and inlets. The huge shells which house the abalone lie in very deep water. Sometimes I worried that our guide was submerged too long, but up he would pop with an abalone shell in each hand. We anchored in a cove and climbed some rocks where he deftly removed the slimy creature from its haven and tossed the shell over a rocky ledge among thousands of discarded shells. Quite obviously, we were not the first to discover this site. He then placed the abalone on a flat rock, squirted it with lemon juice and salt, and let it "cook" in the hot sun. We were offered the result for our lunch. Bill, who could eat anything, loved it—I did not. That evening, he developed ptomaine poisoning and was nauseated all night long. For a few hours, so desperate was his condition, that I wondered if I might be widowed on this remote speck of the earth.

ʔ   ʔ   ʔ

In the spring, Joni was chosen for a starring dance role in the musical, *Tom Sawyer,* which newspaper reviews praised as "delightful, nostalgic, bright, sparkling." Under the direction of a Belles Artes teacher, performer and choreographer, Alonzo Vargas, she gained a great deal of stage experience. Best of all, Vargas took an interest in Joni and elected to continue teaching her privately. A graceful man with chiseled Indian features, he came to our house almost every day during the ensuing weeks. Not only did Joni's artistic and technical ability strengthen immeasurably, but she began to think seriously about a future career in dance.

Meanwhile, Channing graduated from Briarcliff College a year ahead of schedule. She had doubled up on courses and, during the summer of 1968, had earned credits at the University of the Americas in Mexico City. A Columbia Business School graduate named Carl Thieme had come on the scene, and they planned to get married after her graduation in May. The wedding took place in Taxco on July 5 at the beautiful sixteenth century Hacienda del Chorrillo, but this time, I reserved all twelve guest rooms for family and out-of-town guests. We hired a mini-bus to transport the guests to Taxco. Margy, Bill, Jr. and Joni drove with Bill and me in our two cars, loaded to the gills with the wedding cake, two gross of white gladiola in bud, a brass cross and candlesticks from Christ Episcopal Church in Mexico City, and Channing's wedding dress. We five stopped along the way for a picnic of turkey sandwiches, caviar, crackers and wine, left over from the civil marriage ceremony, required by law, the night before.

The sixteenth century outdoor chapel, the site of the ceremony, was bedecked with gladiola, palm branches and tall white candles. A small hurdle was cajoling the marimba band into playing Mendlessohn's "Wedding March." To keep them on track, the *dueña* of the inn, Nancy Sullivan, solved the problem by singing "da-da-dada" loudly.

In spite of the unchurchly strains of the marimbas, the service was beautiful. Channing wore a gown of white Mexican lace, a short veil which fell from a crown of orange blossoms in her hair, and carried a bouquet of white orchids. Joni was maid-of-honor in yellow lace with a wide brimmed lace hat that remained a bit cockeyed throughout.

On Sunday, the rains descended in torrents causing major landslides along the highway. Several wedding guests, returning to Mexico City, were stranded for hours. My older brother's car was unaccounted for until 8 A.M. the next morning. Completely blocked by a landslide, he and the driver had managed to ease the car over the median strip, crash through a hedge, and backtrack to Cuernavaca where they found lodging. Telephone lines were down and they were unable to call.

After a honeymoon at the emerging resort of Zihuatanejo on the south coast of Mexico, without benefit of luggage lost in transit, Channing and Carl, a brilliant man who would turn out to be a good provider and father, settled happily in Boston where he was a research economist with the John Hancock Insurance Company.

ᒕ   ᒕ   ᒕ

Joni finished the eighth grade at her school, and in early September, went off to St. Catherine's, a girls' boarding and day school in Richmond, Virginia. The last fledgling had flown the nest.

Bill and I thought it best to send Joni back to the States to boarding school, mainly because it was known that the American High School in Mexico City had teenage drug problems. We chose St. Catherine's, not only for its excellent reputation, but because Joni would have permission to continue her dance studies at the Virginia Ballet Theater in Richmond. She would also have relatives nearby. My youngest brother, Bill, and his family lived but a few blocks from the school.

Not only did Channing get married and Joni depart for boarding school, but in mid July, Bill, Jr. received a grant from the Health, Education and Welfare department (HEW) to do field work for his Ph.D. in anthropology on a tiny island in the New Hebrides in the faraway South Pacific. Before leaving in November for fifteen months, he and Margy came to Mexico for a two-week visit, dotted with trips to our favorite spots—San Miguel de Allende, Guanajuato, and Taxco. Bill and I were delighted for them, but with the thought of my children going off in every direction, I simply sat down and cried.

· —— Chapter Sixteen —— ·

OUR LITTLE BROTHERS AND SISTERS
(Los Pequeños Hermanos)

As BILL AND I WERE CRESTING THE EMPTY NEST
SYNDROME, we were invited to visit an orphanage called
Nuestro Pequeños Hermanos, (Our Little Brothers and Sisters),
located at the old hacienda of Alcomán, some twenty-five miles
north of Mexico City. Instead of the expected cold, grim,
depersonalized institution with high walls and rigid discipline,
we found healthy, happy children, ranging in age from infant to
early teens, living in an atmosphere of security and unconditional
love—a huge family brimming with smiles and bouncy good
humor. So infectious were these children and their needs so great
that Bill and I decided to help wherever we could.

In her article about NPH, "From Prisons to Playgrounds," in
the National Catholic Magazine, *Sign,* Jean Dorcy wrote, "Here
is proof, if proof is needed, that love is contagious. You can catch
it from someone who really has a good case of it."

჻   ჻   ჻

It all began in 1954 when a young Roman Catholic priest,
William Wasson, was asked to testify against a hungry street

233

boy who had robbed the poor box in his church. Instead, the priest petitioned the judge to remand the abandoned child to his care. A week later Father Wasson took on eight more homeless boys, and at the end of the year he had thirty-two. By 1969, his family had grown to a thousand.

Father Wasson was an extraordinary man. He was a taskmaster, yet capable of infinite love which embraced all of his children. In other words, these kids were not homeless nor fatherless. They were his and no one could take them away from him.

To be accepted at NPH, mothers had to be dead and fathers either dead, unwilling, or unable to support their children; all siblings of a family under sixteen years old had to enter together; all had to come from impoverished backgrounds.

Father Wasson's philosophy of child rearing was based on four principles: security, love, work, and responsibility. The kids were secure because they knew they were accepted unconditionally, would never be asked to leave, and could not be adopted. They were loved and loving because each was treated as a person of worth. As a family, they shared the work load. Every child was required to perform chores typical of any household—cooking, cleaning, maintenance, washing, ironing and sewing.

Erich Fromm in his book, *Our Little Village,* describing NPH wrote, "What is remarkable is not only the absence of major behavioral problems, but the presence of a spirit of cooperation and mutual responsibility. The boys and girls feel themselves to be members of the 'family' and are proud of this membership . . ."

Fromm also said that something happened here contrary to professional opinion. Many psychologists, sociologists, and educators would say that the enormous success of Our Little Brothers and Sisters was impossible. Father Wasson didn't agree and proved them wrong, insisting that the success of his orphanage all boiled down to one concept—love.

During the years we were in Mexico, NPH was located at four separate donated sites: younger children lived at Acolmán, older boys were housed in an old brewery and older girls in a large house just outside of Cuernavaca. All of the older *pequeños* had the experience of spending time at Miacatlán, twenty miles south of Cuernavaca. There they learned to farm the rich soil, raising fruits, vegetables, and livestock to improve the diet of a thousand brothers and sisters.

Schooling at the orphanage, from kindergarten through high school, received superior ratings from the Mexican Department of Education. Co-curricular activities included sports, art, music and native dancing. Upon completion of high school, each pequeño was required to give a year of service to his "family." These young graduates became counselors, cooks, drivers, farmers, gardeners, painters, builders, paramedical and administrative assistants.

Our interest in NPH was almost all-consuming. Both Bill and I became members of the Mexican Board of Directors, he as director of the food and agricultural program, and I as chairman of the scholarship program. I became an ardent fund raiser and job seeker for those graduates going on to technical, secretarial, language, nursing, or trade school, or to a university to pursue a professional career. I was also a member of the Womens' Auxiliary. We collected clothes, raised money for items such as medicines, shoes, sports equipment, musical instruments, or whatever was most needed. I even set up a little barbershop and cut hair.

Through Bill's agricultural contacts, he was able to augment the orphans' diet with produce which didn't meet U.S. export standards. One American contact was so impressed with the operation that he persuaded his company to give funds for window glass in the huge dining hall at Acolmán, originally used for grain storage.

In the early days of NPH, providing food for his pequeños

was Father Wasson's greatest worry. Rice, beans, and corn tortillas were the backbone of the daily diet. Sometimes the food problem was solved miraculously, such as the time there was almost nothing in the larder to eat. The hungry hoard of boys, with their distressed father, went into the chapel and prayed. They were still there when a benefactor knocked on the door. These small miracles seemed a part of the legend of Father Wasson.

A board member and supporter of NPH whom we already knew was our dear friend, Helen Hayes. One day she, Father Wasson and our new American ambassador, Bob McBride, met in our living room to discuss ways to raise funds for the orphanage. Suddenly Helen piped up with, "I have an idea. John Wayne loves Mexico. Let's invite him to premier his new movie *True Grit* in Mexico City. Here, I have his private phone number. Bill, go to the telephone and call." Why Helen felt that Bill should call instead of herself, I cannot fathom, but Bill happily carried out her order. Pilar, John's Peruvian wife, answered the phone, and after Bill explained who he was, heard her shout, "Hey Duke—telephone!" Bill remembers that the Duke's first word was a drawn out—"Yeah?"

And so followed a memorable conversation in which John Wayne approved Helen Hayes' suggestion and gave Bill the number of his agent in New York to arrange a suitable date.

John made a big occasion of his trip to Mexico. He, Pilar and his four-year-old daughter, Melissa, cruised from Los Angeles to Acapulco in his converted Navy mine-sweeper and then flew to Mexico City on the appointed date. Bill and I escorted them to the Camino Real Hotel, where an impressive suite had been reserved with its own swimming pool, garden terrace, kitchen, dining room and bedrooms. There was a full staff of servants including a gourmet cook. I doubt if the actor paid a peso for all this luxury. John Wayne was an icon in Mexico, perhaps because of the numerous pictures he had made south of the border. The Mexicans adored him.

The following morning, Bill and I arrived early at the hotel to escort the Wayne family to the orphanage at Acolmán. Raquel Welch was also in Mexico City making a TV special and had offered a generous gift to the orphanage. She knew John Wayne and wanted to get in on the act, so she too was waiting at the hotel to join the entourage. Bill had requested a couple of embassy limousines. He and I and John rode in the first, and Raquel and others followed. Although Bill had warned John that there was no pit-stop on the twenty-five mile trip, about halfway along there was a urgent plea from the front seat where John had elected to sit—"Gotta go, Bill."

Bill knew of a very rundown gas station but was horrified at the thought of subjecting the Duke to its appalling facilities.

When John got out of the car, I decided that I too had to go, and the two of us went around to the back of the station where there were two corrugated iron stalls about five feet high. From my vantage point, I could see the Academy Award Winner's head and hear his tinkle, a one-of-a-kind situation which I look back on with vast amusement.

When we arrived at the orphanage, we "notables" were met at the gate by Father Wasson and proceeded to walk the length of the driveway banked with orphans clapping and cheering. Several of the smallest tots grabbed our hands and walked with us. After much picture taking by the press and TV cameras, we took seats in the big open courtyard and enjoyed a program of singing and native dancing by the children. Both John Wayne and Raquel Welch were emotionally touched by the experience. After the performance, as they greeted many of the orphans and hugged the little ones, tears streamed down their faces.

Later, John Wayne commented, "When I came to Our Little Brothers and Sisters, I expected to find children who needed love—but I found instead children who had love to give."

When we returned to his hotel suite early in the afternoon, John was tired and ready to relax. First he removed his false hairpiece and tossed it across the room, then he unlaced his corset and breathed a exuberant sigh of relief as his anatomy reverted to its natural state. Finally he ordered himself a drink and settled back contentedly in an easy chair.

Later that day, there was a reception for John and Raquel at the ambassador's residence followed by the premier of *True Grit* at one of the city's movie theaters. Before the show, a master-of-ceremonies announced winners of gifts raffled off by various prestigious stores in Mexico City, followed by on-stage appearances by the two celebrities.

Seated next to John Wayne during the movie, I was amused at the novelty of my position. There he was on the big screen larger than life, yet the man beside me was authentic. I thought— nobody will believe me.

With John Wayne

As we were downsized to one child for Christmas 1969, Bill, Joni, and I decided join in the festivities at Nuestros Pequeños Hermanos in Cuernavaca while lodging nearby at one of our favorite inns, Hosteria Las Quintas.

On the evening of December 23, we went to the orphanage for a Christmas posada and party put on by the kids. The Mexican posada always starts off on a solemn note with Joseph leading Mary on a donkey and others following on foot with lighted candles. As he knocks on doors, everyone sings the traditional posada song in which the wanderers ask for lodging, and at each doorway, a group inside answers, "No, no, you can't come in." Finally, on the fifth or sixth try, the answer is, "Enter, enter," and everyone bursts forth in a joyful finale.

After the posada the party started with *piñatas,* clay pots artistically covered with paper, generally in the form of animals, and hung out of reach on a clothesline or pole. A Mexican tradition, the fun begins when one child at a time is blindfolded, and, to the great merriment of the others, he or she tries to break the swinging piñata with a stick or club. Finally a good whack breaks it and out cascades a plethora of small sweets, followed by a mad scramble to stuff pockets and mouths with the booty. The orphans insisted that Joni have the first go at the piñata.

On Christmas Eve we visited friends for a feast of suckling pig, wassail, turkey, and all the trimmings, then picked up Helen Hayes, also in Cuernavaca for the holidays, to go to midnight mass in the courtyard at the orphanage. Under a full moon, a group of *pequeños* played guitars and sang the mass, followed by traditional carols. The setting was beautiful, but the night had turned cold and we didn't have warm wraps. Bill gave Helen his jacket, and I had the benefit of his arm around my shoulders.

The day after Christmas, Joni, Bill and I set out for Oaxaca, a long tortuous drive along winding mountainous roads which made the traveler feel as arid and craggy as the countryside. At dusk, we stopped in a dusty pueblo, where we found a little x-rated hotel and wondered about bedbugs and ptomaine poisoning before falling asleep.

Oaxaca, which we had visited nine years before on our Pan American Highway trip, was in a festive mood. The Mexicans were unequaled when adorning and lighting up their cities at Christmas time. Both Indians and locals were out in all their finery, chatting and laughing. Here and there, little groups of wandering music-makers competed with the piping whistle of a hot-tamale wagon. At an outdoor cafe, we were amused watching the vendors peddling their rebozos and serapes to a group of tourists. In spite of the "no's" and head shaking, most of their quarries succumbed to their good-natured persistence. We even tried *bunuelos* at a stand in the zocalo. These were big fried pancakes made of flour and sugar upon which was poured diluted honey from a black pot, a Christmas tradition in Oaxaca. Delicious! When consumed, we copied the locals by making a wish and throwing the pottery plate over our shoulders.

જ   જ   જ

Early in the New Year, 1970, Joni returned to Virginia and Bill and I set off on a 4,000 mile business and pleasure trip. We headed due west to Guadalajara, then turned north and followed the west coast to visit old friends in Tucson, Arizona. On the return trip we traversed the center of Mexico.

Mexico is a land of contrasts where enchantment and beauty vie with melancholy and despair. At one moment, an oasis—beautiful, prosperous, content; at the next, a wilderness—barren, impoverished, dejected; at one moment, stately homes sequestered behind imposing walls; at the next—poverty-stricken hovels and squalor; at one moment, the delicate scent of flowers; at the next—the acrid smell of exhaust fumes.

While the Mexican's aesthetic sense is highly developed and scores of its people can create lovely objects, the masses prefer the plastic trinkets which flood markets and stores. Although numerous Indian dialects are spoken, Mexico prides itself on well-spoken Spanish. Many of its citizens are cultured, cosmopolitan and wealthy while others still move in the dark world of poverty and superstition. Mexico's domain stretches from high volcanic peaks and lush rain forests to endless miles of desolate wasteland.

The Mexicans have a keen sense of family. Poor or rich, they take their children with them wherever they go. Not only children, but aunts, uncles, siblings, and grandparents are fused into the family circle—a close-knit unit against the world. Although the world is ever changing, women, for the most part, lead carefully protected lives, and daughters of the upper and middle classes are chaperoned until they are married. Men enjoy a greater freedom. The "casa chica," or little house—an extramarital establishment maintained by the male for his mistress—is common at all levels of society, but it does not seem to impair the sanctity of the home. Parental discipline is mixed with prodigal affection. Except for the indigent, children are kept immaculately clean. There is a fascination with the macabre. One of the most popular holidays is the Day of the Dead when deceased ancestors are ceremoniously honored, and children are given candy skulls to eat. At the opposite pole, there is the love of life, fiestas, and lively music. No sound is muted, no edges dulled. Everything proclaims itself boldly, whether in the etched shapes of the landscapes, the oversized creation of its statues, ancient gods and murals, or in the vivid beauty of its flowers.

ॐ   ॐ   ॐ

There was a string of abductions and murders of diplomats in Latin American countries during the spring of 1970, and American embassy officers were warned to be on guard. We made several trips into the country with Ambassador and Mrs. McBride, but after the murder of the German ambassador in Guatemala, security went into high gear, especially for ambassadors. On one trip to the annual Strawberry Festival in Irapuato, we had the excitement of speeding along in the official Cadillac with an escort of motorcycle cops and secret service men.

Our schedule was fine-tuned to the minute and included a visit to Del Monte and Birdseye freezing and packing plants, an inspection of fair grounds with a rear-view review of show cattle, a *charreada* (Mexican rodeo), a banquet in the garden of a tobacco factory, and a bullfight. Because of security, we had to leave before the sixth bull, but the five we saw were ferocious, brave beasts. One came charging into the ring and jumped right over the guard rail into the moat causing great frenzy and injuring several spectators. When you see two tons of beef go sailing over the fence, it's unnerving, even if you are out of the line of fire. I was sitting next to the ambassador who was an "aficionado" and obligingly answered all of my dumb questions. Thank God we were spared a scheduled cock fight. The ambassador refused to go.

ॐ   ॐ   ॐ

Bill and I made another trip in 1970 to the emerging but still unspoiled coastal resort of Zihuatanejo with our friends, Lucy and Dick Kleinhans. Our hotel was built on a cliff overlooking the bay. Steps led down to the beach, with its never-ending procession of burros carrying incredible loads, natives shouldering the inevitable machete, and happy *niños*. Nondescript dogs ran in and out of the surf, and a colorful, if pitiful, array of hippies lived in grass shacks in the brush.

We four must have appeared "ultra establishment" to the hippies who turned their heads when we passed. What a pity that these young Americans were wasting precious years doing absolutely nothing! Two boys did break through the sound barrier and spoke to us. One confessed that he was sick, so Lucy and I, feeling motherly, took him some pills. The next day he was both better and grateful. We felt that everything they told us was what they wanted us to hear, not exactly the truth. They called themselves vagabonds and said they were dropouts from San Francisco State University. Possibly they were evading the draft, or hooked on drugs (although this wasn't apparent), or just trying to find their footing in a messed-up world. At that time, there was great unrest on college campuses throughout the United States, and we wondered if they had witnessed or had even been involved in the rioting at San Francisco State University in which students were killed. As a final gesture, Lucy and I took our two young friends stamped postcards which they promised to send to their mothers.

The flight to and from Zihuatanejo in a small twin-engine aircraft was studded with uncertainties. The plane held twelve passengers, and during the flight, everyone became forever friends. I was not sure whether this was the result of a feeling of shared uneasiness, confined quarters, or the fact that there was a serve-yourself bar with free sandwiches, beer and Coke. A darling little girl of about ten assumed the role of stewardess. The pilot needed all of his wits and skill just to maneuver his craft over and between the mountains, and to finally bring it down on a postage stamp air strip in the middle of a jungle. At one stage, he called to the young stewardess to bring him a sandwich and left the cockpit door open. We could see him poring over a common, everyday road map which added to our insecurity. After the plane finally landed to rousing applause from the passengers, we endured a hair-raising taxi ride along a dirt road edging cliffs to a spot where a descent of about a hundred steps led almost vertically down to the hotel. "Oh God!" exclaimed Lucy. But we finally made it to our rooms, and when we walked out onto the veranda, the sun was beginning to set on the distant horizon.

ॐ   ॐ   ॐ

Our anthropologists, Bill and Margy, sent us fascinating tales of the South Pacific. Their special island was Aoba in the New Hebrides. I cannot say they blended into native life as they were the only Caucasians in residence, but I can say that they were unconditionally accepted. Both were adopted into Aoban families and entered into all the rights and privileges of a primitive, tribal society. Meanwhile, Channing and Carl had settled into young-married rhythm in their apartment in Boston where Channing was testing her talent as a free-lance artist. She continued to show a keen sensitivity to the world about her as shown in her art work in later years, a sensitivity to God's creation through nature. Despite her passion for justice, and talent for loving, Channing has always been slightly charmed, strangely detached. Our teenager, Joni, had adjusted well at boarding school and had joined the Virginia Ballet Theater, later to become the Richmond Ballet. We missed them all!

The summer of 1970 was home-leave time again. Joni returned to Mexico from school, and our niece, Mimi, arrived soon after. In late June, we four took off on a *Travels With Charley*-type trip rediscovering America. I had found a wonderful little travel booklet called *The Farm and Ranch Guide* and plotted our course covering twenty-two states and an equal number of hamburgers. Our trip of more than 5,000 miles took us from ranches in Texas and Arkansas to fishing villages in Maine. We were in no hurry as we had almost three months before returning to Mexico.

ॐ ॐ ॐ

Several of Joni's plane trips to Mexico were noteworthy. In May of 1970, she left Richmond at 8:45 A.M. routed through Atlanta and New Orleans to Mexico City. Scheduled arrival time, 1:40 P.M. When she failed to get off the plane, seven desperate hours followed—telexes, messages and telephone calls to Eastern Airlines offices and terminals were to no avail. How could they lose a fifteen year old when written permission was required to allow a minor child to travel? It turned out that because of air traffic in Atlanta, Joni had been rerouted to Houston, then put on Air France for Mexico City arriving at 9 P.M. Neither her parents nor the Eastern office at the airport had been informed. Bill and I were irate!

Because of this fiasco, when the following Christmas vacation came along, in order to allow more time for connections, Bill and I decided that Joni should fly Delta Airlines from Dulles Airport in Washington, D.C., with a change to Eastern Airlines in New Orleans arriving Mexico at 11:53 P.M. This time, Joni herself called from New Orleans to say that Eastern had scheduled her on a flight that was nonexistent. An Eastern clerk then came on the line and said, "Sorry, but don't worry, your daughter will be put up at the Hotel Hilton, given breakfast money, car fare, and put on a plane arriving 2:40 P.M. tomorrow with a first-class

Joni in 1970, age 15
Pueblo of Tepozotlán, near Mexico City

ticket as there is no room left in coach." And Mom thought, poor little "Jonikins," all alone in that big hotel, missing one whole day of vacation because bloody Eastern goofed up again! And bloody Eastern got even bloodier the next day when I checked her new arrival time and found the plane was four hours late.

Unknown to us, however, the little drama had taken a serendipitous turn. Upon arrival, when Joni finally disembarked—lithe of step and full of smiles—just behind her was a handsome, uniformed plebe from the Naval Academy carrying her bundles of Christmas gifts. The goof-up in New Orleans turned out to be the making of her holiday.

Tom had also been scheduled on the nonexistent flight. He and Joni had met at the airport in New Orleans and went together to the Hilton where they dined and danced, and met the next morning for breakfast. And for the next two weeks, our sixteen-year-old was swept off her feet. Tom's father happened to be the general manager of the Marie Isabel Sheraton Hotel in Mexico City where there was a first class night club, swimming pool, and various dining rooms—and Tom just happened to be able to sign the chit. He also had a Jaguar. As Joni's wardrobe wasn't up to all this elegance, she and I had to rush about Mexico in search of suitable outfits.

The comedy of errors increased on Christmas Day when Joni met Mark, our doctor's son, who decided that Joni compared favorably with the Holy Grail. In spite of Tom, Mark was persistent and his status improved as Joni decided he was really very sweet and not to be brushed aside. He also had a car which was pretty cool even if he couldn't afford Café Diablo.

The second act of this little comedy found Mark and Joni in our living room with Tom expected any minute and Joni not knowing how to get rid of Mark. When the front door bell rang, Joni wished the floor would open up and swallow her, but the comedy continued—not as expected. A third young man named Brian who had fostered a crush on Joni ever since she danced in

Tom Sawyer, had arrived on a bicycle. So, we had a bicycle and a Datsun parked out front, and a Jaguar about to roll up. Forgive me, but I was back in my room peeking out the window and chuckling.

The final act ended happily as all good comedies should. Datsun and bicycle departed just in the nick of time, and Mr. Annapolis sauntered in to the love theme from Tchaikovsky's "Romeo and Juliet," a new Christmas LP.

And guess who was at the airport at 8 A.M. the following morning to see Joni off to school? Mark!

᠍᠍᠍᠍᠍᠍᠍᠍᠍᠍᠍᠍᠍᠍᠍᠍

Casey died soon after Joni's departure. Quite suddenly, his back gave out and he could no longer walk without dragging his hind legs. I was sure that the forty-eight marble steps at the Cow Palace were partly responsible for his infirmity. He was only nine years old. In that time he had flown across an ocean from Australia to America, and traversed a continent from Virginia to Mexico. Always an obedient and loving little dog, he had given us untold pleasure.

᠍᠍᠍᠍᠍᠍᠍᠍᠍᠍᠍᠍᠍᠍᠍᠍

Early in the new year, we took a momentous step and bought a small *quinta* (villa). A visiting acquaintance from Virginia had asked us to take her to look for a vacation home in Cuernavaca, and we dutifully complied. After viewing several expensive houses with an estate agent, Bill asked if he happened to have any inexpensive listings. The man thought a minute, then said, "Yes, as a matter of fact I do," and took us to a charming little quinta on the outskirts of town—price $20,000! It seemed practically a gift, and what a lovely place to escape to on weekends from smoggy Mexico City! Also, my creative juices started flowing as I mentally pictured what this small Eden could become with TLC and imagination. The house had two bedrooms and a bath, and a lovely big veranda off the living-dining area. Part of the veranda was covered, making a cool, shaded spot for dining outside. In front of the veranda was a small, tiled swimming pool and a garden of brilliant flowers and shrubs. To one side stood a majestic royal palm. Down a path from the pool was a guest house, one big room, bath and small kitchen. Both house and guest house were equipped and furnished attractively. A tall Aztec wall surrounded the entire property. But, as happy as we were to own this little Camelot, we only needed to look over the wall to be reminded of the dichotomy of Mexico. No more than a few hundred yards away was a squatter settlement where ragged children and skinny dogs romped, and women washed threadbare clothes in stone troughs after carrying heavy pails of water from miles away.

We named our acquisition "Quinta Tecolote" after a large painted ceramic owl which we had bought in Guadalahara some months before, and set him on a pedestal at one end of the pool. Each weekend when diplomatic life closed down, we set out after work on Friday and arrived at the quinta in time for supper. Whenever possible, I spent extra days there, or even a week at a time supervising improvements, painting small objects, or copying the Mexican art of bark painting which intrigued me. In time, we added two bedrooms to the guest house and decorated them with handsomely carved doors and furniture. Mosaic tiles, colorful bedspreads, and curtains of Mexican cloth added accents of color and charm.

A handsome young Mexican named Armando, and his wife, Imelda, came to work for us. Imelda did the cooking and housework while Armando did yard work and repairs. As with most Mexican peasants in their childbearing years, Imelda was perpetually pregnant, but Armando would take over her chores when necessary. He seemed able to do anything, including play the guitar and sing. Whenever we had guests, Armando, sitting at the edge of the pool in the moonlight, serenaded us with song.

I was obsessive about "Quinta Tecolote." I couldn't get enough of it. To me it became a jewel of perfection in an imperfect world.

ᴣ   ᴣ   ᴣ

Bill, Jr. and Margy flew directly to Mexico on their return from the New Hebrides. Dividing our time between Quinta Tecolote and Mexico City, they stayed for ten glorious days, entertaining us with fascinating tales of Aoba, their tropical isle, the original Bali H'ai. James Michener had been inspired to write *Tales of the South Pacific* during World War II when he was stationed on the island of Spiritu Santo, and could see Aoba across the water. When the film, *South Pacific,* was made, the filmmakers substituted the island of Morea, near Tahiti, as Bali H'ai. It was closer to Hollywood.

ᴣ   ᴣ   ᴣ

Our friendship with Helen Hayes blossomed with renewed energy during our weekly trips to Cuernavaca. Her home and ours were less than a mile apart, and she and I became constant companions, like the relationship of a beloved aunt and niece. She had turned seventy in October of 1970, and depended on Bill to meet her at the airport and facilitate passing through customs, then drive her to her home in Cuernavaca. She and I loved to play card games and scrabble, or drive to outlying pueblos to wander through the colorful Mexican markets. When she had to be in Mexico City, she stayed in Joni's room and I escorted her to civic and charity functions, clubs, and universities where she spoke eloquently. Inevitably she would be asked to recite an excerpt from her famous stage role as Queen Victoria in *Victoria Regina.* She was always thinking of how she could please others rather than giving in to the weariness of advancing years. Her biggest fault, she often commented, was her inability to say "no."

I was continually impressed by the great actress's intellect, compassion, and insight into things human and divine. She had an uncanny sense of the world about her, never lofty, but a down to earth understanding of her fellow man. At times, she could be acerbic and critical—on several occasions I was taken down a peg or two. Her knowledge of two of her favorite subjects, history and anthropology, was impressive. She could also be witty, and draw from her file of memories an endless dialogue of amusing anecdotes about the theater which she loved, and Hollywood which she often scorned. On occasion I answered her phone to find I was speaking to such notables as James Stewart, Jack Benny, or Lillian Gish.

One of the shining moments of my life came during the summer of 1971 when she called to ask if I would be available to come to her home each morning for about two weeks to be her prompter in memorizing the role of Mary Tyrone in Eugene O'Neill's play, *Long Days Journey Into Night.* The play, scheduled to open in Washington in the early fall, would be her final stage appearance. At almost seventy-one years old, she didn't want to broadcast the fact that her memory wasn't what it used to be. She went on to explain that actors get so adept at memorizing their lines that often they don't bother to learn them until rehearsals begin. She too did that in her younger days, but now she felt uncertain. She also said that every *if, and,* or *but* of O'Neill's plays had to be on target—with some playwrights you could fudge a little on small words, but never with O'Neill, and *Long Day's Journey* was a four-hour play.

This was an interlude so special in my life that I find it hard to describe the joy, almost rapture, that I felt sitting on Helen's veranda while the First Lady of the American Theater walked back and forth, back and forth, speaking her lines. Only occasionally would I have to prompt, and she would say, "Thank-you."

In a letter to her son, James MacArthur, during a long stage wait, she wrote her feelings before the final moments of the play:

> Elation, that's what I feel. Just think. I no longer need worry how I feel physically, whether my voice is right, whether my costume is secure, whether I'm going to trip, make a false move. I have feared these things for as long as I can remember, since I was a child of five. . . . They have ruled my life and daily thoughts, always the performance just ahead, always the fears of the endless things that can go wrong. Now I'm free of them, or about to be, and what I'm feeling as I wait for this last moment of mine before a stage audience is sheer elation!

ॐ   ॐ   ॐ

Joni's roommate, Mary Ball Ellett, visited us that summer. At Quinta Tecolote, they stayed in the guest house and loved the freedom of their own quarters away from the eagle eyes of prefects and dorm mistresses. Older boys at Nuestros Pequeños Hermanos swarmed around them like bees to honey.

At the end of her visit, we four drove west to Veracruz on the Gulf Coast where Cortes had launched his conquest of Mexico. We continued up the coast stopping for the night near Tuxpan. Nearby were the ruins of El Tajín, the beautiful old city of the Totonacs, which lay hidden in a flow of green hills. At the site, there was no one to take money or act as guide. We were completely alone. As evening settled, Joni remarked that she had an eerie feeling that unseen ghosts of long ago might jump out from behind the ancient walls.

ॐ   ॐ   ॐ

After Mary Ball's departure, Joni worked at the NPH orphanage at Alcolmán during the month of August, the summer of her sixteenth year. Volunteers were lodged in a small compound of trailers. As hers was the smallest, Joni lived alone. Her special job was to teach swimming, especially concentrating on children with rickets or other ailments affecting mobility. When it rained, or when she wasn't busy at the pool, she invented games to play, taught simple dances, told stories, or played her guitar. The children followed her about like downy ducklings. Her long blond hair was irresistible to these young Mexicans, and she let them brush it or braid it to a chorus of happy giggles. I visited her once, bringing with me a special dinner to give her a break from the staple diet of black beans and rice, and spent the night on the sofa in her tiny trailer while she slept on the floor. I marveled at our child's ability to teach, to communicate, to spread happiness, and to give unreserved love.

৵   ৵   ৵

Antonio, the bedraggled little Indian, who became our house boy just after we arrived in Mexico City, inched his way into our hearts. He continued his schooling until completing sexto grado. Bill and I were proud *padrones* at his graduation. Fortunately, his small stature meant that he didn't tower above his younger classmates as he marched down the aisle in his navy blue suit, his black eyes sparkling with triumph. His accomplishment had not been easy; he could barely read and write when he came to us. Each morning when he brought my breakfast to my room, he would sit cross-legged on the floor by my bed and we would go over his homework. We also talked about many things—courtesy, loyalty, honesty, religion, morals, the future. He was attentive and bright. I remember telling Antonio that someday when he was grown and married how wise he would be to limit his family to two children. (He had been one of eleven.) In later years, he

252

must have remembered what the Señora had said for sure enough, he had two and gave them Anglicized names, Paul and Nancy. Even though life had treated him harshly as a child, he was fiercely proud of his country and loved to read about the great Mexican heroes: Morelos, Hidalgo, Cuauhtémoc, Juárez, Zapata. His pride knew no bounds during the 1968 Olympics when Mexico made such a fine showing as host country.

After his graduation from *sexto grado,* Antonio attended a three-month course in television and small appliance repair, and another in auto mechanics and chauffeuring. He became an excellent and careful driver. Bill and I then felt satisfied that our Mexican surrogate son now had skills which would stand by him all his life.

🙢 🙢 🙢

Upon his return from a business trip to Washington in mid-August of 1971, Bill broke the news that F.A.S. had offered him an assignment to London, but he had doubts as to whether he should accept. He knew how much I loved Quinta Tecolote which we had only bought in February of that year, fully expecting to be in Mexico for two more. As Washington wanted an answer by the end of the week, we had to make a decision. My reaction, however, surprised my husband. It was almost immediate and one of pure elation. Perhaps if he had said Tokyo, New Delhi or even Rome, I would have balked—but London? Fantastic!

And the more he thought about it, the more Bill felt obligated to take on this assignment. His civil service career had given him twenty years of background experience in the foreign service, and a chance to see the world along the way. He also knew that the Court of St. James was the optimum post to cap off his career. The United Kingdom bought millions of dollars of agricultural products annually from the United States, and at that time was about to join the European Economic Community (EEC). This would require important and delicate trade negotiations in order not to lose part or all of that market.

When Bill called Washington, the administrator of FAS said he was glad to hear of our decision because transfer papers to London had already been signed by the Secretary of Agriculture and were now at the White House. We never really had a choice.

Just as we were building up a head of steam over our move to England, Bill and Margy called to inform us that we would become grandparents in early February, about the same time as our transfer. They were living a frugal married life in an apartment near the University of Chicago where Margy was working on a masters degree and Bill on the final stages of his Ph.D., both in anthropology. A few months later, they planned to move to Hamilton, Ontario, where he had accepted a position as an assistant professor at McMaster University.

During the autumn of 1971, Bill yo-yoed between Mexico, Washington and London. We decided to rent rather than sell Quinta Tecolote and found a neighbor to manage the property. Arrangements were made for Armando to take care of the grounds. Upon retirement, somewhere down the road, we hypothesized, our quinta would be a welcome retreat from cold winters at home, wherever that might be.

ふ　ふ　ふ

Bill left Mexico in early January 1972 for briefings in Washington, then on to London where he settled into bachelor living until my arrival in March. I was again left behind with the task of picking up stakes and the sundry decisions that accompany a move between countries. Then on to Chicago for the birth of our first grandchild, Sean Stewart Rodman, on a bleak Chicago afternoon, February 8, 1972. I had a new little boy to love.

· —— Chapter Seventeen —— ·

ENGLAND
January 1972 to July 1980

ST. JAMES, LONDON

OUR FLAT IN LONDON WAS ON THE FIFTH FLOOR
OF AN IMPOSING APARTMENT BUILDING called Arlington
House in the heart of St. James off Piccadilly. Overlooking Green
Park, the view from our windows crossed green lawns to
Buckingham Palace. Theaters, shops and traffic jams were close
by. Though muffled somewhat by the height and concrete of our
building, the screech of sirens sounded continually. In 1972,
England was besotted with political problems, inflation and
strikes. Every so often, apartment living became challenging due
to strike-induced electrical outages—no lights, no heat, no
elevators, defrosting refrigerators. On the outside, theaters and
cinemas closed and the underground shut down. At dusk, the
city became aglow with candlelight. It was cold! But, in true
Spartan style, the Brits just put on another "woolly," They could
grumble aplenty over little setbacks, but in a crisis, they rallied,
and maintained a sense of humor along with the proverbial stiff-
upper-lip—the same stiff-upper-lip that was in part responsible
for winning the second World War.

I was quite overwhelmed when I saw Arlington House for
the first time. A tall doorman in full regalia called me "madam"

and ordered his underlings to scamper for my luggage and lead us to our flat. The rooms, tastefully furnished by the U.S. Government, were large except for a small kitchen containing what I considered an inadequate gas stove which the English called a cooker. Happily for Bill, the American Embassy was within walking distance via Mayfair and Audley Road. Rain was constant. Taxis were reasonable. I had heard of London fog and chill, but was far from prepared for that first winter of crippling strikes and atrocious weather. Few things amaze the English as much as a spell of sunshine. On the first sunny day of spring, droves of Londoners made a dash for the parks to cast themselves prone upon the grass.

I took on the city of London with the zeal of a crusader vowing not to miss any of its wonder and brilliance. But most of all, I grew to love the feel of London—the pulse of its heartbeat.

There is little doubt that I had embarked on a love affair with a city. I had only to walk out of the front door to set my passion ablaze. Disregarding fashion, I ordered hiking boots from L. L. Bean, and roved, by foot, by bus, by underground, until London's network of streets was possessively familiar. I loved the wide avenues, alleyways and arcades, helmeted bobbies—two in stride—flowers, markets, and historical bounty. I dawdled in front of theaters to read the critics' comments, and look at pictures of scenes and cast. I ambled into old churches, art galleries, and museums. The great auction houses excited me and the peaceful parks restored me. I enjoyed the cool elegance of Regent and Bond Streets, and the trendy abandon of the Kings Road. My curiosity was boundless. Sometimes I boarded an underground train to ride to a stop with an compelling name to explore a new area—Cockfosters, Elephant and Castle, Petticoat Lane, Bethnall Green, Blackfriars. I fully agreed with Samuel Johnson's apt remark to his friend James Boswell:

"No sir," he said, "When a man is tired of London, he is tired of life; for there is in London all that life can afford."

When spring came to London, the parks sprang to life awash in golden daffodils, red tulips and white narcissus. Municipal bands in freshly painted bandstands played familiar music, verbose men and women mounted their soapboxes at Hyde Park Corner, and children sailed little boats in ponds where ducks and swans swam to the rim for handouts of bread and crumbs. Along the streets, a cheerful array of bloom added beauty and charm to window boxes, and nannies wheeled their charges in perambulators. After the chill and damp of an English winter, it seemed that the world was created anew in springtime and I enfolded myself in the magic of it.

On weekends, Bill and I roamed the countryside, stopping at wayside inns or guest houses for the night. We enjoyed mingling with the locals in pubs, and poking into antique shops. We visited National Trust properties, and ate in small cafes and tearooms in little villages, continually being awed by the antiquity of houses and buildings canted and creaky with age. We journeyed by car, bus, train, and along footpaths through that green and pleasant land, marveling that so many miles of it were still unspoiled and unpopulated. Trees had a magic quality all their own. In winter, without foliage, they were etched and round, like an old woodcut engraving, and in summer they became plump and green like a little child's crayon drawing. We went north, south, east and west, sometimes along narrow sunken roads of Roman origin, but always off-the-beaten-track.

Few people on earth rival the British in love of pageantry or in skill in staging it. Fanfare and color distinguished every parade and ceremony. Being very close to the Mall, which led from Buckingham Palace to Whitehall, Bill and I could walk down St. James Street to watch the Queen leading her household cavalry during the annual Trooping of the Colors, or watch the panorama of a royal coach, drawn by six white horses, proceeding slowly down the Mall on such festive occasions as the wedding of Princess Anne to Captain Mark Phillips in 1973.

In our area of the city there were no markets, butcheries or fruit and vegetable stands. In fact, Fortnum and Mason, with its famous clock and exotic foods, was my neighborhood grocery store—just fine if you wanted to buy pâté-de-foie-gras or Russian caviar, but hopeless when it came to catsup and baked beans. I found out in time that such ignoble items were actually available, but it took a lot of nerve to ask one of the swallow-tailed attendants to descend to the basement to retrieve them.

Many people envision men's clubs in London as austere places where pompous old men, served by stodgy old waiters, languish in overstuffed brown leather armchairs, sip brandy and immerse themselves in the *London Times*. Bill couldn't quite picture himself in that role, but for diplomatic reasons he accepted membership in the distinguished Farmers' Club in southwest London overlooking the Thames, thus disproving the saying that to become a member, a gentleman must own a hundred acres of downtown London or have been "on the land" since 400 A.D.

In one respect, the Farmers' Club had broken with tradition— in one carefully screened off section of the dining room, women were allowed on certain nights of the week. Bill introduced me to his new club one evening, but contrary to a dark and inviolate atmosphere, I found it cheerfully decorated, flowers on the tables, delicious food.

The Naval and Military Club on Piccadilly, just around the corner from Arlington House, was referred to as the In and Out Club because, quite logically, on its gateposts in large letters were the words "IN" and "OUT." During a spate of bombings by the Irish Republican Army (IRA) in 1974, a bomb, thrown through a window of the club, brought down the ceiling, damaged some valuable pictures, and, in the words of a member, "wrecked some bloody good port." Another club member recalled how, "The wretched thing came crashing through the glass and landed at the feet of one of our best generals. He looked at the thing— it was some sort of bottle—and said, 'Oh ——it!' He seized his sherry and wandered down towards my end of the bar. He was only a few feet away when the damn thing went off. It really made a mess. The general looked pretty dazed for a moment. Then he sat down and returned to sipping his sherry."

An old world air of formality still hung about the west end of London. Many businessmen, with the *London Times* tucked under one arm, wore bowler hats and carried black umbrellas; ladies wore fashionable English hats and met for tea at the Ritz. The English were too polite to honk car horns, and bills were tendered in the most delicate manner. For example, we received a doctor's bill worded as follows:

Dr. Jerome Sturridge
presents his compliments
to Mr. W. L. Rodman
and begs to say the amount
due to him for Professional
services rendered is
£5.00

ॐ　ॐ　ॐ

I was surprised when the Women's Liberation Movement became such a hot issue in the United States. To me it was a paradox. Although I am a firm believer in women's rights if it means equal opportunity and equal pay for doing the same job as a man, I also believe that the biological differences go beyond sex. We are not as strong; our bodies are soft; our breasts aren't muscled; we cannot run as fast or jump as high; most of us can neither lift heavy weights nor withstand the rigors of warfare. We are not physically constituted to be stevedores or construction workers. We are constituted, thank the Lord, to be wives and mothers. Supporting our men as help-mates and gracious hostesses overseas was a very important role, and our actions and conduct as representatives of our country were as much on view as our husband's. A great deal of diplomatic representation was expected, and the necessary hostessing was intense. If a visiting official was accompanied by his wife, we were at the airport with our husbands, often at an ungodly early hour, to welcome them to London, and act as guides on sightseeing or shopping excursions. In the evening, we hosted dinners and receptions in their honor. Sometimes, there were hotel arrangements to be sorted out: one bed instead of two, two beds instead of one. Fingernail polish might need repair, transport arranged, or occasionally, a doctor summoned. Not entirely jokingly, we diplomatic wives avowed that we were unpaid civil servants and that the U.S. Government was indeed fortunate to get two for the price of one.

It therefore came as a shock to many hard-working foreign service wives in 1972 when, with President Richard Nixon's approval, the Secretary of State decreed that attendance was no longer required at Embassy Wives' Club meetings, nor would wives be included in an officer's "efficiency report," and representational entertaining was up to the individuals concerned. In other words, wives of officers were liberated from responsibility and could conduct their lives however they pleased, including taking on a job. Very few of us agreed entirely with the new policy and continued to consider ourselves a team with our husbands. Besides, I enjoyed being called "madam" and the accompanying manifestations of British gallantry, so diametric to women's lib.

✲   ✲   ✲

Soon after my arrival, Bill and I were invited to a black-tie dinner at the Savoy Hotel in honor of Peter and Sally Nixon, dear friends from our Australia days when he was a back-bencher in parliament, but now elevated to Minister of Transport and

Shipping. Our hosts were Edmund Vestey, President of the Blue Star Shipping Line, and his wife, Anne. Aussies never forget a friend and when the Nixons were asked if there was anyone special they would like to include on the guest list, Peter said, "Yes—the Rodmans." This would be my introduction to the British gentry at its most preeminent, and despite my training as a diplomatic wife for twenty-one years, I felt somewhat restive.

The private dining room at the Savoy was set with sparkling silver and china under glistening chandeliers for twenty-four guests. Behind every other velvet and gilt chair stood a waiter in livery, tall and silent with shoulders thrust back. During a short period of small-talk before being seated, Bill asked a portly gentleman about his interests:

"Oh," said he, "I'm into boats."

"Ah, said Bill, "You enjoy sailing?"

"Yes," he answered, "I bought the Q E II yesterday."

Another snippet of conversation with a second gentleman went something like this after the same query:

"I like horses," said he.

This was a subject Bill could warm to and he asked, "Ah, do you raise horses?"

"Yes," came the answer, "And I have two running in the Grand National next weekend."

And so went the evening. I was on my best behavior.

As we were saying good night to our hosts, Anne Vestey said we must come to visit them in the country some weekend. That, I thought, would be the end of that, but a few months later, she called to invite us to spend the weekend of the Puppy-Hound Judging Contest at their country home, "The Waltons." I declined politely because that was a weekend when Channing would be with us for a visit and Joni would be home for the summer. But Anne would not be put off and invited the girls as well. Later I would be somewhat embarrassed when I thought of my response. I accepted but, thinking that four members of the Rodman family would be an overload, I suggested the girls stay at a country inn or guest house.

"Oh no," she exclaimed, "Lots of room. Do come along, and by the by, we've invited some guests for dinner and the dress will be informal."

When we arrived at Ashdon in Suffolk, Bill stopped the car along the side of the road to ask a man directions to "The Waltons."

"See this wall on your left, guv'ner?" he said. "Just follow it along for 'bout a mile 'til you come to the gates."

"Uh, oh," Channing commented, "This is no simple country home!" and we continued on in our dirty mustard-colored Plymouth. No sooner had we parked in the forecourt of the brick mansion than a butler came running out to assist with the bags. His face bore a "Who are these country bumpkins?" look. Anne met us in the living room where we had tea before going to our rooms to dress. She explained again that company would be arriving for dinner at 7:30 and the dress would be informal. That was the night I learned that "informal" meant black tie and, "formal" meant white tie! Obviously we were ill prepared.

The Vestey house, built by Edmund as a gift to his bride some twenty years before, was baronial. The rooms were furnished with fine Georgian furniture and decorated with priceless objects d'art and paintings. Among the treasures was a dinner service which had belonged to Queen Victoria, and paintings by such notables as Constable, Corot, Holbein, and Turner. On a lesser scale, we enjoyed mahogany toilet seats, heated towel racks, linen bed sheets, and flower arrangements in our rooms. Our suitcases were unpacked by the chambermaid, beds were turned down at night, and a manservant named Adrian brought us early morning tea and "digestive" biscuits.

The following day was the Puppy-Hound Judging. My wardrobe fared better on this occasion as I knew to bring a hat and white gloves, the accepted dress for ladies at country functions. For their first year, foxhounds, I learned, were individually parcelled out in foster homes where they were "walked." This meant that they were exercised, fed, and taught manners. After that, they were brought to the show grounds and judged on confirmation and obedience. The English weather didn't let us down. It poured.

That evening while we were enjoying before-dinner drinks in the living room, a British nanny paraded two darling little pajama-clad boys in to say good night to their parents. James was eight and Robin, five. Edmund explained that James would be going off to boarding school in September in preparation for Eton when he was thirteen. My American motherly mentality had difficulty absorbing the fact that the norm among the British gentry was to wean little sons from the nest at such a tender age.

ॐ   ॐ   ॐ

In spite of our few wrong steps and some friendly disagreement on raising children, Anne and Edmund became cherished friends.

At another time, Anne and Edmund, devotees of fox hunting, invited us to their hunting lodge in Braunston, Rutland, to observe the renowned Cottesmore Hunt, frequented by royalty. The lodge was comprised of two adjoining houses, one for the family and the other for assorted grooms, chauffeurs and caretakers. Well-appointed stables were close by. The weather did everything that English weather is capable of doing in rapid succession—cold, rain, sleet, snow, fog, and sun. Undaunted, the hunt proceeded on schedule with a field of 120 horses and riders. These included earls and postmen, baronets and barbers, all looking very smart in the proper gear. What is it about "pink" coats, white breeches, polished boots, and hunting derbies that make the plainest of mortals look dashing?

Bill and I followed the hunt in a car with two women: Sheila, now crippled with polio, but a keen fox hunter before her illness, and Penelope, an octogenarian who had given up hunting the year before, "only because her horse had gone lame." When Shiela stopped the car to give us a panoramic view, Penelope would leap out of the car before you could say "horse," jump the ditch, and climb the fence in order to get a better view. I couldn't believe her eyesight! At a distance of three fields, she could recognize every rider, and pointed out such remarkable details as the dent in Rodney's crash helmet.

෴   ෴   ෴

Joni danced relentlessly all summer. Except for two weeks at the Russian Cecchetti School of Ballet in Shropshire, she took the underground to Covent Garden each evening after supper to attend classes at the Dance Center on Floral Street, returning home about 9:30. We did not worry about her going off alone; London seemed a safe city in 1972. One evening, looking very beautiful in a long evening dress with her hair done in a swirl atop her head, she went off on a date with one of Bill's young assistants to see Rudolph Nureyev and Margot Fonteyn in *Romeo and Juliet* at the Royal Opera House. After the performance, the ovation lasted for twenty minutes and flowers showered the stage—a tremendous thrill for a budding dancer.

In dance, Joni felt a sensitivity beyond her years. Dance was her focus, her form of self-expression. She was more certain than ever the path her future would take.

Before returning to St. Catherine's for her senior year, Joni auditioned and was accepted at the prestigious London School of Contemporary Dance for the fall of 1973. She was also looking into other colleges and universities both in England and the States where she could pursue a fine-arts degree in modern dance. One possibility was the United States International University (USIU) which had a campus in Sussex some thirty miles from London. Bill and I could think of nothing better than to have Joni near us again.

ॐ   ॐ   ॐ

Joni, Bill and I had an amusing time getting dolled up for the Queen's Garden Party in mid-July. Bill looked debonair in his rented morning suit and gray topper, while Joni and I looked somewhat comical in frilly hats.

This, however, was a minor event compared to our next date at Buckingham Palace in the autumn of 1972. Bill and I, along with four other couples from the American Embassy, were presented to Her Majesty and other members of the royal family at an evening diplomatic reception. Just how we were chosen for this honor, I'll never know, but we wives flattered the four men by saying it was done by height (each was over six feet), and good looks. Hollywood couldn't have matched that evening, simply because it takes at least 900 years of history to produce the patina of such an occasion.

Bill and Joni getting ready for the Queen's Garden Party

The evening started out with an elegant dinner given by Ambassador and Mrs. Walter Annenberg at the embassy residence. We were then chauffeured to the palace, where we entered the Grand Entrance and mounted the Grand Staircase under the Grand Dome. Passing through a series of splendid rooms, we arrived at the massive Picture Gallery where we were lined up in prearranged pecking order. Around the room were representatives of other countries in their own little groups, each diplomat dressed in his or her own native finery. The American men wore white tie and tails with decorations, and ladies their most stylish evening gown.

When the queen appeared on the stair landing, there was a hushed silence. "Her Majesty, the Queen," a stentorian voice called out. She was dressed in heavy white satin with a blue sash draped across her bodice, a diamond necklace of three strands and a bejeweled tiara. She was undeniably royal and surprisingly tiny in stature. Elizabeth was followed by Prince Philip, the Duke of Edinburgh, walking two paces behind, straight and handsome, in a naval admiral's uniform adorned with decorations and medals. The third in line was the Queen Mother, the beloved "Queen Mum" of formidable charm, in a blue gown and a small tiara on her head. She was followed by assorted royals including Prince Charles, Princess Ann, and the stunning Princess Alexandra with her husband, Angus Ogilvy—all in all, a pretty good tally of royalty for one night.

The regal procession moved slowly encircling the room and each royal had a word or two to say to each and every diplomat after first being introduced by his or her ambassador. Gentlemen bowed slightly; ladies, a full well-practiced curtsy. Queen Elizabeth asked Bill if this was his first time in England to which he briefly answered that he had spent nine months in Somerset before the invasion in World War II. "Where in Somerset?" she asked, and he replied, "In Wincanton, your Majesty." She smiled broadly and moved on. Prince Philip, emanating charm, walked with his hands clutched behind his back. I told him I had last seen him in 1968 running up the steps at the Olympic Village in Mexico City, to which he responded with a chuckle, "Shhhh! I'm not supposed to run up steps in public." The Queen Mother was almost jolly. She asked one of our fellow presentees if he still "made those wicked martinis?" She was adorable.

After the diplomatic introductions, Bill and I feasted on canapes and drank champagne in the State Dining Room, wandered through the great halls and reception rooms admiring centuries' old treasures, danced to music from *My Fair Lady,* and resisted a temptation to sit on a pair of chairs which looked like thrones in the Throne Room. "All that glitters really is gold," turned over in my mind in this fairy tale setting, and me with my Prince Charming at my side!

A postscript to this event happened a few days later. While wandering the streets of London, I stopped for a pub lunch. As there were more customers than space at tables, strangers sat together. I was still so blown up over my night at Buckingham Palace, that I blurted out the story to the gentleman opposite me, a Britisher in the navy blue uniform of a bank guard. He listened patiently while consuming his sausage and mashed potatoes. At the end of my tale, he looked up and said quietly, "I've been to Buckingham Palace too. Every year the queen gives a party for the palace staff. My best friend, one of the queen's butlers, is permitted to invite two outsiders to the party—my wife and I have been going for the past five years."

He was not trying to prick my balloon, but I learned a lesson in humility—I wasn't the only commoner who had danced at Buckingham Palace!

ઝ   ઝ   ઝ

The English are courteous, but reserved, often taking a good bit of time before committing themselves to friendship. It was therefore of the utmost delight to make my first close friend at the basement lunch counter in Simpsons of Piccadilly, a renowned clothing store. I was sitting at the counter next to a proper looking English lady with whom I exchanged a few pleasantries. She had come to London by train from her home in Leiscestershire for a day of shopping. As we were finishing lunch, I noticed she was rummaging through her hand bag with increasing agitation, obviously searching for her billfold. Unintentionally, her arm swept the dishes on the counter sending both hers and mine flying. With the crisis at hand, I tried to calm her down with something like, "It's OK—happens all the time. Please let me pay for your lunch. It would be my pleasure." This I did, with great reluctance and embarrassment on her part. A few days later, a note arrived:

I am so thankful that I was unBritish enough to talk to you at the Snack Bar at Simpsons today—otherwise I might now be looking out from behind bars! . . . Please will you come and have lunch with me next time I am in London and I will try not to throw the crockery about! Thank you again for your kindness.

Yours very sincerely,

Biddy Bennion

֍   ֍   ֍

On another occasion, it was my turn to lose my wallet. In a shop called The Needlewoman on Regent Street, I was attempting to match some yarn for a needlepoint pillow. As the shades of yarn were in cubbyholes on the wall, I placed my pocketbook on the floor for a few seconds while I reached up with my sample to match the color. When I looked down, I was horrified to find my pocketbook open, and my wallet gone.

At a police station nearby, I registered a complaint, but the policeman in charge shook his head. "Forget your wallet, madam—whoever took it is miles from 'ere by now. You can 'ave one phone call." I rang Bill, but, being late afternoon, he had already left the office.

"Could you lend me some money to get home on the underground?" I asked. I was miles from home.

"Sorry, madam, against policy."

Coming into the police station I had noticed a scruffy looking teenager with long hair sitting on a bench. A hippie in trouble, I decided. Feeling miserable, I sat down beside him. After introducing himself, he told me he was Canadian and was there because he had lost his luggage, but he still had his wallet and would I please accept a one-pound note? When I answered that I only needed fifteen pence for my tube fare, he replied that I just might need some extra along the way. And when I asked him for his address, he said, "No. If I give you my address you will return the money and that will ruin the whole thing."

✺   ✺   ✺

One morning, on my way to a hair appointment, I found myself walking behind a man whom I thought I recognized as the actor, Alec Guinness. I followed him down Jermyn Street and into a little side street where the salon was located. Sure enough, he went up the six or seven steps, entered, and stopped at the reception desk to give his name.

"Alec Guinness," he said politely. "I have an appointment at ten o'clock."

Although London is full of surprises, I never dreamed that one day I would follow the famous actor into a beauty parlor. He was Sir Alec by then but his demeanor was that of an ordinary citizen. I remember he had on a gray felt hat rather than the more dashing bowler so ubiquitous in London's West End. The English don't glorify their superstars as we too often do in the United States. They can lead quite normal lives and are not mobbed or hounded for autographs.

ॐ　　ॐ　　ॐ

Inflation was rapidly climbing in England in the seventies. During our eight and a half years in London, we would watch prices double and triple. In the early seventies, however, we couldn't believe our good fortune to find theater tickets, country lodging, and public transport still very reasonable. We took advantage of all three. Theaters in the Piccadilly area and on Haymarket Street were within easy walking distance of Arlington House, and we indulged our theatrical appetites with a musical or a play at least once a week. On my "walkabouts," I often dipped into some enticing matinee on the spur of the moment. We saw many of the English greats— John Gielgud, Lawrence Olivier, Alec Guinness, Peggy Ashcroft, Maggie Smith, Deborah Kerr, and many superstars of the American stage and screen—James Stewart, Henry Fonda, Ingrid Bergman, Ginger Rogers, Angela Lansbury, Yul Brynner, and many more making for a virtual Thespian feast. Inside the historic theaters I found another world of velvet-draped boxes, palatial gilt, and ghosts of dramas past. During intermission at matinees, tea and biscuits could be ordered, or I could chip away at a small carton of ice cream with a tiny wooden spoon.

One evening before a play, Bill and I paused to buy a program and chat for a moment with Winnie, a striking woman in her seventies who might just have walked out of an Edwardian novel. I suspect she was once an actress but now sold programs at the Duke of York's Theater in London's West End. We were both so struck by her beauty and grace that, at intermission, we found her again, not so busy this time, and exchanged a few more words. Then, out of the blue, she asked for our address.

A day or two later, two tickets to the play arrived in the mail with a note, "Thought you might like to give these to a friend . . . Winnie" As I didn't know how to contact Winnie to thank her, I called the box office at the theater and they gave me her phone number. After thanking her, I asked if she would join me for tea. "Maybe someday," she answered. She would not give me her address or surname. At a later date, I again asked Winnie for tea, but she answered with the same "maybe someday," and two more tickets arrived in the post to the Sadler Wells Theater. So, Winnie was not limited to the Duke of York's productions. I would love to be able to enlarge on this story, but Winnie had made it clear that she wanted to keep her secrets hidden.

సౌ   సౌ   సౌ

Of all of our assignments abroad, England was far and away the most formal and demanding socially. Unlike other posts, some of the evening functions were for men only. These could be ultra-formal, and Bill would don his white tie and tails with war decorations dripping from his chest. At first, he put his medals in his pocket, but as the other men wore them, he decided to conform. Other engagements, still formal, were numerous and exquisitely elegant: the Lord Taverners ball at Grosvenor House, the Fruit Importers annual dinner at the Savoy, Australia Day dinner at the Dorchester, the Worshipful Company of Tobacco Pipe Makers dinner at Mansion House—and the list goes on.

Bill and I were often guests-of-honor. At a Fruit Importers dinner at the Savoy, British pomp was at its prime. Those placed at the head table were lined up outside of the banquet hall while other guests were seated. Then the booming voice of the red-frocked toastmaster called out, "Ladies and gentlemen, please be upstanding for the chairman and his honored guests." At this point the orchestra played a rousing march and as many as 500 seated guests stood up and clapped in the "luminaries." As we paraded through the splendid banquet hall with its ceiling of painted clouds and sky, cobalt blue walls, and beautiful chandeliers, I was enjoying a private chuckle. After being seated and the requisite toast to the queen, I had to stifle another giggle when the gentleman on my right introduced himself as Mr. Eroticos, a Greek Cypriot, and proudly told me that his name meant "student of love." After dinner, the chairman made his long and boring financial statement, then introduced Bill, who had a talent for lightening up the atmosphere with a short talk interspersed with humorous remarks.

When we gave dinner parties at home, we pulled out all the stops—gold-rimmed lay plates, finger bowls, two kinds of wine. After dinner, brandy and cigars were offered to the men while the ladies repaired to another room for coffee and cordials. Every course was beautifully served by a whiz of an Argentine cook and her helper. It was a treat to observe her artistry while she prepared and cooked her carefully selected foods. Her timing was flawless. Now, in later years, I look back on the whirl of London's social life with awe. I'm glad I experienced it, but, as I grow older, I'm more than content to stay at home and relax with Bill in comfortable clothes on a cold winter's evening.

·——   Chapter Eighteen   ——·

JONI

JONI RETURNED FROM VIRGINIA FOR CHRISTMAS OF 1972, her senior year at school, so worn out from exams and an exhausting schedule of rehearsals and dance performances, that she was a candidate for any virus that happened to be in the air. The result was a severe case of the flu. Bill and I were glad she was home where we could pamper her with TLC, but sorry that she would miss out on the joys of Christmas in London. We had planned a trip to the west country after Christmas, and a few days at the Yarcombe Inn in Somerset, where we would celebrate Joni's eighteenth birthday on New Year's Eve. As she seemed to feel better by December 28, the doctor said she could travel, so we bundled her into the back seat of our car and off we went.

We were glad to get away. With the Christmas bombing of Hanoi and Haiphong in Vietnam that year, Nixon had brought the wrath of the world down upon the United States with the result that American diplomats in London were receiving protest telephone calls. During the day, the callers were intelligent people who gave their names and wished to express their concern, but at night, between 2 and 5 A.M., there were nuisance calls gauged for every half hour, designed to keep us awake and in a state of turmoil. Usually the caller would hang up as soon as we answered the phone. It was not the harassment that bothered us as much as the big question, "Why?" Why were we bombing Hanoi again with the obvious result of civilian casualties at a time when the media told us that a cease-fire was being negotiated? Why was Nixon remaining silent? What had really happened at the Paris peace talks? So there we were, especially Bill, on the receiving end of a sincere protest with which we sympathized. This was one of the occasions during our diplomatic career when we were in the difficult position of having to support our president while disagreeing with U.S. policy. Later we would have to contend with the deplorable situation of Watergate.

On January 23, 1973, the Vietnam War, that tragic mistake that had plagued four presidents, finally came to an end. The conflict had polarized the country more deeply than any other event since the Civil War and had cost 50,000 American lives. Perhaps its most grievous toll was a profound wound to the American spirit that would live on for decades. And as an irony of history, any celebration of the precarious peace agreement was crushed by the exhaustion of twelve years of a no-win war.

Along with anxiety over Vietnam, the closing months of 1972 had been laden with disaster: soaring inflation and ongoing strikes throughout the United Kingdom; the sickening massacre of the Israeli athletes in Munich during the Olympics; the spate of letter and package bombs in London in which Bill's colleague, the Israeli agricultural attache, had been killed. Now, every piece of mail which came to the embassy had to be monitored and x-rayed. Delivery often took weeks. Our trip to the peaceful countryside of Somerset and Devon was indeed an escape, if only momentarily, from a troubled world.

Joni, however, continued to feel poorly, and we decided to postpone her return to school for a few days. Still feeling shaky, but with the okay of the embassy doctor, Joni departed for school from Heathrow Airport on January 6, 1973. Little did we know that we were saying good-bye for the last time.

ᴓ   ᴓ   ᴓ

Eighteen is such a remarkable age for a girl, suspended between uncertain youth and the full bloom of womanhood. It is like watching the bud of a flower unfurl, knowing that its full perfection is yet to come.

During the winter of their senior year at St. Catherine's School, the students, with the approval of an advisor, were given a three-week minimester away from campus to pursue a special interest. Some became teaching assistants, some medical aides, some studied art and drama, and others concentrated on their own special field. Joni's field, of course, was dancing. She had been invited to spend the three weeks at United States International University in San Diego, California, and audition for the dance program for admission the following September. Arrangements were made by Hugh Terrell, Director of Housing, for Joni to live in one of the dormitory suites with two other students.

After her stay there, she would still have ten days of spring vacation. Her plan was to stop at several other universities for interviews on her way east; then to Hamilton, Ontario, for a brief visit with Margy, Bill, and her little godson, Sean; finally, a stop in Boston with Channing and Carl, and an audition at the Boston Conservatory of Drama, Dance and Music. From her letters and one or two phone calls, Joni was thrilled with this schedule. Bill and I hoped she had gained back some weight as she was very thin, only 106 pounds when she left London, but she had given us no reason to be concerned about her health, nor had the school.

With Britain's entry into the European Economic Community (EEC) coinciding with the end of the Vietnam War, Bill's job of selling U.S. goods to English markets became more competitive.

Now nine countries vied for sales among the partners. One of the avenues to introducing American products to the English trade was by displaying and promoting them at food shows in large hotels in major cities. Both Bill and I were attending such a show in Bristol, England, when we received a call from the officer on duty at the American Embassy in London.

࿓   ࿓   ࿓

Joni died on March 7, 1973, in San Diego, California. She had returned to her suite at United States International University after a dinner date with a young man from Virginia named Bill Trotter. According to Karen, a blind girl, one of her two suitemates, the date had been a great success. Merri, her other suitemate, who happened to be away on an "overnight," had planned to meet Joni for breakfast in the dining hall at 8 A.M. When Joni didn't show up, Merri went back to the suite and found her dead. Attempts at resuscitation failed.

࿓   ࿓   ࿓

There is no more shattering experience than to live through the death of a beloved child. I was overwhelmed by longing, crushed by defeat—my masterpiece wiped out in a single stroke of destiny. I felt cast into what seemed a bottomless pit, and when I tried desperately to crawl up and out, I slipped back into throbbing helplessness. If I did manage to free myself for a little space of time, someone would say, "Are you all right?" And I would smile and nod and brush myself off. But there was no brushing off. I would never be quite all right again, never quite the same.

To this day, we are completely bewildered as to why Joni died. An extensive autopsy was performed which showed her to be a normally healthy young woman. The coroner's report stated that she died peacefully in her sleep at about 3 A.M. of "undeterminable natural causes." After talking to doctors, our best guess is that the flu virus that she had at Christmas never left her system, and that under the stress of dancing, academics, and the trip to California, it had manifested itself by attacking the myocardium, the muscle surrounding her heart, causing arrythmia and death.

Such sudden deaths as Joni's are known to happen in young people, especially in athletes. A renowned doctor in England, Dr. Tunstall Pedoe, made a study which he called "Sudden Death in Athletes." In many of these cases, he found there was a history of a virus several months before the death. By the time the autopsy was carried out, the heart had returned to normal.

When we received the call, Bill and I had just closed the food show and had gone up to our room at about 9 P.M. to retire. As the caller said he was the duty officer at the American Embassy in London, I handed the phone to my husband. From the conversation I realized there was a death in the family, and when I heard Bill ask, "Which one?" I assumed it was one of our mothers, both in their eighties. As Bill began repeating a number in California to call, I knew it was Joni.

The feeling was one of disbelief together with an anesthetic reaction that left me numb and unfeeling, but strangely able to function. Bill and I were on the west coast of England, about four hours from London and somehow we had to get to San Diego, California. Bill's staff arranged for a car and driver to take us to London, and made reservations on Pan American Airlines for the following morning. Those hours are a blur, but I do remember the drive to the airport in an embassy car and Pan Am's kindness in upgrading our coach fare to first class.

We arrived in Los Angeles some fourteen hours later and transferred to another plane to fly the short distance to San Diego. There we were met by Hugh Terrell and Anne Pearson, an old friend of Channing's who was also working at USIU. I guess we went to our motel and perhaps slept—I don't remember.

The following morning, Bill, Jr. and Channing arrived. Hugh had set up an appointment with a funeral home, and, not knowing our church affiliation, had alerted both a Roman catholic and a protestant priest. We also had to go to the Homicide Division at Police Headquarters to talk to the officer in charge about the police investigation into Joni's death. Whenever there was a death from unknown causes, the police had to be notified. We were told that there was no evidence of drugs, and that death appeared to be from natural causes.

Before this was ascertained, however, the police had summoned Joni's date of the night before, and released him after questioning. Not knowing that Joni had died, this was an unspeakable shock to him. Nevertheless, he came to the motel and we were so impressed by his bearing as well as his distress, that we called his parents, Marnie and Jesse Trotter. Their son, Bill, had called them after his date with Joni to say that he had found a wonderful girl. He had then called back the next day to say that she was dead. At that time, Jesse was dean of the Virginia Episcopal Theological Seminary in Alexandria, Virginia.

Merri Whitten, Joni's roommate also came to see us. In a very short time, she and Joni had become close friends. She told us about the many things they had done together and reiterated the fact that there was no indication that Joni was anything but well and happy. In fact, she handed us an unfinished letter from Joni's desk which began, "IF THERE IS A PARADISE ON EARTH, IT IS THIS! IT IS THIS!! IT IS THIS!" the caption on a hunting print which Joni loved in our front hallway.

The appointment at the funeral home that Hugh had arranged for us, created in retrospect, a kind of dark comedy. Like a bad movie, we were greeted by wringing hands and ushered into an office where a black-suited gentleman sat behind a large desk.

Organ music played softly in the background. After seating the five of us (Hugh was with us) in front of him, he handed out a brochure describing what was included in the various expensive package deals they could offer. Each one included flowers, a singer at the church service, and several attendants. When we asked what the attendants were for, he responded that they would be there to catch anyone who happened to faint during the ceremony. It turned out that the singer was the owner's wife.

"Whoa! Wait a minute!" said Bill. "There will only be the family and a few others at the service, and the casket is to go directly to the cemetery. Please step out of the room as we would like a moment of privacy."

After the man left the office, with one accord, Bill, Bill, Jr. and Hugh stood up shaking their heads, and Channing and I followed them out of the building, passing by the befuddled funeral director still wringing his hands.

This was a Friday and here we were in a strange city without any arrangements for burying our daughter. Hugh suggested we look in the yellow pages of the telephone book for a funeral home, so we stopped at a public phone booth, called a number and drove to the address given, a private home in a middle-class neighborhood. The gentleman there was both kind and businesslike, and arrangements were made to our satisfaction for Monday morning. As we had no home base, the simple casket was to be taken to El Camino Memorial Park Cemetery where Hugh had made arrangements for burial after a service of holy communion at a small Lutheran church.

The weekend dragged on forever, but Bill, Bill, Jr., Channing and I shared a feeling of family harmony and great love in an unknown motel in that unknown place.

Bill, Jr. returned to Ontario from California while Bill, Channing and I flew to Richmond, Virginia, where a memorial service in the St. Catherine's School chapel was attended by hundreds of stunned young people. Bill flew back to London, and Channing stayed on with me for a few days while I visited my mother in Charlottesville. I then spent a week with my dear friend, Mary Cam, who had returned home from Florida to be with me. She had lost a son in Vietnam. There is a silent language between two people who have each lost a child. She knew that I needed her.

Before returning to London, I stopped briefly with the Trotters in Alexandria. They too had lost a child. I was desperately searching for answers and I hoped that Jesse, being a priest, could somehow help me.

ॐ ॐ ॐ

On my flight back to London, I began a journal which I called *A Mother's Thoughts*.

> *I am writing in Joni's notebook in which are her notes taken in class on the book* Don Quixote, *choreography notations for the middle school performance of* Annie Get Your Gun, *an unfinished letter, and a few original poems. Joni is dead at eighteen years, two months and seven days, a senior in high school, the youngest of our three children.*
>
> *I cannot accept it. It is not a normal sorrow. It is like a running sore inside my body. A child should not die before the parent. Have I enough courage for a long uphill climb back to sanity?*

The British rally round in a national crisis, but seem to have difficulty dealing with personal tragedy. During the day when Bill was at the office, our apartment was a very lonely place. Our few friends and neighbors in London did not call either by phone or in person. One told me several months after Joni's death that she respected my privacy at such a time and was waiting for me to call her.

I find it hard to talk of the spirit, an elusive word that must have a great deal to do with the heart. When the heart is heavy, can the spirit lighten the load? After the death of a child, can a parent return to a sense of purpose in life? It is obvious that life, so tenuous, does go on. Reason dictates that laughter, music and beauty are still precious and to be enjoyed, but my senses do not take them in.

I believe I might have become unhinged had it not been for Audrey, an American acquaintance whom I had met only once. Six months before she had lost her son in a drowning accident. As soon as she heard I had returned from the States, she was at my door. Except on weekends when Bill was home, she came every day for several weeks, each time bringing something for our lunch. The bond between us was very strong as we cried together and talked endlessly about our beloved children. She also wrote a letter which stabbed at my heart.

It's no good asking 'Why?' It just seems to keep happening and all we can do is endure. They are safe now, our lovely children, home safe. Whatever meaning this life has, it is a consolation to think they have for some little space grown beyond us, gone on ahead as children will, and that in time we will catch them up. It is only time.

For what comfort it may be, we are six months ahead of you now and my days have become liveable . . . God knows what He is doing. Believe this now of all times, believe it fiercely. It is true. We don't understand; we cannot read the future; we are too small to reason with fate, but if we are to find any grace or meaning in life, it lies in that belief.

Letters arrived from all over the world. So many were stunned. So many cared. For most of Joni's young friends, it was a first jolt with death.

> *Oh God how it hurts! Like an amputation without an anesthetic! Each morning I awake with a fleeting hope that Joni's death was only a dream, but reality quickly creeps into my consciousness, and I am again consumed by emptiness. We still do not know the cause of Joni's death which adds bewilderment to grief. Perhaps we never will. The doctors are baffled. She had led an active, normal, happy day, and, after chatting with her suite-mate, went to bed about midnight and died sometime during the night. The bedclothes were not even rumpled. She did not suffer. She simply did not awaken.*

A naturally emotional and sensitive man, Bill became very impassive. He was, I believe, trying to suppress his feelings by carrying on "business-as-usual," and spending long hours at the office. Or perhaps he felt he couldn't let down while I was so snowed by great waves of despair. Our grief was taking different directions, his submerged, mine spilling over. We could not share our sorrow.

I continued to struggle with a thousand questions, searching, asking, almost pleading for answers. I agonized that I could not reach God. One night, in desperation, during the small hours of the morning, I called the Samaritans, a volunteer support group for people in dire need or contemplating suicide. The woman who answered talked to me with calm understanding. She suggested I come to see a man named John the following morning at his office in the ancient catacombs of old St. Stephen's Church on the bank of the Thames. I agreed.

John never mentioned that he was an Anglican priest until I was leaving that Tuesday morning. When I commented on this fact, he explained that people from many different countries and religious persuasions came to the Samaritans for help, and that some could be turned off if they found themselves facing a priest. He therefore wanted to hear my story first. I returned the following day and continued to pour out my soul to this soft-mannered man with kind eyes. When I complained that I could not seem to pray, he remarked, "But that is just what you have been doing for the last two days in my office. God has been listening."

I still battle with the 'whys' of Joni's unexplainable death. I can see her everywhere. Walking down Piccadilly, she is suddenly running toward me with that Joni gait— free, vibrant, blond hair flowing; our front door opens— I give a start thinking she has come home; she calls me in the middle of the night—but she is not there. Then the emptiness engulfs me and I know that she is gone.

When Joni died she was planning a dance program to be given in the St. Catherine's school auditorium toward the end of May before graduation. In a notebook, she had written down some ideas, notes on choreography, and her choice of music. The dance instructor, Lucy Stockdell, and Joni's friends took this material and developed it into a full memorial production entitled, *Joni, Our Dance is Love.* They used her favorite music and choreographed dances reminiscent of three countries where she had spent a good part of her life—Australia, Mexico and England. As these were being performed, blown-up photographs would be flashed upon a large screen. Dancers from the Richmond Ballet would perform a beautiful dance called "The Unanswered Question."

Joni's roommate, Mary Ball Ellett, wrote me about these plans. At first, I wasn't sure I had the courage to attend, but soon realized I not only had the courage, but that I had to be there, and booked a flight to Richmond. Unfortunately Bill could not get away. Besides, I yearned to see Mary Ball.

Mary Ball and Joni had roomed together for three years. How

do I describe this lovely girl? She had already burrowed deep into my heart, but with Joni's death, I needed her love more than ever. In the yearbook, there is a picture of the two girls; Joni's arm is around her friend and the caption in Joni's writing says, "Name what a friend should be, and she is that." Just after the performance, Mary Ball wrote to Bill in London:

"The program went really well tonight. . . . The theater was packed. . . . A spirit of love radiated to every corner of every heart. . . . The last number was fantastic! Everyone on stage sang and danced to "Spring," a happy song about hope and renewal. We sang it twice. The second time we all went clapping and singing down the aisles. When we reached the foyer a cheer, loud enough to shake the rafters, went up—"Joni! Joni! Joni!"

I was so very proud. Thank goodness I was there. In my journal, I wrote:

> *So much kindness and joy glowed out of people who had been touched by Joni's warmth and sparkle. That which she has left behind can never be lost. Nothing is wasted, nothing is lost, merely transformed and used again.*

ॐ　ॐ　ॐ

Since then, Joni's name has been carried on at St. Catherine's School. "The Joni Rodman Dance Theater," (JRDT), organized through the efforts of Lucy Stockdell, Joni's friend and mentor, stands as a symbol of excellence for other aspiring young dancers. At graduation, a gold charm with the initials JRDT intertwined, is presented to a student "who by exceptional effort and dedication, has contributed most to the enrichment and success of the dance program." A three-and-a-half foot bronze rendering of those same initials, a gift from her family, adorns a wall in the theater where she danced. Underneath the bronze sculpture is an engraved plaque:

JONI RODMAN DANCE THEATER
FOUNDED IN MEMORY OF
JOAN STEWART RODMAN
CLASS OF 1973

Take my hands, and let them move
At the impulse of thy love.
Take my feet, and let them be
Swift and beautiful for thee.

The JRDT is Joni's legacy to other young dancers. It is a comfort and a source of pride to us that a living memorial lives on in her name. At St. Catherines, the word "Joni " means "Dance."

Instead of one person, I am two. Outwardly, I appear normal. Inwardly, I am still torn apart. Little by little, however, I think I am beginning to surface, finding a kind of anodyne in motion and involvement. I do not any longer resent the world around me going on as before. My heart tells me that, although I am still very fragile, the pieces are falling back into place.

✺   ✺   ✺

When we returned to London after our leave in the summer of '73, the full wallop of Joni's death hit Bill. Like any delicate instrument, a heartstring can only be pulled so taut, and Bill finally had to let go. About three o'clock one afternoon, he walked into our flat, tears streaming down his face, and proceeded to bloody his knuckles against the wall. We both went to see John at the Samaritans for help.

Bill's faith in both the now and the hereafter had always been strong and he started to lean heavily on prayer and attended church regularly. On the other hand, going to church still left me in shreds and I didn't attempt it. But, we were again able to communicate, talk about Joni, and comfort each other. A corner had been turned.

Another help in turning that corner was the arrival of our friend Eloise Atkinson in September. She was an artist and sculptor from Richmond, Virginia, who had been commissioned by Joni's senior class to sculpt the figure of a dancer for a small memorial garden outside of the theater. I had seen her only twice, but as sometimes happens, the moment I met her I knew the chemistry between us flowed, and I invited her to come to London to do a pastel portrait of Joni. She combined her keen understanding and joy in living with an infectious sense of humor which brightened our lives and made us smile. She also had a sixth sense as to how to handle a delicate situation. When I walked into the living room early one morning, there on the easel was a pastel portrait of Channing, not of Joni as expected. Joni's portrait was done later. With keen insight, she gave us a pair of living daughters rather than a single image of the one who had died.

Eloise somehow made it a little easier to face the busy autumn season in London, but, as Christmas approached, I wrote:

> *It will soon be Christmastime—carols, decorations, shops, gifts, merriment, good cheer. I wish I could shut it all out, not to wallow in my sorrow, but to keep memories from tormenting me.*
> *Joni should be coming home.*

Channing and Bill, Jr. insisted that we come to Boston for Christmas. Little Sean was twenty-two months old and we longed to see him. I had knit mittens for everyone, a little blue outfit for Sean, and an Irish Aran sweater for Channing.

Joni

A New Year has dawned —1974. I am still struggling with fate, but there are longer periods when I feel quite myself, able to take on the world again. I can laugh. I can even count my blessings. For me, Joni's death divided time. I thought in terms of before and after. Before, life had been a smooth continuum—birth, growing up, school, marriage, children. After, life had shocked me into insane confusion. Now I need to rediscover myself and put this long climb behind me, a kind of reentry into life.

Perhaps Joni's life was not interrupted? Could it be that it was completed?

*Joni's senior picture taken in December 1972
just before her eighteenth birthday.*

287

Chapter Nineteen

REENTRY

MY REENTRY BEGAN BY MY PLUNGING MYSELF INTO ART CLASSES at the Chelsea-Westminster Institute, a flagrant example of a typical British postwar architectural disaster. Similar institutes, heavily subsidized by the government, were dotted all over London, and for the ridiculous cost of $3 a term, a student could take as many courses as desired. My introduction into this unknown world is indelibly printed upon my psyche.

When I walked into a fourth-floor classroom after mounting seventy-two steps, the only sound was a tape recording of bongo drums. On a platform, a entirely nude male model did a slow motion dance, and eight or nine rapt students worked at easels—no apparent teacher. After a couple of hypnotizing minutes, someone said, "Take a break," and I was told which easel to look behind for the teacher. I soon learned that the moving-nude-model routine happened on Friday, called "action" day, when the students were supposed to loosen up, be imaginative, let themselves go.

The class was very unstructured, everybody doing their own thing. At first I was disappointed that there was virtually no instruction. Derek, our teacher, who looked like a benign Father Christmas, believed that instruction only hampered whatever was within. Consequently, during those beginning sessions, I spent a great deal of time standing in front of my easel wondering what was within, and how to put it on canvas?

It was quite beyond me to perceive that the soul within felt that tubes of glue, bits of trash, aerosol spray, chewing gum wrappers, and paper clips could make a painting, but that was Derek's style. One day, the students challenged him to do a straight pastel of the model, and he graciously proved to us that he was a good technician. When not hidden behind his easel, Derek walked around offering helpful criticism, but most of what I learned was gleaned from watching others.

I had not painted or drawn for several years, and it felt good to put crayon to paper again. The class was comprised of a heterogeneous group ranging from dukes to chimney sweeps, and nobody cared whether you were a rank beginner or Rembrandt himself. An unwritten rule was no talking except during the breaks for government issued tea and biscuits. The students mingled between the morning and afternoon sessions over brown-bag lunches. For me, the camaraderie between students was not only welcoming but healing. We joked and laughed as we shared our histories and critiqued each other's work.

ঙ্গ   ঙ্গ   ঙ্গ

In early 1974, the "Land of Hope and Glory" was again hurting badly due to soaring prices, fuel shortages and crippling strikes. Lights were dimmed throughout London, giving an eerie glow to nights in the foggy city. The coal miners, however, achieved their purpose and brought the country to its knees. Bitter and relentless political infighting resulted until a sudden call for a general election knocked out the conservative government under

Edward Heath and returned to power a labor government headed by Harold Wilson. In the meantime, after months of agonizing drama in the United States, the Watergate scandal had finally up-ended Richard Nixon, forcing him to resign as president, and Vice President Gerald Ford had taken the oath of office.

In August of 1974, I wrote: "It is unthinkable that a man, who has been President of the United States for five and a half years, should be accused, convicted, and possibly imprisoned for offenses committed while in office. It is even more alarming to think that any man is so special that he is above the law, and that in the end, an agreement can be made to protect him from answering for his leadership in the most disgraceful political scandal in American history.

To even consider immunity from legal action for Richard Nixon shows the forgiving nature of the American people. I admit that I am thinking that way, but it must be wrong. Justice cannot be bent by the winds of the moment."

The mess in both countries posed an interesting political comparison.

☙   ☙   ☙

During the spring, I took a train to Blackpool, an ugly, overcrowded, honky-tonk resort on the Irish Sea to meet Bill, who was involved in a trade show. There we rented a little English Hillman and drove on to Scotland for a week of touring in that jagged and infinitely beautiful land. While London froze over Easter that year, Scotland had a rare case of warm, clear weather.

In the small village of Kirkkudbright (Kirk-coo-bri), a quaint fishing village in Dumfrieshire, Bill and I went down to the docks where an old fisherman invited us aboard his boat. Suddenly and without warning, we were edging away from the dock on our way out into the harbor. When I registered my surprise to Bill, he leaned over and whispered, "Perfect kidnap attempt." In actual fact, it was the Scotsman's way of being friendly. He was giving us a little tour of the harbor, but not about to waste words by explaining his action.

For the first time, we gave rides to backpackers—buoyant, young people from assorted countries. They assembled on the steps of country hotels. Many were wee girls with huge strapped burdens beside them waiting for a friendly tourist, and it seemed the only humane thing to do in that rugged, mountainous terrain. We loved Edinburgh where we walked the royal mile down Princes Street to Edinburgh Castle, sitting high on its volcanic pedestal overlooking the city.

৵   ৵   ৵

I looked forward to my daily walk through St. James Park to the art studio, and found satisfaction and excitement in my efforts at the easel. I grew to love the big-windowed room, the painterly smells, and my fellow students. I experimented with oil paints, a medium I had not tried before. According to Derek, I was lacking in a certain art sense which allowed me to see colors which weren't there. He would say, "Look at all those lovely blue and purple tones in her hair," and I'd be dashed if I could see anything but mouse-brown. But, just to please him I would slash on a little blue or purple. Then he would say, "Be free—be a devil," so I'd whack away at something I wouldn't put on the wall of my attic. One day I drew a model with only one breast, right in the middle. Derek was so pleased that he took a photograph of my ridiculous depiction while all the work that I considered good went unheralded. He didn't understand that I wanted to be an inhibited artist. I wanted to paint pretty pictures of pink and yellow shops in Shepherd's Market, or pastels of little children!

Another teacher at the institute, with the Christian name of Given, was in charge of our Thursday class. She may not have had Derek's flair, but she believed in teaching her students basic guidelines and agreed to give me private lessons in oils. On Saturdays, she rented a studio in Kensington which had been used by accomplished artists, and remnants of their work were tacked or hung in disarray along the walls. At that time, a man named Michael Nokes was painting the royal family, one by one, and most interesting was the fact that they, including the queen, came to this studio for sittings. The portraits were just lying about and I felt like an intruder in a wonderland of royalty. The portrait in progress on an easel was of Princess Margaret. Nokes had also done other celebrities—the Archbishop of Canterbury, Sir Alec Guinness, Sir Laurence Olivier, Sir Ralph Richardson—and, for reasons I did not comprehend, they too were hanging about. They looked finished to me, but were probably studies or rejects.

In early summer I went on a painting holiday with a group of artists including a close American friend, Helen Bennett. Our headquarters was a hotel in Bridgewater, Somerset, and from there we branched out to paint the rocky coast, the Quantock Hills, or a beautiful English garden. There was a freedom all its own in the English countryside. Helen and I ran through meadows of white daisies pausing at the edge of cliffs to watch the restless sea rise and fall into the horizon. During those few sunlit days, I felt alive and ready to take on the world.

ॐ   ॐ   ॐ

When Joni died, I had worried that our inclusion among young people was over, that we would sink into a cheerless middle age without the antidote of youth. She was our late child, a good many years younger than her siblings. But to our delight, Joni's friends continued to write, and send us tapes, assuring us that neither we nor Joni were forgotten. They told us their problems and disappointments as well as their successes and accomplishments at colleges and universities, with boyfriends, with life. They called me "Danny," a nickname that Bill derived from my maiden name, Daniel, when we first met, and I loved being a part of their blossoming world.

After her first year at Vanderbilt University, Mary Ball wrote that she would like to spend six weeks of her summer vacation with us. One thing I have learned from my scant supply of wisdom is that there is no limit to the heart's capacity to love, and I could hardly wait to spill over onto her. Together we tramped the streets of London poking our noses into its nooks and crannies and travelled widely through England, Scotland, and Ireland. All the while we talked as dear friends do, focusing on that person closest to our hearts—Joni.

ॐ   ॐ   ॐ

Our dear Helen Hayes came to London often during our eight-and-a half years in England. She too had lost a beautiful teenage daughter, Mary. We were already close friends, but our mutual heartache spawned further understanding between us and we clung to each other amid our smiles and tears.

Helen was making an absurd film at Pinewood Studios in Buckinghamshire for Disney called *One of My Dinosaurs is Missing* with Peter Ustinov and Derek Nimmo as co-stars. At seventy-four she tired easily under the strong lights and stress of movie-making. When she asked me to be her companion for a few days, I dropped everything. We stayed at the delightful old Burnham Beeches Hotel near Windsor. One evening, we shared a picnic supper on the lawn at Cliveden, the former estate of Lord and Lady Astor, while listening to a concert by the Royal Grenadier Guards. Such lawn picnics are frequented by the gentry and have a uniquely British flavor. A linen tablecloth is laid upon the ground, an elaborate wicker hamper dispenses china, silver and napkins, and another hamper caters the delicious fare, which traditionally includes paté, caviar, and champagne. The guests dress in their finery, and on occasion, such as the country's best-known summer operatic festival at Glynebourne, in evening clothes.

Observing the complexities of movie-making on the studio lot was fascinating. One morning I was passing the make-up room where Peter Ustinov was going through a long and tedious transformation into a chinaman. An incredibly amusing man, all too willing to admit that he craved an audience, he called to me to come in so that he could practice his hilarious Chinese accent. Later, when the movie was previewed at the Disney Studios in Hollywood, something was wrong with the sound track, and both he and Helen Hayes had to fly out there to dub, or "sync" their lines. This meant getting into a claustrophobic little booth, watching the film, and respeaking the lines to "sync" with the mouthings on the screen. Neither actor took kindly to this and wished they had followed the example of Katherine Hepburn, who had also been in England making a film. When told the sound track wasn't clear, she used some apt expletives and told

Helen Hayes

294

them to "bugger off." Poor Helen was already half sick from the dry ice fumes used to simulate London fog, and exhausted from climbing up an eighteen-foot fiberglass dinosaur. And she admitted to me that British comics like Peter Ustinov tended to frighten her with their superior wits.

Helen stated that this would be her last movie, but it was not. She simply didn't know how to say "no" and returned in 1976 to make another Disney film with David Niven and the young actress, Jody Foster, called *Candleshoe*. Again I was her companion for a short period. David Niven later told me about an incident that occurred when filming was taking place at a large country house in Gloucestershire, the home of an aristocratic old British lord. Feeling the inflationary pinch, this gentleman had rented his mansion to Disney, but suddenly realized that he had left a priceless painting over the fireplace in one of the bedrooms. The room happened to be that of thirteen-year-old Jody. The old dear managed to get through security and up the stairs to rescue the painting when Jody came along and, not knowing who this intruder was, tackled him just as he was making his way out of the bedroom staggering under the weight of his masterpiece. They both ended up on the floor in a tussle when Mademoiselle, Jody's companion, alarmed by the commotion in the adjoining bedroom, arrived on the scene and halted what looked like a fight to the finish.

When Helen Hayes was in the room, those around her could feel the almost physical clap of her presence. She loved to come to our flat because she knew that neither Bill nor I would infringe on her privacy. We never asked anyone to stop by unless she had agreed beforehand. Feeling secure and safe and very much at home, she would rest with her feet up on our sofa, and when the time came, we would bring her a light supper. She was forever beautiful. Often, she commented that the lines in her face were proud ones, well-deserved wrinkles. Helen heartily disapproved of all the cosmetic face-lifting that went on in Hollywood.

꿁   꿁   꿁

In England, Derek Nimmo was a star of stage, screen and television. A charming man, he asked Bill and me to his current West End hit, *Why Not Stay For Breakfast,* and invited us backstage after the play before going on to dinner together with his wife, Pat. As we entered the stage door, a case of hysterics emanated from one of the dressing rooms. In a minute or two, Derek came out of his and said, "Helen, it's Katy. Please go in there and see what you can do." Katy Manning was Derek's leading lady and a successful actress, having scored a hit in the *Dr. Who* series on television. I had not met her and felt odd barging into her dressing room, but by now the cries were heart-rending and I guessed there was some sort of need I had to try to fill. Intuition told me that my best course of action was to put my arms around her tiny body and hug her. When she had calmed down, she looked up at me and entreated, "Please come back tomorrow after the matinee."

A matinee and evening performance in one day can be grueling for an actress as unstable as Katy obviously was, and the next day I returned with an armful of roses. In the ensuing weeks, whenever possible on matinee afternoons, I was in her dressing room waiting for her to come off stage. If I couldn't be there, I called her, and a unique friendship developed.

Katy was a five-foot firecracker with a five-inch smile and an interesting collection of personality problems. She was a brilliant actress, but could not seem to "turn off" when the play was over. The character of Louise in *Why Not Stay For Breakfast* was unfortunately more explosive than her own, and much of the time she could not sort out who she was. The combination was pure dynamite. Katy's best friend was Liza Minnelli, her roommate at an English boarding school when they were twelve and thirteen years old. She had visited Liza and her mother, Judy

Garland, in the States, and was present on one occasion when Judy tried to kill herself; this experience had made its mark on her psyche. Katy was still grieving from the death of her father, whom she adored. He had died suddenly just after *Why Not Stay For Breakfast* had opened, and she had not had time to mourn.

When we met Stewart Bevin, he was a handsome out-of-work actor hopelessly in love with Katy. Their personalities were very different—he tall, patient and square—she, tiny, restive, and tempestuous. Nevertheless, he wanted to marry her, but she wouldn't consider such a conventional role as that of wife. Stewart was also a very good actor. Whenever I watched these young actors perform, it was something akin to total involvement, just as it had been when I watched Joni dance.

Later on, another young man named Dean Harris filled out the Rodman trio of young actor friends. Dean was endowed with a resonant baritone voice and impeccable timing on stage. Katy spotted him on TV playing the part of a bank robber, arranged to meet him, and in nothing flat, had him securely tucked under her wing. Poor Stewart was out the window!

One day Katy invited Bill and me to her flat, a stage set in itself of overstuffed Victorian furniture on which a menagerie of dogs and cats were comfortably ensconced. A snobbish King Charles spaniel snarled a greeting. Katy's big eyes were so made up that her tiny face had almost disappeared, and she had a new hairdo—one of those kinky jobs where the corkscrew effect defies gravity by pointing east and west instead of south. She wore a long white frock of cotton eyelet and very little underneath. If you could ignore this outrageous masquerade, a little Katy was still there, sitting on the edge of her seat, rolling her own cigarettes, and talking both aimlessly and intelligently in turns in her gravelly voice. Suddenly Dean, tired of waiting for a chance to break into Katy's ramblings, dropped a bombshell. "We have big news," he announced proudly. "Katy's pregnant. Four months along—twins!"

At that time, Katy and Dean were starring in a new play called *Doctor in the House*. After a nine-week run in London, the play was scheduled to go on tour in Canada. I could not see how Katy could possibly continue the role of a sexy blond, but one doesn't somehow question the implausible Katy—one just rolls with the punches. I was amused at this recent development, but not entirely. When I could get behind the greasepaint, I felt genuine affection for this tiny actress, but I also believed in good mothers and healthy babies, so the news of her pregnancy was like sandpaper to my innate nature.

The twins, Georgina and Jonathan James, were born two months prematurely, weighing in at two pounds each, and somehow survived. At twelve weeks old, the babies were christened at All-Hallows-by-the-Tower Church in London in a well-publicized ceremony with Liza Minelli and Derek Nimmo among the godparents. Although Dean was referred to as Katy's husband, I doubt if they were ever officially married.

On later visits to Katy and Dean's flat, two small babies and several dogs could be found floundering around on an old brown carpet, and both the two-legged and four-legged species were mouthing each others' toys and bones. A happier scene could hardly be imagined.

For a while Katy and Dean continued their active careers as a team, even taking the twins with them on tour, once as far as Rhodesia. Katy later moved to Australia where she found off-and-on work in the theater and the kids grew up, while Dean continued to live in England.

Our little group of special actors are in their fifties now, and over the years we have lost touch. I often wonder what kind of hands life has dealt them?

౯   ౯   ౯

In mid 1974, it had become quite apparent that Regency Properties, Ltd. who owned Arlington House, was trying to "winkle" us out of our flat. After more than a year of noise, drilling, sandblasting, dust, a spate of burglaries and unbearable disruption, tenants were notified of massive increases in rent. Legally, we didn't think this possible because of rent controls, but, because we were diplomatic, the owners felt assured we would not take them to court, and basically this was true. Bill and I didn't want to be the principals in a case of the United States versus Regency Properties, Ltd. So very reluctantly, we started looking for a new flat. The scandal of "winkling out the tenants" of Arlington House, made front page news in the London Times, and was later clarified when the building was sold to the Arabs for eight million pounds sterling.

The Arab invasion of London's West End was creating unbearable tensions for the hard-pressed English gentry. Families who had resided in established neighborhoods for centuries now had to put up with screaming children, all-night parties, laundry hanging out of windows, and a lack of Western toilet training. Properties were being mistreated and prices raised out of all proportion. Arabs could be seen squatting in doorways, lying on the pavement, and dozing on porches. Along Oxford Street white-robed sheiks, yashmakked women, and fat children filed into shops where they produced stacks of bills from bulging attache cases. Limousines, driven by stiffly uniformed Englishmen, absorbed them and their voluminous purchases on prearranged street corners.

A well-known antique dealer told the *London Times,* "They bought two items for £14,000 and extracted two rolls of pound notes in payment from a briefcase." The dealer went on to say that he stared rather obviously at the unavoidable display of wealth within, and while he was wondering just how much money the case held, a sheik volunteered the information:

We cashed a small check this morning for £170,000 before we set out. We have all the money here—and we'll have it all spent before the day is over.

In the manifestation of British dominion, the worm had turned.

ჟ   ჟ   ჟ

In October, during my almost frantic search for a new flat, I received a call that my mother had died. She had been ill with cancer for more than two years, and her death was merciful. I was glad that I had been with her for three weeks in September.

ჟ   ჟ   ჟ

For several years, Bill and I had been thinking about where we would retire. We were considering Charlottesville, Virginia, but had never dreamed of owning mother's house. However, sitting alone in her living room after the funeral, I suddenly realized that this very house was where I wanted to be someday, and hoped Bill would feel the same. My three brothers had houses of their own. I called Bill in London and he quickly agreed that we should buy mother's attractive home. It combined all that we had hoped for—a lovely garden, two downstairs bedrooms, a central location, and best of all, the advantages of a university town. We decided we would rent until retirement, and were able to find graduate students who took adequate care of it. We also knew that when we returned to Charlottesville, we would want to renovate extensively.

Bill and I had thought we would retire in 1976, but, when the time came, Bill was asked to extend until 1980. Jimmy Carter had been elected president, replacing Gerald Ford, and the US government wisely knew that the less stirring up of affairs overseas, the better. On the day before leaving office, President Ford had introduced a bill to lift the freeze on the top three grades of government salaries, and the new president, and Congress, approved it. This meant that Bill's salary raise was so attractive that we simply couldn't afford to retire. It also boosted our retirement benefits later on. Actually, we were pleased about the change in plans, especially when Bill was asked to stay on in London. Perhaps we weren't quite ready to retire and fate stepped in. Bill, now promoted to counselor rank, was considered the dean of the corps of agricultural attaches, and in the perfect post to train young officers.

Bill and grandson, Sean, enjoying the pigeons
in Trafalgar Square, London, England.

◆ —— Chapter Twenty —— ◆

KNIGHTSBRIDGE, LONDON

Bill HAD CLEVERLY FOUND A NEW FLAT WHILE I WAS STILL IN THE STATES and had moved our effects before my return. Wellington Court was in the heart of Knightbridge, two blocks from Harrods, and our fourteen-foot, swag-draped windows overlooked South Carriage Road, and Hyde Park beyond. Like the sounding of an alarm, at 7 A.M. we would be awakened by the clippity-clop of the Royal Household Cavalry trotting to Hyde Park for exercises. Later the horsemen, in their plumed helmets and finest regalia, would again march by on their beautiful bay horses for the Changing of the Guard at Buckingham Palace.

The flat was spacious with lush carpeting and high ceilings replete with molded Adamesque garlands and cupids. It bespoke of gracious Victorian charm. We settled in comfortably and quickly, happy to be away from the frustrations of Arlington House, and I enjoyed having a new neighborhood to explore. Instead of Fortnam and Mason, my nearest grocery store was now Harrods, with its baronial Food Halls.

ॐ ॐ ॐ

London was a booklover's mecca. Bookshops of every imaginable description dotted the city, especially in the area of Charing Cross Road with its amazing Foyles, where a bibliophile like me could get lost for a week. A favorite of mine was Henry Southeran, Ltd., a wonderful, timeworn shop on Sackville Street. Founded in 1640, I could mentally flash back to a bearded and craggy old Henry sitting there among his musty, laden shelves. About every fifty years, old Henry was probably replaced by a next-generation Henry, who, like all the Henrys, felt the way one Cotswold village shopkeeper put it on a slightly petulant sign above his door: "You are welcome to come in and browse, but be quiet and don't try to fool me into thinking you are going to buy anything. Let me read on in peace." Failing all else, I could trot off to the British Museum, fondly referred to as the BM, where massive floor-to-ceiling bookcases stretched on forever, and cozy reading rooms were provided for pleasure, study and research.

৵   ৵   ৵

The I.R.A. kept up their mindless bombings throughout the Christmas season of 1974, shattering public equilibrium. The mood of the big city changed from the festive aura of Christmas to one of anger and fear. Bombs exploded in underground stations, pubs, clubs and restaurants. Department stores were not spared. Within days, a twenty-pounder wrecked two floors of Harrods, and a hundred-pound car bomb exploded in front of Selfridges, its animated Dickensonian display windows all blown to smithereens. A new abomination was the drive-by spraying of machine-gun fire into hotel entranceways. While walking the streets, we became bomb-wary and tried to avoid bus queues and other spots where people gathered. Before we got into our car we looked carefully underneath. Most restaurants frisked customers and searched handbags. We avoided sitting near windows. People were clamoring for the restoration of the death penalty for terrorists.

In spite of these anxious moments, an amusing incident happened one day at Harrods where I had gone with a friend for lunch. Upon entering the store, the security man quickly prodded and returned my rather large shopping bag, but when he examined my friend's small handbag, he registered alarm. We soon found out why—he pulled out three Tampax!

Our amusement was short-lived, however. While having lunch on the third floor, there was an ear-shattering alarm followed by a loud-speaker announcement to proceed out of the building via the escalators. Obviously a bomb scare. One could only be full of admiration for the management and staff, who quickly went to their "battle" stations, and herded an estimated 10,000 people out of the store quietly and efficiently. The voice kept repeating, "Do not panic," and nobody did.

჎   ჎   ჎

Bill had the brilliant idea of spending Christmas in the Cotswolds at our favorite inn, The Shaven Crown, in Shipton-Under-Wychwood. When I called the owner, she said that the inn was closed for the Christmas season, but, as we were not strangers, she would take a chance on our fitting into her special group of fifteen friends who had spent the past twenty Christmases together. Being well versed in the Arlington House variety of English reserve, we hoped that it wouldn't take a pneumatic drill to crack the cement. Our worries were quickly dissipated.

So started an old-fashioned English Christmas in a tiny Cotswold village—a cluster of creamy-golden limestone houses, a fifteenth century church, a village green, a pond with white swans, dry-stone walls bordering layers of fields receding into the distance, and the old inn, once the hostel for a monastery up on the hill. Across the street from the inn was the General AMERY Store which I thought must be named after Shipton-u-Wychwood's most famous son, a General Amery no less. But on Christmas Eve, a certain old woman by the name of Ivy Amery joined our group, red-faced, frowzy, and smashed. Long ago her family had owned the entire area, but little by little the clan had guzzled away their prosperity at the pub, and were now reduced to selling eggs, clotted cream, and post cards. But because of past pride, AMERY somehow got itself capitalized between "general" and "store."

It would take a modern-day George Bernard Shaw to do justice to the characters assembled on this antiquated set, but Bill and I were accepted warmly and our fears of being outsiders were foundless. With so many diverse personalities from assorted backgrounds whom we had never met, the feeling persisted that we could be members of the cast of an amusing play. One of the leading characters on stage was Ted Rodman, a retired executive of Marks and Spencer's galaxy of stores. Our mutual name was an icebreaker and we became instant friends. Later, when kneeling at the altar rail of the village church on Christmas morning, my eye, which shouldn't have been roving, lit upon a marble wall plaque To the Glory of God and in Memory of a collection of Rodmans. Irreverently, I nudged Bill and pointed. Obviously, this tiny bit of England was Rodman Heaven, and we must have been under the spell of its guiding spirit. The dear departed turned out to be Ted's ancestors, possibly our own.

On Christmas Eve afternoon, the village choir came into the Great Hall at the inn singing "Oh Come All Ye Faithful," then assembled on the divided staircase to sing more carols while the villagers gathered below. Candlelight, a blazing fire, and a Christmas tree lighted the big room, and evergreens adorned the windowsills and bannisters. Looking and listening, I thought of the words on a past Christmas card of Joni's:

This is a day that brims with love,
   With all the meaning of devotion,
The warm response,
   The tone that means so much,
So rich, so reassuring
   Endearing and enduring.

Our room was directly over the pub adjoining the inn, and, that night, while getting ready for bed, we heard singing coming from below. Not wanting to miss anything, we reversed our plans and went down. The "Joy to the World" fellowship in that old English pub on Christmas Eve shone from every face. Several lusty voices led the singing, carol sheets were shared, everyone from the lord of the manor to the little kitchen maid was there, and social barriers dissolved.

And so passed a very different Christmas. Because we were with strangers in a new setting with new traditions, the nostalgia for Christmas Past was easier to bear.

ॐ   ॐ   ॐ

As time went on, I became increasingly interested in learning about antiques. One can hardly live in England without the patina of antiquity working its way into the senses. Although I continued to go to art classes twice a week, I immersed myself fully in classes on antique silver, furniture, and porcelain, still keeping time free to prowl antique shops and auction houses, or to meander in museums and galleries. To my delight, Bill too became smitten by the antique bug and happily accompanied me on Saturday trips to antique markets and *fayres,* or we drove out of London to villages and towns, poking about in shops and becoming acquainted with "the trade." Antique dealers were largely people with a deep love of their profession, all too ready and willing to impart their knowledge. A fraternal feeling interfused them. Many became friends. Antiquing offered Bill and me the chance to learn together while enjoying each other's company. As our knowledge grew, we felt more confident to buy, and in time I turned this interest into a small business.

Each Wednesday, I would install myself in the front seat of the top deck of bus no. 73 at 6 A.M. and enjoy a panoramic journey to my favorite antique market, Camden Passage. There I had breakfast with other dealers and bought mostly "smalls" in trade language, to be sold later, I hoped, for a profit. Sometimes I made the mistake of all beginners and bought a hard-to-tell fake, but all the while, I was learning and enjoying this new diversion.

The Portobello Road Market was another preferred haunt on Saturday mornings—market day. Bill and I would spend the morning searching for treasures, then have lunch beneath the cobwebs in an unique English establishment called a "wine cellar." Talking to dealers and handling old objects not only removed the mold from the past, but helped bring history into clearer focus. I developed such an obsession for collecting that two of any one item started a collection.

My first collection was Victorian ink bottles, little crudely-made, inexpensive objects in many shapes and colors. As my interest grew, I added rare and very rare specimens. These could be in many shapes—a teakettle, a cottage, a tent, a boot, a pillar box, or a globe, to name a few. In the 1970s, a rare ink in mint condition was valued at as much as £100. Today it would be far more. A bus driver named Norman who moonlighted by digging for bottles in old rubbish tips and stream beds became a source of supply. Whenever he found a "clean" ink, meaning not cloudy or damaged, he called me rather than selling to the trade. Such a transaction was known as "buying off the end of a shovel." As my interest grew, I researched my little bottles and made a book with three-dimensional drawings of each one. Before leaving England, my collection which had started out with two twenty-five pence ink bottles had grown to more than 250.

Over a period of time, Bill and I acquired other collections: blue and white Staffordshire china, Mason's ironstone, old Sheffield plate, miniature Staffordshire china, and commemorative china. Perhaps our most appealing collection was Staffordshire cottages and castles, crudely made but naively charming little objects often designed as pastille burners to mollify unpleasant house odors during the Victorian period. Seeking out these treasures in auction houses, shops, and markets across England gave us tremendous pleasure.

In the antique business, I learned that it was an advantage for a dealer to do his or her own simple restoration. Not only was it financially expedient, but there was something soul-satisfying about restoring an old derelict. The process of learning restoration was fraught with mistakes because nobody wanted to divulge secrets, and books on the subject were useless. I simply had to knuckle down, get out the meths, turps, shoe polish, beeswax, lemon juice, vinegar, steel wool, sandpaper, salt, and so forth, and go to work. Bill facetiously said he was surprised that there wasn't a use for artichoke hearts and tuna fish!

One morning, at the Kensinton Antiques Fair, a friend asked me to mind her booth while she had a cup of coffee. Along came a Canadian couple who showed interest in a beautiful mahogany slant-top desk from the Isle of Man worth several thousand pounds. I was fluttering about pointing out special features of the wonderful object when my fingers felt a slight movement at the back of one of the small drawers. I prodded further and discovered a panel which could be removed to reveal a secret chamber containing thirty very old Isle of Man pound notes, a numismatist's bonanza. The question was, who should keep the notes—should I, who found them? the antique dealer who was selling the desk? or the Canadian couple who said they wished to buy it, but had not put their name on the dotted line? The final decision among us was that the notes should be left with the desk.

Knightsbridge, London

My first business venture was to rent a stall with my friend, Jill, at a new antiques' market off of Berkeley Square. Sadly, the center closed after about two months. Although disappointing, I had gained a valuable lesson in the tricks-of-the-trade. I had also learned a lesson in patience. An antique market is a very dismal place when the customers don't come.

My second venture was to strike off on my own as a small-time buyer for American clients. By then I knew many dealers personally, where to go to buy the desired pieces, and was given the ten to twenty percent trade discount of a recognized dealer. A new career was developing. I called my business Rodmantiques.

This venture grew bigger when Judy, an old school mate, wrote to say that she planned to expand her very successful gift business, the Whitney Shop in New Canaan, Connecticut, to include antiques, and asked me if I would be interested in becoming her agent in England. To delve further into what she so graciously called a partnership, Judy came to London. We decided that I would accumulate enough items for two shipments a year, each worth between $8 and $12 thousand dollars. My commission would be twenty percent—not a fortune, but an opportunity to probe the antique world spending someone else's money.

Before she returned to the States, Judy and I went to Camden Passage together to start collecting for the first shipment. She was an astute businesswoman, and I think she enjoyed demonstrating her style. No dilly-dallying. Decisions were made with the speed of a comet as she darted about saying, "Negative. Affirmative." She was not a connoisseur of antiques, but she knew exactly what would sell in her shop, and I suspect that is why her business was so successful.

I was launched on a new career and loved every moment. After a day of shopping, I would notify the shipping company, who in turn would collect and pay for the items I had bought and send the Whitney Shop the bill. Judy and I had also set up a joint checking account so that I had funds to buy in markets where it was often necessary and beneficial to pay in cash. The hard part, if I could call it that, was the responsibility that went along with buying successfully for someone else.

Judy sealed our contract with the gift of a lovely little Billston-Battersea enamel box with the words, "All things are sweetened by risk." I hoped that "risk" would not leave her screaming, and it didn't. Our venture was successful.

჻   ჻   ჻

One morning, Antonio, our Mexican houseboy, called. From his past letters, I knew that he was married, expecting a baby, and had a fine job as "man friday" for an executive at Mexico's largest television station. I never dreamed, however, I would receive a trans-ocean telephone call, and queried him. His reply was noteworthy. "Do not worry, Señora—I am at the airport calling from the white Cadillac." He went on to explain that part of his job was to meet important people upon arrival at the airport. Our little Aztec had come a long way from the day a policeman found him sleeping in Chapultepec Park.

Antonio's son, Paul, was born early in 1975 in Mexico City, just before our second grandson, Trevor William Thieme, who was born on the Ides of March in Marlboro, Massachusetts.

Channing's call came late that day, and the following morning I was on my way to Boston to take care of the new arrival. It was my seventh flight across the Atlantic in less than three years. Trevor already had the glint of the devil in him. As he grew into little boyhood, his no-nonsense grandmother had to discipline him on occasion. After a scolding at age four, he declared, "Granddanny, I love you 'cause I gotta, but I don't like you." When he was five, he modified his thinking to, "Granddanny, I love you, and I think I'm getting to like you a little bit." By the time he turned six, we had resolved our differences and pledged lifelong solidarity. I adored him.

⚜ ⚜ ⚜

In the early summer, our friends, the Vesteys, invited us to spend a week at Glen Canisp, their country estate at the northern tip of Scotland. At the height of the gorse, rhododendron, and azaleas, it was surely one of the loveliest spots on earth, and throughout our stay, brilliant sunshine made the craggy landscape sharp and dimensional and magical.

The journey began when Edmund picked us up at Wellington Court in his Rolls Royce and drove to a spot just below the Tower of London where he kept his helicopter. He insisted I sit alongside the pilot for the next leg of the trip to Cambridge in order to have a better view through the plexiglass undercarriage. As we flew just above the tree tops charting the course of the Thames, I watched the river traffic as on a panoramic film, and could almost count the sheep grazing in fields along the water's edge. At Cambridge, the helicopter set down next to an executive jet. Anne was already aboard with two spaniels, Thistle and Faith. We then made the run to Inverness enjoying afternoon tea on board. At Inverness, another Rolls Royce rolled up to the jet and took us on to Glen Canisp Lodge.

The house was large, a veritable manor house of many rooms. The staff had gathered in the forecourt to greet us, the women curtsying slightly and the men bowing. The cook was addressed as Mrs. Nicholson. Two border collies barked their welcome.

The Vestey holding encompassed 110,000 acres and thirty-two miles of coastline, a small domain in Sutherland County at the northwest tip of Scotland. Within the Vestey territory were two towns, a hotel, salmon rivers, miles and miles of rough grazing land for sheep, and a plethora of deer, grouse, partridge, pheasant, and other game—a hunter's paradise.

311

A huge walled garden provided fresh vegetables for the house, and Mrs. Nicholson was a superb cook. We had lobster and salmon, lamb and currant jelly, roast beef and Yorkshire pudding, gooseberry fool and rhubarb pie. A breakfast dish was kedgeree made of salmon, rice, and hard-boiled egg. Asparagus, I discovered, was a separate course, eaten with the fingers. Crisp toast, in a little silver rack, and marmalade were served after the eggs and bacon. How is it that marmalade always tasted better in England or Scotland? I tried to resolve this question by buying a jar of the best English marmalade and taking it on trial to America. Alas! It did not taste as good.

At noon we picnicked, either alongside salmon streams or on the rocky shores of islands to which we sailed in Edmund's launch, the Puffin. One day we went to Handa Island, a bird sanctuary, with dramatic rock formations mindful of old Inca ruins. We saw legions of eiderdowns, razorbills, puffins, guillemots, and kittiwakes, and climbed the rocks to quietly view the nesting eggs. Across The Minch between the Outer Hebrides and the mainland, the islands of Lewis and Harris were just visible.

Bill and I enjoyed fishing in the salmon streams with Charlie, our ghillie, a fishing and hunting guide, who wore plusfours, jacket and cap made from the Glen Canisp tweed. In total, Edmund employed six gamekeepers, five shepherds, five maintenance men, a permanent staff for the hotel on a rocky cliff, three pensioners as gardeners, and the house staff. The overseer of the entire operation was Peter, the factor. Each of the men wore the Glen Canisp tweed, included in the terms of employment, along with a house, three cows, a pair of sturdy boots, venison and salmon. All game had to be reported to the factor when killed.

Edmund too wore the Glen Canisp tweed, and was a kind and respected "lord of the manor."

One Sunday, after a service of morning prayer at the kirk, he drove us many miles across the shire to visit his shepherds and their families in their isolated cottages. He asked after each member, and, if there was a complaint, listened quietly and assured them it would be looked into. I could not help but think that the experience of that wonderful week was analogous to fiefdom in the middle ages.

In the sunshine of those precious clear days, I felt a peace I had not known since Joni's death.

჻   ჻   ჻

Bill and I were due for home-leave in July. Channing had made arrangements for the entire family to spend two weeks at Yoke Pond Camp in Kokadjo, Maine, a favorite fishing spot of the Rodman family for many years. It was a glorious holiday in the beauty of a northern wilderness. Each family occupied a cabin, except for Bill's mother, Granny Rodman, who stayed with Bill and me in our rustic dwelling facetiously known as The Ritz. Little Trevor spent most of his daylight hours tucked into a pack on his father's back, and Sean, then three, ran wild and free among the pines chasing squirrels and collecting small creatures. At one end of the spectrum was Granny, eighty-three years old, the beloved matriarch, surveying her progeny with open pride. At the other end were the two new little boys, proof that the cycle of life was never ending.

჻   ჻   ჻

I was continually amazed at how many small doors opened after Joni's death, giving Bill and me the opportunity to love, and sometimes help. An almost magnetic pull brought us together with young people, many of whom we affectionately called "littleones:"

Jenny was an innocent, about-to-blossom girl of twelve, the

313

daughter of friends from Sussex. Her father had been with us at the hotel in Bristol when we learned of Joni's death and was sensitive to our loss. I think he had it in mind that when the early pain had abated, he just happened to have a little girl that might ease a bit of the heartache. He was right. As Jenny arrived by train for the weekend on a Friday afternoon in her school uniform, I worried that I would overlook this small creature in the late afternoon rush at Victoria Station.

I called Amanda "A-1." Her father, Derek Nimmo, the actor, and his wife, Pat, asked if their sixteen-year-old daughter might stay with us to continue her schooling in London during a three-month period when they would be in Australia. We, of course, said, "yes," but had no idea what a delight she would be.

Brendon and Dinie, an amusing Aussie couple. She was the daughter of our friend Pip Walker at Templemore in New South Wales. They were making a grand tour of the world on a working holiday. He was a great bear of a young man, as mild as a lamb, who had been working on an oil rig in the North Sea, and she at odd jobs here and there. I set about tidying him up by cutting his hair and was surprised to find a gold earring in one of his ears, an adornment of youth that has since become unexceptional.

Hampton, my thirteen-year-old niece, went to school at St. Catherine's and had been like a little sister to Joni. She lightened our lives with her vivacious personality and enthusiastic approach to life.

The list goes on.

Toward the end of our sojourn in London, one of our dearest "littleones" showed up unexpectedly on our doorstep after an interval of thirteen years. It took me a few seconds to realize it was Jillian, Joni's best friend in Australia. I hugged her with a hug that I'm sure was overwhelming. I couldn't let her go. The mental flashbacks were like lightning. Jillian wasn't like others that skirted the topic of Joni. She wanted a complete history of her childhood friend from Australia onward. As a mother, I kept looking at this beautiful young woman, now twenty-four years old, with incredible yearning for an interlude that had been so happy in my life. I could still remember the day in 1962 when, holding hands, Joni had brought her little friend to our home and announced, "This is Jillian, my best friend," and Jillian adding, "I'm Jillian with a J, not a G."

჻   ჻   ჻

For Christmas, Bill and I decided on a fly-drive trip to Spain. Another "littleone," Sarah, the daughter of friends from Virginia, was living in Cambridge at the time with her English husband. Their marriage was shaky, and John had suddenly gone off to Bahrain for six months to teach English at a church mission. Poor Sarah was distraught. Knowing that Christmas would be very lonely, we asked her to join us on our trip.

After landing in Malaga, we quickly decided that the Costa del Sol was a grotty concrete jungle and fled into the interior in our little orange Fiat. There was much to enjoy in Spanish cities. I loved the cobblestoned labyrinth of twisting streets, the flower-decked balconies, many displaying song birds in little wooden cages, the people bartering in open markets, the hidden squares and courtyards, the church bells.

On December 25, we were in Seville, where Christmas day was observed strictly as a religious holiday. As we had to make our own good cheer, we bought bread, cheese, olives, anchovies, and a bottle of good Andalusian wine for a feast in our hotel room. The celebration was further enhanced by a jolly housekeeper and her crew of two delightful little *camareras* who joined us for a sprinkling of good will among nations. We must have made an unusual sight, Sarah and I in evening skirts, and Bill looking very smart in a suit and tie, while big-bosomed Lola wore the ordained black dress, and her two giggly little charges were in black uniforms with white frilly aprons and organdy caps. We all sipped wine, exchanged bilingual "Merry Christmases" with hugs, and clapped loudly when the smallest of our guests jumped onto the coffee table and danced the flamenco.

On Christmas afternoon, we drove on and stopped in a small town close to the Portuguese border. Our lodging was a hostel with no heat. With the temperature near freezing, we warmed ourselves by putting our feet on the edge of a brazier placed beneath a round table over which a heavy blanket had been draped. In this manner we ate our dinner, and breakfast the following morning. Sarah, thinking that we were the only guests, collected blankets from other beds in the hostel. Imagine her chagrin the next morning when she discovered that she had deprived late travelers of warmth! Crime doesn't pay; she awoke covered with bedbug bites.

We didn't stay in Portugal as long as planned due to the political climate. Graffiti in the form of violent slogans—the hammer and sickle, the clenched fist, and "muerte a . . ." (death to . . .)"—was written on walls in red and black paint recording the political furor, and at times the people looked at us as though we were firecrackers about to go off. Dressed in black from head to toe, some with bowed, spindly legs, the women appeared older than their years. I guessed that mourning lasted forever. Men wore black caps and huddled together on street corners and in bars. The atmosphere changed when we retreated to the beautiful Algarve Coast, where we basked in sunshine and picnicked on the westernmost tip of the continent on cliffs that rose high above the sea.

Back in Spain, we made our way slowly back to Malaga over what was called the "route of the white towns." This took us through low country with miles of vineyards, orange and olive groves, and cork trees stripped of their bark, which made them appear oddly naked. In contrast, we also went over high, twisting roads with snow-capped mountains in the distance. A series of beautiful little whitewashed towns were neatly stacked on top of their rugged, rocky bluffs like so many lumps of sugar. Usually, the only road up to the town was not wide enough for two cars to pass. On one occasion, this caused an altercation involving six cars, three on each side. After a period of horn-blowing, the male members of the confrontation got out of their cars and engaged in impassioned gesticulations, a sort of Spanish version of a street rumble. Finally, a lone policeman arrived to umpire the situation, and we were disappointed to find ourselves on the losing team. The lower three cars were ordered to back down the hill, and the game was over.

Ronda was a small miracle of a town because of its rugged mountain setting and the 1,000-foot gorge which cut the town in two. On one side was the "old town" dating back to time immemorial while on the other was the "new town," only four centuries old. The "old town" was an up-and-down enclave hidden behind ancient walls, of winding alleys and white houses with decorative wrought-iron balconies—a striking contrast of black against white enhanced by the interplay of sun and shadows—an artist's eden.

ॐ   ॐ   ॐ

Back in England, an interesting excursion was to Winston Churchill's war cabinet rooms three stories underground, which had remained untouched since they were vacated in 1948. In its maze of rooms and corridors some 300 persons, men and women, lived and worked and breathed dank air between 1938 and 1948. In spite of this large staff, the War Rooms were kept a closely guarded secret. Our guide pointed out that wives and families might live within walking distance and never know that a loved one was there; the wife would be told that her husband was in France when all the time he was a decoding clerk forty-five feet underground in London.

In addition to the chambers, twenty-three miles of

subterranean tunnel, through which messages were relayed by bicycle to Buckingham Palace and Parliament House, zigzagged below the busy city, and, should the Germans invade, elaborate escape measures had been charted. Only ten visitors were permitted at a time as the corridors were narrow, and unlit except by flashlight. In some of the rooms we had to bend over to keep from bumping our heads against the ceiling and I wondered if they had drafted very short people for duty down there. Plumbing was nonexistent, necessitating an almost continual bucket brigade moving up and down the narrow stairs—a miserable mole-like existence.

I felt very fortunate to have seen this painful bit of history and held great admiration for the invincible British spirit. When I sat in the great man's chair in the Cabinet Meeting Room while our guide gave a short talk, my imagination soared in true Walter Mitty fashion. Churchill's pencils, notebook, letter opener, ink, pens, and water glass were still right there in front of me—even cigar ashes in his ashtray! I wondered about that as we were told that Churchill, being both untidy and unmannerly, would toss his butts and ashes over his shoulder. He also had a habit of waddling around in the nude, and liked to ring a cow bell instead of a siren when he was driven in his car through the streets of London. But with all his well-publicized eccentricities, he had the uncanny ability to lead and to inspire his country to victory.

ॐ   ॐ   ॐ

Before returning to the New Hebrides for anthropological fieldwork, Sean, Margy, and Bill, Jr. visited us in the spring of 1976. While his parents enjoyed a quicksilver week of theater, museums and browsing in bookstores, six-year-old Sean was captivated by the more basic offerings of London such as double-decker buses, the Underground, Harrod's toy department, and spaghetti for lunch. His favorite spot was Trafalgar Square, where he could buy a small bag of crumbs to feed the pigeons, and his favorite song was "I Got a Luvly Bunch of Coconuts" (Sean's spelling), which he learned at a band concert in St. James Park. One day Sean and I went into the garden to play. He had a new glider, which attracted a bunch of little Arab children dressed in their long white nightshirts. I tossed the glider with Granddanny enthusiasm, and it landed like a shot duck with a broken wing. Sean looked dismayed as the kids retreated into the bushes. I said, "Don't worry, Sean, we'll glue it." But Sean knew better. It was made of Styrofoam and wasn't glueable. Being kid-oriented, his upset was because of the disappearance of prospective playmates.

Channing's visit later that year was equally delightful. She brought Trevor, nineteen months old, an alert, happy little guy with blond curly hair and a pixie grin. Helen Hayes called him our Sir Joshua Reynolds' grandson. Each day, Trevor and his doting grandmother would bundle up in woollies and trundle off to Hyde Park. He was smitten with the ducks on the Serpentine, and loved the horses along the dirt path that edged the park called Rotten Row, a corruption of Rue de Roi when the kings and queens of old used that route as a thoroughfare from Kensington Palace to the city.

ॐ   ॐ   ॐ

In England, where 200 years is but a drop in the bucket, I was glad and proud when the United States celebrated its bicentennial on July 4, 1976. In spite of violence on television and films in America, and screaming newspaper headlines of crime and terror, I believe that the quintessence of an American is kindness and courage. Few words are written about the majority who go quietly about their own business neither criticizing nor complaining, but are ready and willing to help others. They love America deeply for its uphill and gallant struggle for freedom.

• —— Chapter Twenty-one —— •

A FAT FARM IN ENGLAND
AND
ALL CHARACTERS GREAT AND SMALL

HEALTH HYDROS, OR IN THE VERNACULAR, "FAT FARMS," were numerous and inexpensive in England. In the States, they were generally called spas, and financially designed for the rich and very rich, but on this fair isle they were reasonable enough to be within the price range of a wider public.

It seemed a curious way to spend the 1976 Christmas season, and some of our friends thought we were altogether mad, but Bill and I enjoyed an occasional dose of the unconventional, and wanted to see what the "curative genius of Mother Nature" could do to relieve the "stresses and distortions of modern living," as one brochure put it. Another brochure told me that our bodies needed "detoxifying," and assured us that if we gave ourselves over to their care for two weeks, we would reap such benefits as "unflagging energy, rejuvenation, tranquil minds, trim bodies and mental alertness."

Therefore, as Bill and I were both considerably out-of-shape, and bound to be riddled with a half century of "toxic accumulations," we set our sails for Inglewood Health Hydro, some fifty miles west of London in the Berkshire Downs.

Inglewood was once a monastery dating back to the

320

Doomsday Book (1085). During the crusades of 1199, it had been used by the Knights Templar, and during the reign of Henry VIII became the Royal Falconry. We arrived at 6 P.M. on December 22 and, upon completion of a tour of the building, were interviewed by the director, known as "Captain Kirk," and a nurse who checked us over and put us on an immediate fast of hot water and lemon. Before we went to bed, Bill and I reviewed the rather odd situation in which we found ourselves with Christmas only two days away, and made a pact to be brave—a tragicomedy of sorts.

The following morning there was a knock on our door, and, before I even had time to remove my crooked hairnet, a giant red-headed man burst into the room with the first of our six daily cups of hot lemon-water. After drinking this woeful concoction, I struggled up from my granite-like bed, donned my bathrobe, and descended to the therapy area. My masseur was the same redhead who had awakened us at 7 A.M. As I had the old-fashioned notion that ladies massaged ladies and men massaged men, I had expected a female. Not at Inglewood. Bill and I had the same guy.

A sauna came next, then a shower which hit me from all sides with alternating hot and cold water. Pure agony! Then a dear little Indian girl gave me a manicure followed by a seaweed bath for my joints and skin. This was taken in a regular tub in water a bit darker than that which comes out of rusty pipes, and a lot smellier. Bill's "bath-of-the-day" was called a "moor" bath. He said it was sodden peat moss, and just as smelly as my seaweed.

In the afternoon, I had two exercise sessions with a big, handsome Northumbrian, and a swim in the heated pool. We were instructed to take a shower or a sauna after every treatment or exercise period.

On Christmas Eve morning, our second full day of that disgusting lemon and hot water fast, I awoke feeling very weak, but determined to carry on. We each had several appointments, one right after the other, and were introduced to two new treatments, the "S/tone" and the "G/5." The first was an electric shock treatment. After an attendant placed rubber disks on the fatty bits of my body, she turned on a machine that looked like the controls for a space ship, and POW! I was launched! For half an hour, I lay there wired and helpless while the disks squeezed and grabbed, and little electric currents gyrated through my body.

In comparison, the G/5 was quite pleasant—a big, standing machine with a spongy attachment at the end of a hose which vibrated my flesh with the intention of breaking up fatty tissue so that exercise could remove the fat more easily.

The "bath-of-the-day" was a "wax bath." I was told to lie down on a large piece of aluminum foil, naked, of course, while an attendant poured hot wax over me, wrapped me up in the foil, placed two heavy blankets on top of that, and finally put a cool little piece of gauze on my forehead. It crossed my mind that the next step might be to insert a meat thermometer. The wax hardened as it cooled and I was encased, mummified. After about thirty minutes, an attendant returned to unwrap me, and the wax was peeled off in great sheets, rather like peeling a grape. Never again!

I was beginning to flag by that evening, but made it to the midnight service in the ancient Inglewood chapel. For this occasion, I dressed in a skirt and blouse, and Bill wore his blue suit, but generally we wore blue and white warm-up suits or terry-cloth bathrobes all day long.

On Christmas Day, we were given a choice of breaking fast in favor of a Christmas dinner, but when told this would undo all the good we had done, we decided to struggle on, and reluctantly accepted our fate. Our goal, set by strict Captain Kirk, was four full days of lemon and water. As hard as it was to believe, Bill and I were very cozy and happy on Christmas morning, opening presents and listening to carols on the radio.

Around midday, we dressed properly and drove twenty-five miles to Winchester where we walked about the old city pausing in front of every restaurant to read the menu and drool. Later, we attended evensong in the majestic cathedral, lighted entirely by candles except for an enormous glittering Christmas tree at the far end of the nave. I am convinced that the most perfect sound on earth is that of a men and boy's choir in the right acoustical setting. The Winchester Cathedral choir, along with Kings College choir at Cambridge, were considered the finest in England.

While the choristers were robing, we chatted with a woman sitting next to us, the mother of one of the young men in the choir. Her son had quarters in the cathedral close and she invited us to join them for sherry after the service.

The cozy little house nestled in the center of a well-tended garden. Pheasants were already in the oven for Christmas dinner, and nuts and sweets were spread about. Our hostess was kind enough to understand our folly and gave us hot lemon-water, but the easy accessibility of the nuts was a bit too much. Bill ate seven and I ate one—a Brazil nut!

Winchester Cathedral had its own choir school where boys were chosen from all over Great Britain, more for their intelligence, character, and feel for music, than for their ability to sing; vocal training was taught at the school. The boys entered at eight years old, and, by the time they were eleven, each could play an instrument well and sight read any piece of music, no matter how difficult. Tuition was free. Although I was told that they loved it, I couldn't help feeling a pang over the fact that those little fellows were not at home for Christmas. It was a tremendous honor to be admitted to a leading choir school. About one in 200 applicants were accepted.

On Boxing Day I crashed! All night long I suffered a booming headache and nausea—three days worth of lemon water and one Brazil nut. If I hadn't felt so rotten I would have searched out the lemon hatchery to confiscate everything therein, and would have kicked the director on the way.

Captain Kirk was a naturopath and osteopath, really a very nice young man who ran a pretty tight ship. When I called him about my sorry state, he actually said, "Good! Your body is throwing off all that rot and rubbish—just bear with it and you'll feel better tomorrow—later today we will break your fast." The broken fast consisted of a bunch of green grapes for lunch and another for dinner.

The following day I felt utterly debilitated but my headache and nausea were gone. The Captain worked on my neck where he suggested I stored up tension. His method was to get a stranglehold from behind and gently move my body from side to side until he felt me relax; then came the crunch and something in my neck went c-r-a-c-k, a rather frightening experience, but the pain was relieved.

I also began to realize that most of Inglewood's prophecies had come true. I would never have believed that I could drink only lemon-water for four days and eat only grapes for two more, and not feel hungry. I was only ravenous at the beginning of the fast. By the time I was allowed grapes, I felt quite satisfied and stronger.

Captain Kirk apologized for his seemingly callous attitude regarding my acute indisposition on Boxing Day, but said he knew that if he could keep my cooperation, and not give in, I would end up transformed and feeling like a million pounds sterling. I told him that he started out the villain in my story but might end up the hero. He never had any problem with Bill, who leapt about like a young kangaroo throughout the ordeal of that first week.

In his evening lectures, Captain Kirk explained that when a person is ill, the body's rejection of food was nature's way of saying, "Let me take over." Animals and babies know this instinctively. People conditioned to fasting such as Buddhist monks can go for as long as three or four weeks at a stretch on water or other liquid.

The miscellaneous assortment of people at Inglewood ranged in size from hippos to sylphs. Some had arthritis, asthma, anorexia or a problem with obesity. Others were neither fat nor thin nor ailing and simply wanted to get away from the pressures of the office, or perhaps of life, or wife. We had an Arab princess with two bodyguards and a lady-in-waiting, and a pair of rotund Kuwaiti diplomats in bright red track suits whom I called Tweedledum and Tweedledee. Among the other personalities present were a fashion editor, a dope addict or two, a jockey, an opera singer, a rabbi, a couple of actresses, and a sprinkling of nobility. Lastly, there was one just plain jerk who went swimming in his underwear until caught by Captain Kirk. Like the couple in the sauna, he picked the wrong hydro.

On New Year's Eve, we graduated to chicken broth, yogurt, and a lovely boiled egg for breakfast. Our batteries were recharged, our vitality renewed. Before going to bed, we hugged tightly and promised each other a loving and happy 1977. We thought of our loved ones, especially Joni, who was born just twenty-two years before on another New Year's Eve in Argentina.

꙳ ꙳ ꙳

On New Year's day, with the sun shining brightly over the frozen earth, Bill and I drove to the nearby town of Hungerford. It was a day when the mind perceives the world in perfect focus.

As we were wandering through an antique market, an elderly woman walked up to within inches of Bill and said clearly, "You have the face of a very kind man—you're beautiful." He looked so startled that she felt it necessary to add, "Yes, I mean you. Happy New Year," and off she went. One of life's charming little vignettes, the kind that tends to be lost forever unless written down. How many hundreds have we lost?

Later, when Bill and I reflected on this unique holiday, we agreed that Inglewood was a cross between boot camp and paradise. I lost fourteen pounds and Bill, twelve. We were pummeled, pounded, steamed and starved into new shapes, and could now face the long mirror sideways with some degree of satisfaction. In fact, we probably had become vain and introspective, but would surely get over it when reality grabbed us, and we were again plunged into the "stresses and distortions of modern living." I also hoped that I had learned something about how to slow down my usual comet-like existence.

I wrote a letter to our anthropologist son, Bill, Jr., at McMaster University in Canada about our romp at Inglewood and received the following reply:

> As resident expert on witchcraft, I would like to inform you that methods used at Inglewood bear a distinct resemblance to techniques employed by Inquisitors in the sixteenth century. Accused witches were often deprived of food for prolonged periods of time, beaten, then made to exercise vigorously. Strikingly, witchfinders in rural England usually dunked suspects in a pool to determine whether or not they would float. Repeated dunkings probably account for the observation made by many contemporary observers that accused witches acquired a "cleare complecktion." In addition, it is said that many victims of the Inquisition lost fourteen pounds. Witches often became vain, obsessed with their personal appearance: It is a little known fact that many men and women accused of witchcraft went to the gallows issuing enthusiastic endorsements for their persecutors.

ᣠ   ᣠ   ᣠ

After our fling at Inglewood, I decided I mustn't allow my efforts to go to waste, and signed up for a "body-beautiful" exercise class three times a week. As the class was held in the building across the alley from Wellington Court, it was easy for me to scoot over in my leotards and coat. I always migrated to the back of the class where I could observe the young participants in front of me, many of them actors and models, and placed myself next to a sagging beauty named Ava. She and I were the oldest in the class and soon our grunts and groans turned into friendship. When I told her I lived at Wellington Court, she responded that she lived just two blocks away in Ennismore Gardens and often walked her dog to Hyde Park via the alley that ran by our back entrance.

The following day, the buzzer buzzed, and it was Ava, little dog in tow, asking if she might come in for a cup of coffee. We sat in our living room chatting amiably when she noticed a photograph of Helen Hayes and said, "There is a lady I admire as a fellow actress but have never had the good fortune to meet." This remark should have clued me in, but it wasn't until later when the conversation had turned to Hollywood and a singer named Frank that a bell rang in my numbskull, and I realized that my friend was Ava Gardner.

After that, we met frequently for coffee or lunch, always at my flat or hers. Ava was pleased to find another lover of antiques, and on several occasions, Bill and I picked her up for excursions to antique markets. She wore dark glasses and a scarf around her head hoping to remain incognito, but sooner or later someone would recognize her and our carefree jaunt was over. For a while she accommodated the autograph seekers, but as soon as possible, we escaped by car or sought refuge in a restaurant or wine cellar. During lunch one day, Bill, remembering her hair color as black, asked her when she had changed to red. Her answer was something like: "When Frank and I were married, we fought like tigers; his hair fell out and mine turned gray; been red ever since," a statement heavily punctuated with expletives. Every now and then, Ava would vanish without explanation, and I learned that, almost routinely, she had disappeared to a health hydro to get back her equilibrium after a bout with the bottle.

ॐ ॐ ॐ

We enjoyed the well-known personages we encountered during our career in the foreign service, but the unknowns who moved fluidly in and out of our lives were of equal importance.

Major Rutherford was one who lived in the next flat at Wellington Court. A dashing colonial officer who had served with honor in Her Majesty's Service in India, he was the epitome of Gilbert and Sullivan's "very model of a modern Major Gen-er-al." At eighty-three, he still had the glint of the devil in his eye, but the years had taken their toll. Bill and I became his support system. Every Friday, he and I walked the short distance to his favorite pub for lunch at a painfully slow pace, but as this was the brightest spot of his week, I tried not to let him down.

Emily was a dignified English lady who came two mornings a week to clean our flat and we became friends. She spent more time sipping tea and nattering than chasing dust. Bill used to tease me that I would hustle to clean the flat before she arrived.

Tommy, once a cockney "barrow-boy" at the Smithfield Market, was now an official for a meat-packing company. He loved taking our guests through the meat stalls in Covent Garden at six in the morning, then treating them to a completely carnivorous breakfast at the meat vendors' pub.

ح ح ح

One evening, we watched a noteworthy "Skating Spectacular" on television featuring John Curry, who infused the combined art of Nureyev and Astaire into figure skating. Curry went on to win the "Sportsman of the Year" award presented by Lord Mountbatten. As he stood at the podium holding his trophy, he gave a teary little "thank-you" to the assembled audience. All of Britain's leading gold medalists were there. Although Curry was deserving, Bill and I had thought that the skater didn't stand a chance of winning. The British are so bloody physical-minded, and a sportsman should epitomize the brawn and strength of manhood, not the grace and artistry of a figure skater.

A word here about the British regarding sport. They love it—everything from croquet to rugby. No matter how impossibly the tide goes against them, they keep hoping for a miracle. The sportscasters come out with such commentary as, "Brenden is now next to last in a field of twenty. What ho! Wait a minute! I believe he is—yes—he is catching up to number nineteen, the man from the Outer Seychelles!" Or you might hear, "In the marathon, our fine runner from Manchester came in fiftieth in a field of sixty. He was only six miles behind the winner." I do love the British. They may have lost an empire, but they haven't lost their competitive spirit.

ॐ   ॐ   ॐ

To quench my long-standing desire to see Florence, Italy, I impulsively signed up for a course offered by the University of London called The Renaissance and Its Precursors in Tuscany. When I filled out the application form asking for my qualifications in art and architecture, I wrote in "none, but willing to learn," and received the following answer: "Dear Madam, Although it is very irregular, the committee has decided to accept you because we haven't met our quota of qualified students."

As the departure date drew near, I became more and more paranoid. Bill had to use utmost diplomatic persuasion to get me onto an Alitalia plane at Heathrow Airport on a rainy spring morning. I had been told that my roommate would be a Miss Primrose Bloomfield, but did not see anyone who fit that floriated description.

Unknown to me, I had signed up for a master's degree course in art history consisting of seventy-two hours of lectures by our indomitable leader, Miss Shirley, on the "cuatrocento " period of the early Renaissance. Out-of-my-depth? I was in the middle of a cyclone in the South Pacific Ocean without water wings! As an example, the group of about twenty would stand transfixed in front of the *duomo* in Florence listening to a lecture on a single panel out of twelve on the Ghiberti doors, then move across to the baptistry to do the same on the Donatello doors, then compare the two while waiting for the famous doors to open. And so it went all day long— frescos, columns, carvings, paintings, minutely examined while the class stood the entire time except for the lunch hour.

At the end of the first week, while the group was gathered in front of an enormous fresco in the famous duomo, I noticed a group of clustered tourists with guide looking intently at something some distance from our group. Ever curious, I snuck off to investigate, and there in front of me was one of Michelangelo's most beautiful *pietás*. As our class was strictly a study group, Miss Shirley would not have pointed this out because Michelangelo worked in the early sixteenth century, not in our small point of reference. From a combination of overexposure and osmosis, I learned a little about the subject, but, by the second week I realized that I would have to break away from the group to get the broader view of the Florence I longed to see, and made my apologies to Miss Shirley.

In Italian, the city is called Firenze, which somehow smacks of Valhalla and the fiery furnace, whereas Florence sounds like a beautiful woman wearing just the right perfume. In any case, Florence was wonderful. I strolled along the Arno River at sunset, zigzagged along narrow pavements, zigging to avoid getting side-swiped by reckless drivers or speeding motorbikes and zagging to avoid kids and the mess of irresponsible dogs. I shopped in the outdoor markets, bargained for treasures along the Ponte Vecchio, was introduced to capuchino coffee and pizza, and grew accustomed to the noisy confusion of the city. All the while, I marvelled at the genius, beauty, and antiquity that was everywhere. I even wormed my way for an entire morning into the art restoration laboratories where I saw masterpieces by Rubens, Boticelli, Van Dyke, and others that hadn't been on view for years. Many had been damaged during the disastrous flood of 1966, and the slow restoration process was still in progress. Several of the study group accepted my odd-man-outmanship and became friends. To my joy and surprise, there were ordinary people underneath the pedantic facade and frenzied note-taking for impending exams. I did not envy them.

Best of all, however, was my very own roommate, Miss Primrose Bloomfield. Her first question to me when we found each other at the airport was, "Do you drink?" a damned-if-you-do and damned-if-you-don't question. To my innocuous answer which was something like "moderately," she exclaimed, "Oh, good! Now we can have our plonk with dinner." Plonk, I learned, was the term for cheap Italian red wine, generally served in a carafe with bits and pieces of unknown origin floating about on top.

Primrose had been an officer in the British Ministry of Overseas Development, had travelled widely, and had never been to a hairdresser; little scissors lopped off unruly strands of hair pulled back into a ponytail. Her prominent ears protruded like two handlebars. She saw no need to buy new clothes when her deceased mother's would do, spoke Italian, missed her budgie, was not swatting for exams, and was delightful company. In addition, she had brought along soap and towels which our "poor-student" brand of hotel did not provide, plus marmalade and digestive biscuits to replace the hotel's unappetizing breakfast.

৵   ৵   ৵

Our third grandson, Carl Brandon Thieme was born during home leave December 8, 1977, a healthy, happy baby. I again had the privilege of being chief of the "diaperpin brigade" while Bill went to Washington for consultation.

Chapter Twenty-two

EARLS COURT, LONDON

THE QUEEN'S SILVER JUBILEE CELEBRATIONS IN 1978 seemed to put a new spirit into her subjects long fed up with strikes, inflation, and political turmoil.

And then the bad news. The owners of Wellington Court sent us notice that we had to move when the lease ran out. Although they claimed to want our flat for their own use as an office, I suspected they were thinking of selling the building to the Arabs. The Arab takeover of so many buildings in London continued to vex the British, but land and building owners were greedy to make their fortunes. As before, it was useless to try to fight the order. After being winkled out of Arlington House, it seemed unfair that the same thing could happen again.

I thought that finding a third suitable flat in the city of London was going to be as difficult as before, but ran into a stroke of luck. In the waiting room of an estate agency, I met an attractive Danish woman who had just come in to register a flat for rent on the Old Brompton Road. In quick succession, I called Bill, who called the administrator of embassy, and we all met at the flat within an hour. We were impressed, and before the day was over, we had a new home, our third in London.

The new flat was located in a large apartment complex called Colherne Court, not quite so elite a location as Knightsbridge or St. James, but still in London's West End. Although it lacked the Victorian charm of Wellington Court, it was spacious and attractive.

Later Colherne Court became newsworthy when it was known that Prince Charles was courting a young woman by the name of Diana in a flat in the same building. We had a nodding acquaintance with Diana and her two attractive room mates. Once, I had knocked on their door seeking a baby-sitter for our grandson, Sean. One of the girls obligingly came on the appointed evening. She was pretty, blond, and tall, but was she the Princess Di to be? Neither Bill nor I are certain, but I like to think that she was the future Princess of Wales.

The Earls Court section of London where Colherne Court was located was a hodgepodge of nationalities and races. I shopped in Pakistani food stores, French bakeries, and Greek delicatessens, dined at excellent Italian and Chinese restaurants, and went to a Swedish hairdresser. Homosexuals, eccentrics, and ethnic mixed-matches felt an openness to express themselves in this section of London. This was their preserve and to hell with what the rest of the world thought.

And so we went from haughty St. James, to fashionable Knightsbridge, to Bohemian Earls Court, three distinct areas in London's West End, each with its own vibrant personality. Once I had recovered from the difficulties of moving, I had new realms to explore in my now shoddy L. L. Bean boots. My art and antique classes were no longer within walking distance, so I changed to the Buckingham Gate Institute. It was a wrench to exchange kind, placid Derek for a persnickety female art teacher who often made me feel that such a non-talent as mine might do better in the sewing class down the hall.

ง   ง   ง

My gynecologist had his surgery at the Wellbeck Street Nursing Home. He was referred to as Mr. Buckle, he explained, because in centuries past, physicians considered themselves far superior to surgeons, then referred to as barbers. This hubris was so insulting to the surgeons that they refused to be called doctors. And, to this day, many surgeons in England prefer to be called "Mr."

The "Plastic Age" had not erased the old world charm of the Wellbeck Street Nursing Home. On two occasions I was admitted there for minor surgery, the kind that today would be in-and-out, but in England in the '70s, still worthy of two nights in hospital. Both times, my large comfortable room looked out on a private garden. Within, I enjoyed a fireplace with an Adamesque mantelpiece, an oriental carpet, a mahogany commode beside my bed, and a crystal chandelier hung from a baroque ceiling. Even the wheelchair to take me to the operating room in a rickety cage elevator was made of fine mahogany. Only the hospital bed was out of sync with the Victorian splendor. The food, brought by assistant nurses in starched blue and white uniforms, was delicious, and tea time, both mid-morning and afternoon, was a pleasant ritual. Obviously, this had been someone's beautiful home in the "Upstairs-Downstairs" era, and I would have loved a longer convalescence in that comfortable spot. Instead I had agreed to attend the Three-County Agricultural Show in Worcestershire on the coming weekend.

Our nephew, Dabney, had been studying at the University of Seville in Spain and arrived in time to accompany us to Worcestershire. Along the way, he showed an interest in meeting the British in their own setting, and found that the best way to do this was to dart into a pub for a quick chat while his uncle and aunt darted into antique shops. At the show, he had a chance to observe us in our "VIP" roles, as Bill and I were special guests, and sat on the bandstand with the three lord-mayors and their ladies who, in the finest of medieval dress, marched in followed by their retinue to the tune of the royal trumpeters. The British did love a bit of pomp.

ॐ   ॐ   ॐ

During our eight-and-a-half years in London, Bill and I had visitors of all shapes, sizes and descriptions. There were the VIPs from Washington, our "littleones," and in between, many wonderful friends. Two such friends were Jody and Art Brinkley, whose story prior to their arrival on our doorstep is well worth the telling.

When Jody's marriage to my cousin Jimmy failed, she started immediately to rebuild her life by studying to become a paralegal. Soon she met Art, a wealthy businessman considered one of Richmond's most eligible bachelors. They fell in love and were married to the delight of all. Their honeymoon was to be especially grand—a voyage to England on the Queen Elizabeth II and a tour of several of the greatest cities of Europe.

But, alas! alack! alarm! When Jody and Art arrived at New York harbor to board the mighty ship, his passport was found to be out-of-date by one day. As it was Sunday, there was nothing poor Art could do. But Jody, having never been to Europe, decided that this impasse was not going to stand in her way of crossing the ocean aboard the beautiful ship, and she waved farewell to her new husband, still on shore.

Via the proverbial grapevine, word spread quickly throughout the ship that a charming forty-year-old bride occupied the bridal suite without a husband, and Jody soon became the toast of the QE II. She found herself caught up in a whirlwind of concern over her plight, and showered with invitations to dine, dance, and take part in shipboard activities. In short, she had the time of her life.

Meanwhile, a sad Art, back in New York city, straightened

out his passport problem and flew to England in plenty of time to meet his bride dockside at Southampton.

مر مر مر

In early 1979, all of Great Britain experienced its worst weather in forty years—penetrating cold and frequent snowstorms plagued the country. To make matters worse, an epidemic of strikes again engulfed the country like lightning. It seemed astounding that trade unions could be so powerful as to bring an entire nation to the brink of economic disaster. One after the other—truckers, trainmen, hospital staff, civil servants, post office workers, ambulance men and grave diggers—walked off the job. When the dustbin collectors joined the fray, mountains of rubbish piled up along the sidewalks of London emitting rotten smells.

Strikes even hit the theater world. Our young actors were out of work. In the case of Katy and Dean, their contracted tour with the comedy, *A Doctor in the House,* was cancelled because the scenery could not be transported.

Into this pandemonium came a strong voice, that of Tory leader, Margaret Thatcher. Like an electric surge, she promised drastic measures to put the country back on its feet, and was elected prime minister on May 4, 1979, the first woman in the western world to hold such a position of power. Dubbed the "Iron Lady," she ruthlessly went to work to stabilize Britain by introducing austerity measures, and taking a firm stand against the strikers, as well as the terrorist tactics of the I.R.A.

I added my two-cents to the fray by writing the following whimsical poem.

The English forget not the Empire they had,
To think that it's gone is ever so sad,
But they still march about as if nothing had happened,
Forgetting their map has been greatly unmapped.

There are demos and strikes and a zooming inflation,
And frightful disputes in this tattered nation.
But one great plus is their lovely Queen,
She's as lovely now as she ever has been.

Thank God that we have their Royal High-ness-es,
Who balance the scales of the British mess
Created by politics, unions, and such,
Without them the Englishmen wouldn't have much.

So long live the Princes, the Duke, and the Queen!
And all those that come in betwixt and between,
But while you are at it, please God, take a note,
Try to go further. KEEP ENGLAND AFLOAT!

But in spite of strikes, unemployment and zooming inflation, diplomatic life went on as usual. Entertaining at the various embassies was often lavish. Wingfield House, the imposing official residence of the American ambassador, sat on its own twelve-acre spread, surrounded by the 525 acres of Regents Park. During our time in London, four ambassadors occupied this beautiful home: Walter Annenberg, art collector and wealthy owner of the *Philadelphia Inquirer* and *TV Guide;* Ann Armstrong, White House counselor to two presidents; Elliott Richardson, U.S. Attorney General fired from his post by President Nixon during the Watergate scandal; and Kingman Brewster, former president of Yale University. Each entertained in his or her own way, but always tastefully and often with gilt-edged magnificence. Many of their guests were titled; some, members of the British royal family. The Duke and Duchess of Kent were frequently the royal guests. I remember one evening how stunning the duchess looked in a silvery gown and a necklace of diamonds almost the size of robins' eggs which swung down to an emerald almost the size of a goose egg. England might have lost an empire and be floundering in economic ruin, but it hadn't lost its crown jewels nor its glitter.

๛   ๛   ๛

In the fall of 1979, the Foreign Agricultural Service asked Bill to stay on in London for another two years after his present tour of duty was over. We were tempted, as we not only loved England, but my job with the Whitney Shop was going well in spite of inflated prices. On weekends, we looked for antiques in the London markets instead of combing the countryside. With petrol up to $3.20 per gallon and the cost of lodging tripled, we were thankful to return in the evening to our own comfortable flat. London was not quite the enchanting city that it had been. With Margaret Thatcher's stringent measures to curtail expense, the government had cut down on street cleaners and park attendants, and the traffic was getting more impossible every day. Unemployment was at an all time high, and public transport at an all time low.

With much vacillation to and fro, we made the decision to retire in July of 1980. We had spent almost thirty years in the foreign service and Bill was tired of receptions, early morning trips to the airport, bureaucratic redtape, reports, political junkets, and representative entertaining. I could not blame him. He had loved his career, but now he deserved a change where he could build his life in other directions in a more tranquil setting.

For me, it would be very hard to leave this beloved city. And the thought of moving to our house in Charlottesville, Virginia, gave me pause. Our effects, plus our carefully accumulated antiques, were spread from London to Mexico, and it seemed that it might take the rental of a gymnasium to sort them out. On the positive side, change can be stimulating, and I looked forward to being "home" where I could easily pick up the phone to call our children and grandchildren, and see them more often. Margy and Bill, Jr. were expecting another child, and we hoped for a granddaughter.

ॐ   ॐ   ॐ

We spent our last English Christmas in Devonshire at a lovely inn on the edge of the Exmoor Plain. This is the time of year when I am most aware of the changes that life brings. Although it is a time of rejoicing, it is also a pensive time when I long for Christmas Past and the days when our family was together. I especially remember the build-up to Christmas, that best of all holidays from school: decorating the house, trimming the tree, excitement in the stores, carols, the joy of buying gifts for others, and the anticipation of that moment when a certain gift will be opened to make someone happy. Closing my eyes, I can almost hear young voices bantering:

"I'm warning you—don't anyone look in my closet!"

"Don't you dare come into my room!"

"Has anyone some paper and ribbon I can borrow?"

"You're going to love what I got you."

And the unbelievable wonder of it all when the Christmas tree was lighted.

ॐ   ॐ   ॐ

Preparations to leave London were exhausting. We had tallied more than a dozen major moves during our foreign service career and each became more difficult than the last. I find it upsetting to say a final good-bye, or to look upon something that has become familiar for the last time—a street, a neighbor, a home, a way of life. And London was a place that I had loved so well.

In the hustle-bustle of leaving London a happy note was sounded—a granddaughter, Channing Spring Rodman, was born on April 16, 1980, and I paraded off to buy a little smocked dress at Liberty's.

· —— Epilogue —— ·

IN ORDER TO KEEP FROM FLOUNDERING AFTER
JONI'S DEATH, I developed a one-day-at-a-time philosophy.
Sadly I had learned that tomorrow may never come. A framed
needlepoint hanging on my wall reminds me that "Today is the
tomorrow that worried you yesterday—and all is well."

Although my goals are generally on my daily list, I keep an
open mind to new ideas be they spiritual or secular, and am
grateful for any little breakthroughs or insights I collect along
the way. I feel very fortunate that mind and body are in working
order.

I have observed life from the poorest sections of Mexico to
the opulence of Buckingham Palace. Little barefooted Elena in
Argentina, Antonio in Mexico City, and the orphans of Alcolman
are my treasures as well as Helen Hayes, Ava Gardner and other
luminaries. I have churned butter and grown potatoes on a
working farm in Virginia and experienced the extravagance and
eliteness of diplomatic life. I have known extremes of climate
from equator heat to Canada's winters, from humid rain forests
in Central America to arid plains in Australia. Traveling by ship,
train and plane, I have seen the sun rise across the circumference

340

of the earth. In spite of a wandering gypsy life, I have watched our children grow to maturity in the security of home, free of social, provincial or local prejudices. I have known great sorrow and great happiness. And all the while, I have had my husband by my side.

One must adventure endlessly in loving, and my orbit has been the world.

February 1991
Dover Beach Hotel, Barbados